Ann Ferguson

MANUSCRIPTS DON'T BURN

MANUSCRIPTS DON'T BURN

MIKHAIL BULGAKOV 1891- 1940
A Life in Letters and Diaries

J. A. E. Curtis

The Overlook Press
Woodstock, New York

First published in 1992 by
The Overlook Press
Lewis Hollow Road
Woodstock, New York 12498

Library of Congress Cataloging-in-Publication Data

Curtis, J.A.E.
    Manuscripts don't burn : Mikhail Bulgakov, a life in letters and
diaries / J.A.E. Curtis.
    p. cm.
      Includes bibliographical references and index.

    1. Bulgakov, Mikhail Afanas 'evich, 1871-1940. 2. Authors, Russian—
20th century—Biography. 3. Bulgakov, Mikhail Afanas 'evich, 1871-1940—
Correspondence. 4. Bulgakov, Mikhail Afanas 'evich, 1871-1940—Diaries.
I. Title.
PG3476.B78Z64 1992
'891.7'84209—dc20   92-8863
[B]   CIP

ISBN: 0-87951-462-0

All photographs reproduced by kind permission of the Museum of
Pushinsky Dom (Soviet Academy of Sciences), Leningrad

First Edition

*This book is dedicated to Professor Tony Cross
and to my colleagues in the Department of Slavonic Studies,
as well as to the Warden and Fellows of Robinson College,
in gratitude for my happy years in Cambridge.*

ACKNOWLEDGEMENTS

I would like to record my thanks to the British Academy for supporting me with a Post-Doctoral Research Fellowship, and with awards under the Academy's Exchange Agreement with the Soviet Union, during the period when most of the research for this book was completed.

I would also like to thank Marietta Chudakova, Violetta Gudkova, Irina Yerykalova, Grigory Fayman and Viktor Losev, as well as the late Lyubov Yevgenyevna Belozerskaya-Bulgakova, for their help and encouragement. I am very grateful, too, to the staff of Pushkin House (the Literary Institute of the USSR Academy of Sciences), the Saltykov-Shchedrin Library and the Cherkasov Theatre Institute in Leningrad, as well as to the staff of the Library of the Union of Theatrical Workers, the Moscow Arts Theatre Museum, the Central State Archive for Literature and Art, and the Manuscript Section and Reading Rooms of the Lenin Library in Moscow. I have collected and collated the material for this book from numerous archives, both State and private, and Bulgakov's second wife Lyubov Yevgenyevna was particularly generous in this respect. Bulgakov very often retained copies of the letters he himself had written, which means that some archives hold copies of documents published by another. This has enabled me to compare texts with publications, particularly those by Marietta Chudakova, Violetta Gudkova, Grigory Fayman, Yelena Zemskaya and Viktor Losev and, occasionally, to suggest variant readings. Viktor Losev and Viktor Petelin are the editors of the most comprehensive – though far from complete – collection of Bulgakov's correspondence, which was published in 1989. I am grateful to Viktor Losev for permission to work on Yelena Sergeyevna Bulgakova's diaries in the Lenin Library in 1990.

Special thanks are due to Lesley Milne; to all my colleagues in Cambridge; and, as ever, to my parents and family.

Without Ray, none of this would have been possible at all.

CONTENTS

PREFACE

Mikhail Bulgakov is a Russian writer whose reputation has been growing steadily over the past decades, until he now stands amongst the giants – Akhmatova, Tsvetayeva, Mandelstam, Pasternak, Solzhenitsyn and Brodsky – of the Soviet period. Bulgakov's story, however, is a particularly unusual one, for he was scarcely published at all, either in the East or in the West, in his own lifetime, and his plays reached the stage only with great difficulty. He was indeed defeated by the stranglehold imposed on Soviet literature during the Stalin period – and yet he would not give up. Time and time again we see him coming up with fresh inspiration and settling down to write new works, as soon as he has overcome the shock of yet another banning of a play or refusal to publish a work.

We talk of the indomitable spirit of certain writers, and in Bulgakov's case this is especially apt. Throughout the 1930s he devoted his nights, as well as other spare snatched moments, to writing in complete secrecy a novel, *The Master and Margarita*, which is generally regarded as his finest work, and as a precursor of that international tradition of 'magic realism' to which Marquez, Kundera and Salman Rushdie have all made contributions. The novel is an extraordinary blend of comic satire, set in the Moscow of the 1930s, with a profound and intense retelling of the encounter between Christ and Pontius Pilate. Its starting-point is the visit to Moscow of an elegant Devil, Woland, who is working

ix

for the forces of good; but the book is also a love story, and an account of the artistic integrity of its writer-hero, the Master.

Although Bulgakov occasionally succumbed to dreams of its publication, there could be no question of publishing *The Master and Margarita* in the USSR of the 1930s. When Bulgakov died of a hereditary kidney disease in 1940, his wife Yelena Sergeyevna Bulgakova, following in a distinguished tradition of great deeds performed by Soviet literary widows, was left to preserve and guard his heritage until a time of greater freedom. It was not until over a quarter of a century after his death that the first publication of *The Master and Margarita* was permitted, in a text abridged by the censors, in the journal *Moskva* in 1966 and 1967. The full publication of the novel in 1973 in a volume with two of his other novels, *The White Guard* and *A Theatrical Novel*, was the literary sensation of the late Thaw period in the USSR, and this coveted volume was soon changing hands on the black market at approximately fifty times its cover price. The cult of Bulgakov and his works which has developed since has established him as one of the most genuinely popular writers of the Soviet era.

During the Brezhnev period some of Bulgakov's works were published, but others were not, even after editions had become available in the West, and the obstacles placed in the way of scholars seeking access to his archives became a *cause célèbre*. During the 1970s and early 1980s the combined efforts of Soviet and Western experts gradually uncovered more facts about Bulgakov's life, but it remained very difficult to establish the authenticity of both texts and biographical materials. With the advent of *glasnost'* things began to change, although rivalries between archivists and scholars and the continuing determination of some Soviet literary historians to present an 'authorized' portrait of Bulgakov have hindered progress. Some access to archives was granted for the first time to a limited number of scholars in 1989, and there is now, at last, a genuine prospect of collaborative publications and studies of Bulgakov by Western and Soviet scholars, something that only a few years ago would have been unthinkable. The 1991 centenary of Bulgakov's birth therefore falls at a very propitious moment. The texts of all four of his novels, several novellas and some fourteen plays have become available to the Soviet public (although considerable work remains to be done to establish the correct versions of some particularly contentious texts, such as his prose biography of Molière, *The Life of Monsieur de Molière*, and his novella *The Heart of a Dog*). Publications of his correspondence have been emerging piecemeal, while extracts from the texts of his own diaries and those of his third wife, Yelena Sergeyevna, have also begun to be published.

Bulgakov's works have been the subject of a considerable number of analytical studies, while his biographers, who particularly in the early years had to work with fairly sparse information, have served him well despite the difficulties. All Bulgakov scholars, both in the East and in the West, owe an especial debt of gratitude to Marietta Chudakova, who fought a tremendous battle for *glasnost'*, with regard to literary history in general and to Bulgakov in particular, long before the term became politically fashionable. Her efforts culminated in the publication in Moscow in 1987–88 of her extremely detailed and thoroughly-documented chronicle of Bulgakov's life, *Zhizneopisaniye Mikhaila Bulgakova* (*The Biography of Mikhail Bulgakov*), which I have drawn on extensively for the background material in this book. In the West, Bulgakov has found energetic biographers in A. Colin Wright (1978) and Ellendea Proffer (1984); and the magisterial study by Lesley Milne (1991) has been able to take into account many recent archival finds and scholarly analyses. These are the works to which the reader should refer for a comprehensive account of Bulgakov's life; the purposes of the present volume are somewhat different.

It is now more than ten years since I began to collect Bulgakov's correspondence – which is held in both private and State archives in the Soviet Union – and to collate these letters written by him, and to him, with the numerous, scattered and very fragmentary publications that have appeared from time to time in Soviet and Western journals and books. More recently, I have been particularly fortunate in being granted access to the full text of a diary kept at Bulgakov's request by his third wife, Yelena Sergeyevna Bulgakova, who wrote in it almost daily from September 1933 until his death in 1940. Yelena Sergeyevna subsequently prepared a special version of this diary for possible publication, and since I have had access to both the original and her reworking of it, I have occasionally blended together entries from both versions for this book.

I have been equally fortunate in being permitted to read the full text of a diary Bulgakov himself kept in the early 1920s, shortly after he had set up in Moscow as a writer. An extraordinary story attaches to this document, which everyone, including Bulgakov, had supposed to have been destroyed over sixty years ago. In 1926 Bulgakov's apartment was searched by the OGPU (a forerunner of the KGB) and his diaries were confiscated, along with the text of *The Heart of a Dog*. Since Bulgakov was on this occasion only marginally implicated in a case being mounted by the secret police against one of his acquaintances, he soon began to make official complaints demanding that the manuscripts be returned. He finally got them back some three years later, in 1929, whereupon he immediately burned the diaries and resolved never to keep a diary again. Since that time, it had been assumed that the diaries were lost, until the advent of *glasnost'* prompted the KGB to admit that, in fact, the OGPU had made a copy of at least part of the diary back in the 1920s, and this was still sitting in the KGB's archives. The text was published, virtually in its entirety, in 1989–90. The fate of Bulgakov's novel *The Master and Margarita*, which was published after being kept secret for a decade while he was alive, and for a further twenty-six years after his death, together with this astonishing re-emergence of his diary sixty years on, has lent a peculiarly prophetic force to a phrase from *The Master and Margarita* which defiantly proclaims the integrity of art: 'Manuscripts don't burn.' This is the phrase from the novel most frequently quoted in the Soviet Union today.

In this book I have alternated extracts from letters to and from Bulgakov with entries from his own diaries of the early 1920s and from Yelena Sergeyevna's diaries of the period 1933 to 1940, selecting the material from my own collection of documents, which amounts to some 1,600 pages. The resulting documentary chronicle does not cover the whole of Bulgakov's life by any means; very few documents in any case survive from his childhood and youth, and it is not until Bulgakov was in his early twenties that the letters he wrote and received appear to have been preserved. What the surviving material provides, however, is a vivid and immediate account of what it was like to be a 'conservative' writer struggling to make a career in the 1920s and the 1930s in the Soviet Union, particularly under Stalin.

The correspondence and diary extracts collected here cover a period from almost exactly the time of the October Revolution in 1917 through to 1940. Above all, they allow Bulgakov, his wife and his friends to speak in their own voices. They open with Bulgakov, newly qualified as a doctor, spending World War I and the Revolution in the remote provinces, practising medicine but wishing he were elsewhere. His feelings of revulsion against his chosen career, against being stuck in the backwoods, and against Russia's new political destiny, were so strong that during a period spent in Vladikavkaz in the Northern Caucasus, from 1919 to 1921, he concealed his medical qualifications and embarked on a new career as a dramatist. Later on he even travelled south to the Black Sea in an attempt to emigrate. But the story charted in these documents really begins with Bulgakov's abandoning that plan and settling instead in Moscow, determined to make a great literary career. He was to succeed in gaining real fame with his stage adaptation of his first novel, *The White Guard*, which as *The Days of the Turbins* was one of the great successes for Stanislavsky's Moscow Arts Theatre in the 1920s. However, political pressure then led to the banning of his plays in 1929 and to the repeated frustration of his further attempts to be published or performed.

The documents dating from the 1930s give an authentic impression of what it was like to be a member of Moscow's cultural élite, moving in the circles of the Moscow Arts Theatre and the Bolshoy Theatre, and having an entrée into the glittering social sphere of the American Embassy. But at the same time they show how a writer could figure as the mouse in one of those terrifying cat-and-mouse games Stalin was wont to play with artists such as Shostakovich, Prokofiev and Pasternak – the artists who were allowed to survive. Bulgakov's letters and Yelena Sergeyevna's diaries record a stream of arrests and deaths amongst their friends and acquaintances during the Terror, and they give a shocking picture of that period, when Stalin, through the Central Committee of the Communist Party, exercised the closest possible control over every writer. A series of spies was forever befriending Bulgakov on behalf of the secret police and the Party, always trying to manipulate him by tantalizing him with the prospect that his fortunes were about to take a turn for the better. A barely suppressed hysteria can be detected in the couple's writings as Bulgakov's neurotic fears gave way at the end of the 1930s to the grave illness that in 1940 ended his life.

I

1917–1921

The writing of Bulgakov's first novel, *The White Guard*, consti-
tuted an act of grateful homage to his family and to the happy
childhood and upbringing he had enjoyed in the Ukrainian
capital, Kiev. In the novel, a family of young adults – one
sister and two brothers, who have recently lost their mother –
is depicted against the background of World War I and the
Revolution in Kiev. The focus of the story is the house where
they live, situated on such a steep hill that what looks like the
second floor from the bottom end, out in the street, becomes
the ground floor by the time you have climbed round the
building to the courtyard and the main entrance at the back.
Behind its cream-coloured blinds, the warmth of this home
glows as a safe haven from the violence and uncertainties of
the successive political coups outside, as battles are fought for
control of Kiev between the pro-Tsarist White Russians, the
occupying German armies, the Ukrainian peasant nationalists
led by Petlyura, and the Red Soviet forces. 'The inhabitants of
Kiev reckon that there were eighteen changes of power. Some
stay-at-home memoirists counted up to twelve of them; I can
tell you that there were precisely fourteen; and what's more, I
personally lived through ten of them,' Bulgakov was to comment
subsequently.

Bulgakov's fictional family, the Turbins (the surname was a
family name on his mother's side), are sustained with their

I

friends through all these upheavals by values that are characteristic of their class and of their political inclinations. Foremost
among these are domestic values such as love, compassion, an
instinctive decency and a concern for right and wrong which
derives from a natural and discreet religious faith. The Turbins
enjoy laughter, flirtations and late nights like any young people,
but their sense of honour comes to the fore as soon as someone
or something they respect is in danger: Aleksey and his younger
brother Nikolay do their duty fighting in the Tsar's name until
the battle becomes hopeless. When Nikolay's hero Nay-Turs is
killed, he makes it a priority to find his family and inform them,
and then undertakes a gruesome expedition to retrieve the body
from the morgue – predictably at the same time falling in love
with his hero's sister. The Turbin family has been brought up to
be loyal to the Tsars, and at the close of the novel it is difficult
to imagine that they are going to adapt to the future Soviet
regime with any passionate commitment; such a transformation
could have been achieved only in a propaganda novel of Soviet
Socialist Realism, which Bulgakov's *White Guard* emphatically is
not. But the Turbins will survive, for in the end the novel shows
political power to be only a transient phenomenon: the family
is sustained by eternal values which will persist regardless of the
political system. These values are, first, a religion which I have
described as 'discreet' because it is concerned less with practice
and worship than with a sense of a higher destiny governing the
affairs of men and adjusting the balance between good and evil;
secondly, art, which in the shape of books, and of music played
and sung around the piano, offers the Turbins solace and joy;
and thirdly, family affection and loyalty, which provide security,
an ideal to defend, and standards to live up to.

The White Guard, written between 1921 and 1923, is one of
the more explicitly autobiographical of Bulgakov's works; not in
every detail, by any means, but certainly in mood and in spirit
it is an evocation of Bulgakov's own feelings about his family
and their experience of the events of the Great War, Revolution
and Civil War period. Mikhail Bulgakov's own family was in
reality much larger than the one he describes in his novel: he
was born in 1891, the oldest of a family of seven children, all

2 brothers
4 sisters

of whom thrived. His siblings were Vera (1892), Nadezhda (Nadya, 1893), Varvara (Varya, 1895), Nikolay (Kolya, 1898), Ivan (Vanya, 1900) and Yelena (Lyolya, 1902). Their father, Afanasy Ivanovich (1859–1907), came from a family of priests, and himself pursued a career as a theologian. He became a professor of comparative religion at the Kiev Theological Academy, and wrote numerous articles on topics relating to Western European religion, from Catholicism to Methodism. Afanasy Ivanovich lived at a number of addresses in Kiev with his young wife Varvara Mikhaylovna (1869–1922) and their growing family, but in the autumn of 1906 they moved into a large apartment at number 13 Andreyevsky Hill, the house that is described in *The White Guard* as number 13 Alekseyevsky Hill. In that same year, however, Afanasy Ivanovich fell gravely ill with a kidney disease, and he died in 1907 at the age of forty-eight, leaving the fifteen-year-old Mikhail (Misha) to help his mother care for his four sisters and two brothers. The same disease would eventually carry off Mikhail himself, and at more or less the same early age (forty-nine). Bulgakov would always remember his father with love, and with admiration and respect for his scholarship; Afanasy Ivanovich knew Latin and Greek, as well as French, German, English and the West Slavonic languages such as Polish and Czech. 'The image of a lamp with a green shade is a very important image for me. It derives from my childhood impressions of the image of my father, writing at a desk.'

Russian, & 7 langs

Family life at 13 Andreyevsky Hill continued to be full of fun and laughter, even if the family's income became rather more limited after Afanasy Ivanovich's death. Three assorted cousins lived there for much of the time, adding to the lively, youthful atmosphere; these included Mikhail's cousin Konstantin, to whom he was particularly close as a young man, perhaps because his own brothers, Nikolay and Ivan, were seven and nine years younger than him. All the children received good educations, thanks to their late father's colleagues in the clergy who helped them obtain scholarships, and several went on to pursue academic careers; they were widely read and very musical, and frequently went to the theatre and especially to the opera to hear, amongst others, Chaliapin. They also enjoyed amateur dramatics, and put on their own plays for the benefit of family and friends either at home or at their dacha outside Kiev at Bucha. Mikhail was particularly ingenious when it came to thinking up comic verses or devising sketches and charades for these occasions. He was indeed tempted to take up a career in the theatre or as a singer, but in the end decided in 1909 to enter the University to study medicine. This was a profession he knew about partly through his mother's two brothers, both doctors, and through the family friend Ivan Pavlovich Voskresensky, who would eventually become his stepfather and to whom all the Bulgakov children became very attached. As a route into a literary career, as it turned out to be, medicine offered distinguished models in the figures of Chekhov and Vikenty Veresayev, the latter an older man who was to become a friend and collaborator of Bulgakov's in Moscow. The move towards science also satisfied Bulgakov's new interest in Darwinism, which, according to his sister Nadya, had by 1910 led him to break with religion and in the ensuing years became the subject of fierce family debates, with Mikhail's views finding support in the atheism of Ivan Pavlovich Voskresensky, Varvara Mikhaylovna's future husband.

Bulgakov's progress as a medical student was not entirely smooth, largely because he spent so much time with a young woman called Tatyana Nikolayevna Lappa. He had first met her in 1908, when she was visiting her aunt in Kiev from her home in Saratov, and three years later they began seeing so much of each other that the young Bulgakov failed his second-year examinations in 1912. Tatyana (Tasya) was later to recall that they spent all their spare time together, and went to see Gounod's *Faust* at least ten times that year. Bulgakov was also neglecting his studies for writing: in 1912 he showed his sister Nadya some stories he had written, and told her that he was determined to become a writer one day. Despite the considerable misgivings of the parents on both sides, the twenty-one-year-old Mikhail married Tatyana in April 1913, as soon as he had resat and passed his examinations to get into the third year. They were to spend eleven years together, until 1924.

This carefree period of Bulgakov's life was brought to an end

4

by the outbreak of war in August 1914. The following year, still a student, he was drafted in to treat the wounded in a hospital in Saratov, and by the time he was awarded his diploma as a doctor, in October 1916, he had moved on from working as a Red Cross volunteer to running a small hospital in the depths of the countryside – virtually single-handed, except for the assistance of his wife Tatyana as a nurse. The experience of working in these conditions is portrayed in the stories he wrote which have been collected together as *A Country Doctor's Notebook*. In them he records his horror at the backwardness of the peasant population he had to treat; his vain attempts to limit the spread of syphilis due to sheer ignorance and prejudice; his terror at having to carry out operations he had only once witnessed being performed, as a student; and his longing to get back to his home and to civilization. In one story, which for a long time was not published in the Soviet Union, he also describes the experience of becoming addicted to morphine, something that happened to him as the result of an accident when he was treating a case of diphtheria, and which he did not overcome until he was weaned off, thanks to Tasya's determined help, over a year later.

The first document in this chapter (page 11) dates from October 1917, the month of the Bolshevik Revolution. It is a letter written by Bulgakov to his sister Nadya in Moscow, and sent from the small town of Vyazma, to which Bulgakov had been transferred – to his great relief – that September. At least there he was not entirely cut off from his medical colleagues, although as the events of October proceeded he became frantic at the impossibility of finding out either what was happening in Moscow, or how his family was faring back in Kiev. His anxieties were fully justified: the letter of November 1917 written by his mother to his sister Nadya (page 12) – which I have included here as an exception, since it is written neither to nor by Bulgakov himself – reveals just how close his mother and his brother Nikolay came to being killed in the days immediately following the Bolshevik coup on 25 October. Nikolay was fighting in this instance as a Cadet, a Tsarist soldier. Later on, both he and his younger brother Ivan decided to emigrate with other White groups, eventually finding their way via Yugoslavia to Paris, where

Nikolay (1898–1966) became a distinguished scientist working in the field of bacteriology, while Ivan (1900–1968) followed the more stereotypical path of a White Russian émigré in becoming a balalaika-player and taxi-driver.

Meanwhile, Bulgakov had one more chance of spending time with his relatives in Kiev, for in February 1918 he succeeded in getting released from his duties on health grounds, and made his way back home, having caught unforgettable glimpses in Moscow of the violence and horrors of the Revolution. It is this period back in Kiev from 1918 to 1919 that he describes in *The White Guard*. While the country was in turmoil and successive forces took possession of Kiev, the house on Andreyevsky Hill remained a precious refuge, and Bulgakov, who had exchanged his early interest in paediatrics for a specialization in venereal diseases, set up a clinic in the front room overlooking the street. However, being a doctor turned out to be very dangerous, since each new power entering the city tended to mobilize all medical personnel. Bulgakov managed to escape and return home on one occasion after being mobilized by Petlyura's Ukrainian troops – an evidently traumatic experience which may have involved his being the helpless witness to at least one brutal murder and to the torture of a Jew. At some point in 1919, probably in the early autumn, it appears that he was mobilized by the Whites and dispatched hundreds of miles away, to the town of Vladikavkaz in the Northern Caucasus. We know little about Bulgakov's feelings at leaving Kiev on this occasion; although we can guess that he was fairly sympathetic to the White Army, he must have been reluctant to leave his family and his beloved Kiev once again. What he could not have known was that this departure was to mark a turning-point in his life and his career.

It was only in 1988 that the combined efforts of Marietta Chudakova and Grigory Fayman in the USSR succeeded in tracking down the first published piece that Bulgakov ever wrote, which came out in a small newspaper in the town of Grozny in the Northern Caucasus on 26 November 1919. Bulgakov subsequently concealed almost all trace of this militantly pro-White publication – not surprisingly, since the article, entitled 'Prospects for the Future' (page 16), gives the gloomiest

6

of prognoses for the future of the country under Bolshevik rule. Bulgakov appears to have written it *en route* with the White Army for Vladikavkaz, where he then settled. He gives an unequivocal account of his despair at the damage inflicted on the country by the years of military turmoil, and sees no conceivable hope for the future unless the Whites wrest control of the country back from Trotsky and the other Bolsheviks. While the West rebuilds itself and flourishes, he anticipates that Russia will go on and on suffering internecine struggles. As Chudakova has pointed out, the article is also notable for introducing right at the beginning of Bulgakov's career themes of guilt and inevitable retribution to be suffered by his own hapless generation, themes that would be developed as a central preoccupation in many of his later works.

guilt and retribution

Bulgakov spent the end of 1919 and the beginning of 1920 working as a doctor for the White forces, but he also began to give an increasing amount of his attention to literature, publishing one or two short stories. Then came the news that the Soviet Red Army was advancing on Vladikavkaz, and that the Whites would have to retreat. Bulgakov had already resolved to abandon the career of medicine, which attracted so much undesirable attention from the military forces, and at this point fate supervened to enable him to do so – but at the cost of considerable danger. For as the Whites prepared to withdraw, Bulgakov fell sick with typhus, and for some time he was seriously ill and generally remained unconscious, tended only by Tasya, who had joined him in Vladikavkaz at the end of 1919. By the time he regained consciousness, sometime in March 1920, the town of Vladikavkaz was controlled by the Soviets. The confusion of all these events afforded him a timely opportunity to create for himself a new identity as a writer, although he remained fearful that someone might betray his past at any moment. Bulgakov never practised medicine again.

typhus . . .

The documents in this chapter all date from the first half of 1921, and comprise mostly letters to his relations, particularly his favourite sister, Nadya, and his cousin Konstantin. He was delighted when contact was re-established with Kiev, for he had known little of the fate of his family during this period; indeed, no news was received of his brothers Nikolay and Ivan from the time when they too left Kiev with the White Army in 1919, until Nikolay managed to get a message back from emigration to their mother in Kiev early in 1922. These letters from Bulgakov give a good impression of his feelings about his early steps as a dramatist in 1920–21. In all, he wrote five plays during this period. At the same time he was helping to run the Literary Section of the Department of Culture for the local Soviet administration, which involved him in lecturing and public discussions of Russian literature. He found himself deeply opposed to the iconoclastic spirit that prevailed in post-Revolutionary culture, which often sought to decry the writers of the past on the grounds of their class affiliation, and to reject their works as being of little relevance to the proletariat. Bulgakov became involved in one particularly heated debate, on 26 October 1920, when he defended the early-nineteenth-century poet Pushkin against charges that he was a frivolous, bawdy writer who had behaved in servile fashion at the court of Tsar Nicholas I; but his audience was not easily persuaded, and Bulgakov was subsequently criticized in the local press as a bourgeois reactionary.

The five plays Bulgakov wrote during this period were *Self-Defence*, *The Turbin Brothers*, *The Bridegrooms of Clay*, *The Paris Communards* and finally *The Sons of the Mullah* (written together with a local lawyer). These works were very varied, ranging from farcical comedy to historical drama; and the way in which they poured from Bulgakov's pen in the short space of twelve months was to be characteristic of his remarkable speed in writing and productivity in later years. When he was living in Moscow in 1923 he apparently burned the texts of all these plays, believing them to be beneath serious consideration, even though at least two of them – *The Turbin Brothers* and *The Sons of the Mullah* – were actually staged. But as if to provide a further reinforcement of his own dictum in *The Master and Margarita* that 'Manuscripts don't burn', a copy of the text of *The Sons of the Mullah* turned up in the 1960s. In his story *Bohemia*, Bulgakov comments on *The Sons of the Mullah*, 'We wrote it in seven and a half days, so in other words we spent a day and a half more on it than on the creation of the world.

Nevertheless, it came out even worse than the world.' It is especially regrettable that we no longer have the text of *The Turbin Brothers*, which was clearly a first attempt to interpret his own family's history over recent years. The fact that the play was apparently set in 1905, the year of the first twentieth-century Russian revolutionary uprising, rather than in 1917–21, may have been a deliberate device to defuse the political topicality of the subject. The play *The Turbin Brothers* was being performed in Vladikavkaz during October 1920; by February 1921, Bulgakov had begun the novel about his family that in 1923 was completed as *The White Guard*. And only after this was finished did he go back to the dramatic genre, turning some of the same material that he had drawn on for *The White Guard* into a second play, the highly successful *Days of the Turbins*.

Throughout the letters Bulgakov was writing to his relatives at this time there is a sense of great dissatisfaction with his present circumstances. He is now fired with literary ambition, and his modest successes on the provincial stage are not enough to satisfy him. Part of him dreams of being a successful playwright in Moscow, even if the prevalent cultural ethos there is uncongenial to him; but another part of him is wondering whether to escape into emigration while it is still possible: hence the cryptic remarks about not seeing his family again for a long time, and instructions about what should be done with the manuscripts of prose works he had already begun in Kiev, in the event of his not reappearing after a stated period. Another area of uncertainty for him, evidently, was his marriage: he hints that Tasya's destiny is likely to work out differently from his own, whatever that may prove to be.

In the event, Bulgakov did set off towards the end of May 1921, at first on his own, apparently in search of an opportunity to emigrate from some Black Sea port. He travelled from Vladikavkaz by a very circuitous route, via Baku on the Caspian Sea, on his way to Tiflis (Tbilisi). From there he sent a message to Tasya urging her to join him, which she did, and they travelled on together to the port of Batum on the Black Sea, right down on the border with Turkey. They spent a couple of months or so in Batum during the summer of 1921, while Bulgakov attempted to earn some money by writing for the local newspapers. On more than one occasion he had a conversation with the poet Osip Mandelstam, with whom he became acquainted at this time, about the best way to get a novel published in Moscow. Yet at the same time Bulgakov was also trying to enter into negotiations with the captains of some of the steamers that sailed regularly for Constantinople, to see whether they couldn't smuggle him on board. Towards the end of the summer he sent Tasya to Moscow, while he continued to try to leave the country; and although he assured her that if he succeeded he would arrange for her to join him, she set off in August convinced that she would never see him again. We do not know exactly what happened to resolve Bulgakov's hesitations, but after a couple more weeks in Batum on his own, he finally abandoned his plan to emigrate. He left for Moscow, stopped off in Kiev to visit his family, and towards the end of September 1921 arrived to join Tasya in the capital. From then on he was determined that he would make a career in the Soviet Union as a writer.

3 October 1917. From Vyazma to Moscow
To his sister Nadezhda

Dear Nadya,

I only discovered yesterday from Uncle's letter that you were in Moscow, preparing for your examinations. [. . .] I have been wanting to write to you, but I didn't know your address. Write and tell me when your State examinations are.

And in any case let me beg you to write to me more frequently, if of course you can find the time to do so. For me the letters of my nearest and dearest represent a great solace at this time. Please also write and give me Varya's address. From Mother's last letter I know only that Varya is in Petrograd. I have been intending to write to her for some time to find out how she is living. I have had no news from Mother since the beginning of September. [. . .]

Just now I urgently need to spend some time in Moscow on my own affairs, but I cannot abandon my work for a moment and therefore am turning to you to ask if you could do certain things for me, if that's not too difficult.

1) Please buy Klopshtok and Kovarsky's *Practical Guide to Clinical Chemistry, Microscopy and Bacteriology* [. . .] and send it to me. Find out which are the very *best books* available in Moscow on skin and venereological diseases in Russian or in German and let me know the price and name; *don't purchase them for the moment.* [. . .]

2) Write and tell me, if you know, how much men's boots (good ones) cost in Moscow. [. . .]

I assume that the purchase of the book won't be difficult for you. You would probably have been going to bookshops in any case?

If I can manage it I will probably come to Moscow for a couple of days in about a month's time on more important business. [. . .]

Tasya and I send you a big kiss.

Mikhail.

10 November 1917. From Kiev to Moscow
From Bulgakov's mother to his sister Nadezhda

I can quite understand that you have lived through some anxious moments, since we too have lived through a great deal. Worst of all was the position of poor Nikolay as a Cadet. He has had to live through some real dramas, and I too along with him on the night of the 29th: we were literally a hair's breadth away from death. Ever since 25 October the Pechersk district had been put on military alert, and it was cut off from the rest of the city. For as long as the telephone was working in the School of Engineers we could speak to Kolya on the telephone, but then telephone links were broken off as well. On the 28th the arsenal was pillaged, and the weapons passed into the hands of the workers and various shady gangs of marauders . . .

My anxiety for Kolya grew, so I decided I must go to see him; and I got through on the afternoon of the 29th. I succeeded in getting there; but when at 7.30 that evening Kolya (who had been relieved of his duties for fifteen minutes to see me home) and I made an attempt to go out into the town past the Constantine School, the famous bombardment of the school was just beginning. We had just got past the stone wall in front of the Constantine School when the first shell thundered out. We threw ourselves back and took cover behind a small projecting part of the wall; but when the crossfire began, with shooting at the School and from it, we found ourselves in the firing-zone and the bullets were smacking against the very wall where we were standing. Fortunately there was an officer among some casual passers-by (about six people) who were endeavouring to take cover from the bullets; he ordered us to lie down on the ground, as close to the wall as we could. We endured a dreadful hour: the machine-guns were chattering away as well as the rifle shots, the bullets clattering against the wall, and then they were joined by the thudding of the shells . . . But evidently our time had not yet come, and Kolya and I survived (one woman was killed); but we will never forget that night . . .

In a brief lull in the shooting we managed (following the commands of this same officer) to run back across to the School of Engineers. There all the lights had already been put out, and only a searchlight flashed out from time to time: the Cadets had taken up battle formation and the officers were shouting out commands; Kolya fell in with the others, and I didn't see him again . . . I sat on a chair in the entrance hall, and knew that I would have to sit there all night, that it was out of the question to think of returning home on that terrifying night; there were about eight people like me, trapped by the beginning of the fighting in the School of Engineers. I sat there, recovering from all the agitating experiences, and my heart began to calm down after beating so violently. I don't know how my heart survived that run across the open ground to the School of Engineers; the bullets had begun to whistle past again, and Kolya seized me with both arms, protecting me from the bullets and helping me to run. Poor boy, he was so alarmed on my behalf, and I on his . . .

The minutes seemed like hours, and I was picturing to myself what was happening at home, where they were expecting me; and I was frightened that Vanechka would rush out to look for me and get caught up in all the shooting. And the helplessness of my situation became a torment for me . . . Later we all gradually crept out of the entrance hall into the corridor, and then towards the outer door . . . Here there stood two officers and a Cadet from the School of Artillery who had also been caught on the street, and at that point one of the officers offered to conduct anyone who wanted to go across the sappers' ground to the abattoirs in the Demievka district, which was out of the firing-line. Amongst those who wished to venture on this path were six men and two women (of whom I was one). And we set off . . . But what an eerie and fantastical journey it was, in the complete darkness, through the mist, along some sort of gullies, through almost impassable sticky mud, in single file one after the other and in complete silence, the men armed with revolvers. Near to the School of Engineers we were stopped by patrols (the officer had taken a pass), and near to one gully which we were supposed to climb down the figure of Nikolaychik with a rifle emerged from the darkness . . . He recognized me, grasped me by the shoulders and whispered right into my ear, 'Go back, this is madness! Where are you going? You'll be killed!' But I made the sign of the cross over him without saying anything and kissed him hard, the officer took my hand, and we began to climb down into the gully . . . To cut a long story short, I was home by one o'clock in the morning (the officer who had been my benefactor accompanied me right back to the house).

You can imagine how anxiously they had been waiting for me! I was so exhausted, physically and mentally, that I simply collapsed on to the nearest chair and burst into sobs. But at least I was at home, and could get undressed and lie down, whereas poor Nikolaychik, who had already not slept for two nights, endured two more terrible days and nights. But I was glad that I was with him on that terrible night. [. . .]

Now it is all over . . . Yesterday the Ukrainian Republic was solemnly proclaimed and there was a big parade. They haven't yet decided what to do about the Cadets. They have been dismissed for a month. The School of Engineers suffered less than the rest: four of them were killed and one lost his reason. They have divided into two groups – some have taken leave, while the rest have volunteered to stay behind on guard duty at the School. Kolya has joined the latter, although I would have preferred him to rest at home after all these alarms. But he is so taken up with the School; all these events have only served to absorb him all the more, and he has developed such a sense of duty. I have no more room to write . . .

Your loving Mama.

31 December 1917. From Vyazma to Moscow
To his sister Nadezhda

Dear Nadya,

I wish you a happy New Year, and with all my heart I wish that this new year should not resemble the old one. [. . .]

You haven't written to me or sent me your address, from which I have concluded that you don't wish to correspond with me. [. . .]

I am in despair that there is no news from Kiev. And I am in even greater despair about the fact that I have no means of getting my money out of the bank here in Vyazma and sending it to Mama. I have begun to develop a strong suspicion that my 2,000 roubles are going to be engulfed in the ocean of the Russian Revolution. And, oh, how useful those two thousand would have been to me! But I am not going to upset myself too much by thinking about them! . . .

At the beginning of December I travelled to Moscow to deal with my affairs, and left with no more than I had gone with. And now I am back toiling away in Vyazma, back to working in an atmosphere I detest, among people I detest. I find my surroundings so repellent that I live in complete solitude . . . But on the other hand I have plenty of scope for reflection. And I have been thinking a lot. My only consolation has been work, and reading in the evenings. I have been fondly reading authors from the past (whatever comes to hand, since there are few books here), and I have been revelling in scenes from bygone ages. Ah, why was I so late in being born! Why was I not born a hundred years ago? But that, of course, cannot be remedied! I am tormented by the longing to get out of here to Moscow or to Kiev, where, even if it is ebbing away, life nevertheless still goes on. I would particularly like to be in Kiev! In two hours' time the new year will begin. What will it bring me? I had a nap just now, and I dreamed of Kiev, of familiar and precious faces, of someone playing the piano.

On my recent journey to Moscow and Saratov I saw with my own eyes things that I hope never to see again.

I saw crowds smashing the windows of trains, and saw people being beaten. I saw ruined and burnt-out houses in Moscow . . . I saw hungry queues outside the shops, hunted and pitiful officers, and I saw news-sheets where in effect they write about only one thing: about the blood that is flowing in the south, in the west and in the east . . .

The new year is coming. I send you a big kiss.

Your brother Mikhail.

P.S. I will expect a letter.

26 November 1919
Article published by Bulgakov in the local newspaper of the
town of Grozny (in the Northern Caucasus)

Prospects for the Future

At this moment, when our unfortunate motherland finds itself at the very bottom of the pit of shame and calamity into which it has been cast by the 'Great Social Revolution', one and the same thought keeps occurring more and more frequently to many of us. It is an insistent thought; it is dark and gloomy, it arises in our minds, and compellingly it demands a reply. And it is a simple one: 'And what is going to happen to us now?'

It is natural to raise this question. We have analysed our recent past. Oh, we have studied very carefully almost every moment of the last two years. Many people have not only studied those years, but cursed them too.

The present stands before our eyes; and it is such that one would like to close one's eyes. In order not to see it! All that is left is the future. The enigmatic, unknown future. And, truly: 'What is going to happen to us?'

Recently I had occasion to look through a few copies of an English illustrated magazine. As though entranced, I could scarcely tear myself away from the wonderfully executed photographs. And afterwards I thought about them for a long, long time . . . Yes, the picture there is clear! Day in, day out, colossal machines in colossal factories are feverishly devouring coal, roaring and pounding, pouring out streams of molten metal, forging, repairing and building things . . . They are forging the might of peace, replacing those machines that only recently, sowing death and destruction, forged the might of war. In the West the Great War between great peoples is at an end. And they are now healing their wounds. And of course they will recover, they will recover in no time at all!

And anyone who has come to his senses, and who does not believe that pitiful nonsense about our malevolent disease [Communism] spreading to the West and vanquishing it, can clearly see the powerful upsurge in the titanic labours of peace which will raise the countries of the West to unprecedented heights of power in peacetime.

And we? . . . We will come too late . . . We will come so terribly late that none of our modern prophets, perhaps, will be able to say when we will finally catch the rest up, and whether we will ever do so.

For we have been punished. It is unthinkable for us to build at present. Before us still stands the painful task of conquering and regaining our own land. The time of reckoning has begun. Inch by inch, the heroic volunteers [of the White Army] will tear the Russian land from Trotsky's hands. And everyone, everyone, not just those who are dauntlessly carrying out their duty, but also those who are skulking in the towns of the south in the rear, bitterly deluded into imagining that the salvation of the country will be achieved without them, everyone is passionately awaiting the country's liberation. And the country will be liberated. For there is no such thing as a country that has no heroes, and it would be criminal to think that the motherland had died.

But there will have to be a lot of fighting and bloodshed, because for as long as madmen whose heads have been turned by Trotsky stand with weapons in their hands, pawing the ground behind his sinister figure, there will be no life, but instead a fight to the death. We have to fight.

And while the machines of reconstruction are hammering away over there in the West, from one end to the other of our homeland the hammering will be of machine-guns.

The insanity of the last two years has sent us down a dreadful road, and we will have no pause nor respite. We have begun to drink from the cup of retribution, and we will drain it to the bottom.

Over there, in the West, countless electric lights will sparkle, airmen will thrust through the air they have conquered, over there people will build things, do research, publish and study . . . And we . . . We will go on fighting. For there is no power that can change that. We are going to set out to conquer our own capital cities, and we will conquer them.

And the English, remembering how we covered the fields with the dew of blood, how we battered Germany, dragging her back from Paris, will also give us greatcoats and boots on credit, so that we can reach Moscow as quickly as possible. And we will reach Moscow. The scoundrels and the madmen will be driven out, scattered and destroyed. And the war will end.

And then the country, bloodied and ravaged, will begin to climb to its feet, slowly and heavily. And alas, those who are complaining now of 'weariness' will be disappointed, for they will have to experience even greater 'weariness' . . .

The past will have to be paid for with unbelievably hard work, and with a life of harsh poverty – paid for in the figurative and the literal sense of that word. We will have to pay for the insanity of the March days [the first 1917 Revolution], for the insanity of the October days [in 1917], for the treachery of the Ukrainian separatists, for the depraving of the workers, for Brest [the 1918 Treaty of Brest-Litovsk], for the insane use of the presses to print money . . . for everything! And we will pay.

And only when it is already much too late will we begin to create anything, in order to regain our full rights and in order to be readmitted to the halls of Versailles. And who will see those bright days? Us? Oh, no! Our children, perhaps, or perhaps our grandchildren, for the sweep of history is broad, and history 'reads' decades as easily as it does individual years. And we, the representatives of an unlucky generation, will die like pitiful bankrupts, forced to tell our children, 'You pay, pay it off honourably, and never forget the social revolution!'

1 February 1921. From Vladikavkaz to Moscow
To his cousin Konstantin

Dear Kostya,

I was overjoyed to receive your letter yesterday. At last I have news of the family. [. . .] I cannot express how happy I was and astonished that everyone is alive and well and, evidently, all together.

(Confounded ink!) The only thing I regret is that your letter was too short. I have read it over several times . . . You ask how I am getting on . . . A fine little phrase. I am precisely getting on, but not living . . .

I last saw you just about a year ago. Last spring I fell ill with recurrent typhus, and it tied me to my bed . . . I almost gave up the ghost, and then was ill again in the summer.

I remember that about a year ago I wrote to you that I had
begun to get published in newspapers. My satirical sketches
came out in many newspapers in the Caucasus. In the summer I was performing all the time on stage, telling stories
and giving lectures. Then my plays were performed. First a
one-act humoresque, *Self-Defence*, and then a very hasty four-
act drama written (the devil knows how,) *The Turbin Brothers*.
And heaven knows what I haven't done since then: I've given
lectures, and am still giving them, on the history of literature,
[. . .] I introduce stage performances and so on and so forth.
[. . .]

My life is a torment. Ah. Kostya, you cannot imagine how
I would have liked you to be here when *The Turbins* was
performed for the first time. You cannot imagine the deep
sorrow I felt that the play was being put on in the back of
beyond, and that I am four years late with what I should have
begun to do long ago – writing.

They were bawling 'Author!' in the theatre and applauding
and applauding . . . When I was called up on the stage after
the second act I came out with a troubled heart . . . I looked
unhappily at the painted faces of the actors and at the theatre in
uproar. And thought, 'But this is my dream come true . . . but in
what a distorted way: instead of the Moscow stage, a provincial
theatre, and instead of the drama about Alyosha Turbin, the
thought of which I had been cherishing, a hastily-done, immature
thing.'

Fate mocks at me. [. . .]

But I have gritted my teeth and am working day and night.
[. . .]

And so I am getting on.

I sit at a writing-desk, heaped with manuscripts . . . At night
I sometimes read over those stories of mine that have been
published (in newspapers! in newspapers!) and I think, 'Where
is the collection of stories? Where is my reputation? Where are
the wasted years?'

And stubbornly I work.

I am writing a novel, the only thing in all this time that has
been thoroughly thought out. But as usual it is my misfortune

that I am pursuing individual creativity, just when what seems to be called for nowadays in literature is something totally different.

I spend most of my life backstage at the theatre at the moment, and the actors are my close friends and acquaintances, the devil take them all!

Tasya's been working in the theatre as an extra. Just now they've disbanded the troupe, and she has no work.

I am living in a nasty room [. . .]. I was living in a good room and had a writing-desk, but now I don't have one and I have to write by the light of a kerosene lamp.

What I'm wearing, what I have to eat . . . all that's not worth writing about . . .

What next?

I shall leave Vladikavkaz in the spring or in the summer.

Where shall I go?

It's not very likely, but perhaps I will be in Moscow in the summer.

I'm hoping to travel far . . .

I shall be waiting for your reply with impatience. Write to me in detail. Where and how you are living. [. . .]

I send you a kiss,

Mikhail.

As a small sample of my glorious and extraordinary activities I enclose one of my numerous posters. As a souvenir, in case we don't meet again.

16 February 1921. From Vladikavkaz to Moscow
To his cousin Konstantin

I've ended up in Vladikavkaz in a situation where I can go neither forward nor back. My wanderings are by no means over. In the spring I shall have to go either to Moscow (perhaps very soon), or to the Black Sea, or somewhere different again . . . Let me know whether it would be possible to stay with you for a little while if I have to spend time in Moscow.

April 1921. From Vladikavkaz to Moscow
To his sister Nadezhda

In the event that I should go a long way away, and for a long time, let me ask you the following: a few of my manuscripts are still in Kiev [. . .]. I wrote to Mama and asked her to keep them. I assume that you are going to settle down in Moscow. Have the manuscripts sent to you from Kiev, gather them all together, and put them in the stove along with *Self-Defence* and *The Turbins*. I beg you most earnestly to do this. [. . .]

Burn the MSS

I send you a kiss.

Your loving Mikhail.

I am sending you some cuttings and programmes. [. . .] As a souvenir of me in case I go away and we don't see each other.

26 April 1921. From Vladikavkaz
To his sister Vera

Dear Vera,

Thank you very much for your detailed letter. [. . .]

I am very touched by your good wishes and Varya's concerning my literary work. I cannot tell you how agonizing things are for me sometimes. I think you will understand that yourselves . . .

I am sorry that I cannot send you my plays. In the first place, they are too bulky, in the second place, they've not been printed, but exist only in typed copies, and in the third place they are rubbish.

The thing is that my work is sharply divided into two parts: genuine and forced. [. . .] Ah, if only we could all see one another again sometime. I would read you something amusing. I dream of seeing the family. Do you remember how we used to laugh sometimes at number 13? [. . .]

I send you a kiss.

Your loving Mikhail.

26 April 1921. From Vladikavkaz to Moscow
To his sister Nadezhda

Dear Nadya,

A friend of mine, Olga Aristarkhovna Mishon, is going to Moscow. I have given her a letter in which I ask you to pick out the best of my things and some essential linen: the white trousers, and Tasya's stockings, and the white dress, and to give them to Mishon, who will be coming back to Vladikavkaz. [. . .] If her journey is likely to be easy, then give her more, but if not, then at least a small bundle of essentials. I am very short of underclothes.

I have been writing less lately – I am completely exhausted. [. . .] And no 'medical' conversations with Mishon; I have had no such conversations since graduating in natural sciences and taking up journalism. Impress this upon Kostya. He's inclined to astonishing liberality when it comes to *faux pas*.

I kiss you very warmly.

Mikhail.

Mid-May 1921. From Tiflis to Vladikavkaz
From Nikolay Pokrovsky (formerly a journalist in the Caucasus)

I shall be setting off in the very near future. If you have not changed your mind, come as soon as you can. I should be glad to have a travelling companion such as yourself . . . I think you will meet up with your brothers again in the very near future . . .

Late May 1921. From Vladikavkaz to Moscow
To his sister Nadezhda

Dear Nadya,

Today I am leaving for Tiflis and Batum. Tasya will remain in Vladikavkaz for the moment. I am setting off in a hurry, so this will be very short. [. . .]

If you hear nothing at all from me for more than six months, beginning from the moment when you receive this letter, throw all my manuscripts into the stove. [. . .]

In the event of Tasya's turning up in Moscow, don't fail to give her a family welcome and advice to begin with as she arranges her affairs.

Greetings to Konstantin. And to everybody. *I don't know* for how long I shall be travelling.

I kiss you, dear Nadya.

Mikhail.

2 June 1921. From Tiflis to Moscow
To his cousin Konstantin and sister Nadezhda

Dear Kostya and Nadya,

I am sending for Tasya to join me from Vladikavkaz and will leave with her for Batum as soon as she arrives and as soon as it is possible. Maybe I shall end up in the Crimea . . .

I am reworking *The Turbins* into a large drama. So throw it into the stove. [. . .]

I send a kiss to everyone. Don't be surprised at my wanderings, there's nothing to be done. There's no other way. That's fate for you! That's fate!

2

1921–1925

The Moscow in which Bulgakov settled in September 1921 was
a city exhausted by seven years of political and social turmoil.
The three years of fighting in World War I that preceded the
February and October revolutions of 1917 had already taken
a considerable toll of the country. Civil war in various forms
then meant that fighting continued until 1921 along a whole
range of fronts: against the White Tsarist forces; against nation-
alist insurrections; and against foreign intervention. Meanwhile,
other battles were also being fought, apart from the specifically
military operations conducted by the Red Army. During these
years attempts to retain alternative political groupings were
suppressed, leaving the Bolsheviks' Communist Party under
Lenin in effective dictatorial control. The Party's dictatorship
had been proclaimed in the name of the proletariat, but when
representatives of these working classes, or indeed of the soldiers
and sailors who had supported the October Revolution, began
to express doubts about the Bolsheviks' undemocratic methods,
they too had to be quashed – as, for example, in the brutal
suppression of the rebellion at the Kronstadt naval base by
Marshal Tukhachevsky in March 1921.

There was also the problem of the peasants, who soon discovered that the promises of more land and bread were translated
in reality into the forcible requisitioning of their crops for the
cities, and the forbidding of any kind of market trading that

might enable them to prosper. The peasantry responded with uprisings, and eventually by withdrawing from participation in anything much beyond subsistence farming. The cost of final victory for the Bolsheviks in 1921, then, was terrible famine and a catastrophic drop in industrial production, in a country over which they had now achieved more or less complete control, and for which they therefore carried complete responsibility. Faced with a grave crisis which threatened to sweep away all the Bolsheviks' hard-won achievements, Lenin decided to introduce what was to become known as the New Economic Policy (NEP): grain-requisitioning would cease, and as a consequence a considerable amount of private trading would have to be allowed again, not just in agriculture but also in consumer goods, although heavy industry, banking and foreign trade would remain under State control.

When Bulgakov arrived in Moscow in September 1921, NEP – which was in fact pursued for seven years, until it was replaced by the first Five-Year Plan in 1928 – was still coming into force. Numerous State-run organizations were being closed down, including the Literary Section of the Department of Culture where Bulgakov obtained his very first job in Moscow, and being replaced by private enterprises governed by market forces. In a long letter sent to his mother in November 1921 Bulgakov writes of the bleak prospects for the winter of 1921–22, which he and his wife Tasya spent struggling to subsist against difficult odds. Had they not been given the opportunity to live in a room rented to Bulgakov's brother-in-law, Nadya's husband Andrey Zemsky, they might well not have survived. Bulgakov cordially detested living with a dozen or more other people in this communal apartment at number 10 Bolshaya Sadovaya Street, where once again he was forced to confront the ignorance and the lack of culture of the Russian people at large. He was to write a number of angry satirical sketches about drunks, wife-beaters and other loutish characters in the setting of a communal apartment much like the one he inhabited.

But that winter Bulgakov was also confronted with much more urgent problems, of how he and Tasya were to eat and how they could remain adequately clothed. He no longer had the advantages of his background in Kiev, which had permitted him a relatively secure, if modest, lifestyle. In Moscow, with the return to private trading, there was a conspicuous re-emergence of the comfortable bourgeois lifestyle for some, with furs, good food, jewellery and smart cafés; and these people, whose prosperity aroused fury amongst those who thought the Revolution had done away with such social inequalities, came to be known as NEP-men. For others, however, such as Bulgakov, who had arrived in Moscow empty-handed, the struggle to survive was an all-consuming task; and he could only contemplate the smug satisfaction of the NEP-men with a distaste tinged with envy. The other marked consequence of the reintroduction of private trading was galloping inflation; in his letters Bulgakov refers to the two different currency rates in force during this period, one of them counted in tens of roubles, the other eventually in tens of millions of roubles. The letters he wrote to his relatives provide a unique record of the early days of NEP, offering not just statistics about inflation and the price of bread, for example, but also a striking impression of the feverish pace of life in Moscow.

Bulgakov's multifarious endeavours to scratch an income together took him for the most part into journalistic work. Writing for the *Trade and Industry Herald* provided some sort of security for a brief period, although the newspaper soon went bankrupt. Bulgakov picked up whatever casual work was going: he seems to have hoped for some sort of job connected with the flax industry, tried working as a compère and joined a group of actors, and through Andrey Zemsky's brother Boris he also did some work for a Scientific and Technical Committee associated with the Air Force. But all the time he was pushing ahead at night with the writing of his own works, determined to succeed in the world of literature. He considered an idea for a play, which he never actually wrote, on the subject of Tsar Nicholas II and the murder of the priest Rasputin in 1916, but for the most part he was developing his writing skills in the realm of narrative prose. After his five Vladikavkaz plays, the period from 1921 to 1925 shows Bulgakov concerned almost exclusively with this form, while the subsequent phase, from 1925 to 1929, would once again be dominated by drama.

In an important move towards establishing himself specifically as a writer of fiction rather than a current-affairs journalist, he joined the staff of two newspapers with contracts to write humorous sketches for them. The first of these contracts was with a Berlin-based publication called *On the Eve*, which was set up in 1922 by the émigré community to re-establish some contact with the Soviet Union and with the Bolshevik government. The latter welcomed the initiative, since the philosophy of the newspaper was that, whether or not one sympathized with Marxism-Leninism, the *de facto* authority of the Bolsheviks had to be recognized as the only force capable of governing the country. A number of writers who had emigrated because of the Bolshevik Revolution began to return to the USSR during these years, including the novelist Aleksey Tolstoy, whom Bulgakov later came to dislike intensely on account of his role as an apologist for Stalin. That Bulgakov still regarded the Bolsheviks with the scorn he had shown for them in his 1919 article 'Prospects for the Future' is very evident from his diaries of the early 1920s, which also suggest that he found the naïvely pro-Soviet attitudes of those associated with *On the Eve* increasingly unpalatable. Between 1922 and 1924 Bulgakov wrote about twenty-five pieces for *On the Eve*, some of them quite substantial, and some of them carrying the seeds of more extended works for the future. He also nourished hopes that the publishing section of *On the Eve* in Berlin would publish his autobiographical *Cuff-notes*, although in the end they failed to keep their promise to do so. In many of the sketches published in the newspaper, however, his principal aim was to give a light-hearted impression to his readership in Berlin and at home of the way Moscow was developing, and of the crazy atmosphere under NEP.

The other newspaper Bulgakov worked for was a very different publication altogether – *The Hooter*, which was the official organ of the Railway Workers' Union. Nevertheless, it attracted some of the most distinguished authors of the day to write comic pieces for its back page, and many of the contributors who got to know one another through working for the newspaper went on to become important figures in Moscow's literary circles during the 1920s. These writers included Isaak Babel,

Yury Olyesha, Valentin Katayev and the duo of Ilf and Petrov. Bulgakov's speciality was the concocting of absurd short letters, purportedly sent in by simple-minded readers, about the effects of the introduction of NEP or about life in the depths of the provinces. Between 1923 and 1926 Bulgakov wrote over a hundred of these miniatures. He once confessed, 'Let me just reveal a secret here: the composition of a seventy-five- or hundred-line sketch used to take, if you include time for smoking and whistling, from eighteen to twenty minutes. Then getting it typed up, if you include time for having a giggle with the typist – eight minutes. So all in all, the whole thing could be wrapped up in half an hour.' Although in later years he was to bemoan the time he had wasted at *The Hooter*, which he would rather have spent on more serious writing, many of these little vignettes are very witty, and display his characteristically sharp ear for dialogue.

By 1922, Bulgakov was beginning to consolidate his position in Moscow, and was energetically establishing himself in literary society. After he had been to listen to a lecture given by Vikenty Veresayev, the author of medical tales similar to his own stories in *A Country Doctor's Notebook*, Bulgakov went to call on him. Veresayev befriended him and did much to assist him in the early 1920s. In 1922 Bulgakov also published an announcement that he was collecting information on modern writers for a biographical dictionary; later he was listed as one of the authors for a projected collective novel. Although neither of these projects came to anything, they reflect Bulgakov's eagerness to make a name for himself. He attended the meetings of a number of literary clubs, and he was an avid reader of contemporary Russian literature. Such involvement presents a contrast to his behaviour once he had become established as a writer, when he participated as little as possible in the literary life of his contemporaries.

And all the while, Bulgakov was writing. Between 1921 and 1925, besides his journalistic sketches, he wrote several important works, including the autobiographical *Cuff-notes*, which humorously retraces his first steps in literature in Vladikavkaz and his early months in Moscow. The nineteenth-century master of the grotesque, Nikolay Gogol, who was one of the authors Bulgakov most admired, provided him with the inspiration for *Diaboliada* and *The Adventures of Chichikov*. Both are reworkings in a Soviet setting of classic Gogolian subjects, the former being concerned with the concept of the double, and the latter with Chichikov, the scoundrelly but endearing hero of Gogol's *Dead Souls*. *The Fateful Eggs* is a science-fiction nightmare in the manner of H. G. Wells, about an experiment that goes horribly wrong and unleashes monsters to ravage Russia, while *The Heart of a Dog* is a brilliant fantasy about a medical experiment to transplant the organs of a dead man into a good-tempered mongrel, which results in the creation of an appalling new proletarian man with criminal tendencies, a garbled devotion to Communism and a fondness for chasing cats. This latter tale was quite rightly read as a satire on the claims made by Marxist ideology that a new kind of man would be created by Communism, and it was deemed unsuitable for publication by the Soviet authorities for sixty-two years after it was written in 1925.

The documents in this chapter give no more than a glimpse of the endless negotiations Bulgakov entered into for the publication of his works, almost all of which ended in failure. His major achievement during his early years in Moscow was the completion of his novel *The White Guard*, referred to at earlier stages as *The Yellow Banner*. The publication of the first part of the novel at the end of December 1924, together with the publication by the Nedra publishing house in 1925 of five of Bulgakov's stories under the collective title *Diaboliada*, seemed to prove that Bulgakov had finally achieved his goal of becoming an established writer. What he could not have foreseen was that the publication of *The White Guard* would be interrupted and never completed, because of the closing down of the journal *Rossiya* by the Soviet authorities; nor could he ever have imagined that, with almost all of his finest writing still to come, these were the last publications of any significance he would see in his lifetime.

The years from 1921 to 1925 also witnessed great changes in Bulgakov's personal life. His first letters to Nadya, who was back in Kiev with Andrey Zemsky while Bulgakov and Tasya were occupying their room in Moscow, bespeak Bulgakov's comfortable relationship with his sister. He writes affectionately, and with concern for her well-being, but also with a brotherly briskness when it comes to trying to help himself and her by getting her to be his newspaper's Kiev correspondent. His letter of November 1921 to his mother suggests the closeness of their relationship also, and he must have shared her delight at the news which finally reached Kiev early in 1922 that his brother Nikolay, who had not been heard of since 1919, was safe and sound in Yugoslavia. Tragically, however, by the time news reached Kiev a couple of months later that her youngest son Ivan was also safe and living abroad, Bulgakov's mother was no longer alive. She had gone down with typhus at the end of January 1922, and died very shortly afterwards. This was an enormous blow to Bulgakov's sense of the security of his home background, and the letters he wrote to his siblings in the following year or so are filled with concern that they should maintain the harmony created by their mother, forget whatever differences have divided them, and rebuild a happy household which is to include their stepfather, Ivan Pavlovich Voskresensky – whom all the Bulgakov children evidently held in great respect and affection. The opening of *The White Guard*, with its scene of the Turbins' mother's funeral and burial alongside their long-dead father, takes on an added poignancy in the light of the knowledge that Bulgakov added this passage to the text in the course of its composition; in real life, he had been unable to get to Kiev to attend his mother's funeral.

Bulgakov's marriage was meanwhile once again suffering from the tensions that seem to have threatened it during 1919–1921. Once the most difficult first year in Moscow was past and he began to make his way in the literary world, it seems that the new sophisticated Bulgakov no longer found his wife Tatyana an adequate companion. Her own accounts of the growing gulf in their marriage suggest that she was very much left at home to run the household while he was busily earning a living – and also becoming caught up in a new circle of friends. He seems to have acquired something of a reputation as a flirt, in any case; and then, early in 1924, he met at a party a woman called Lyubov Yevgenyevna Belozerskaya (1894–1987). She had recently returned to Moscow from emigration, along with a number of other people who had fled the country after the Revolution, but who had now come back in the expectation that things had settled down. Lyubov Yevgenyevna had lived in Constantinople and Berlin, and had visited Paris, and was very vivacious and attractive.

Bulgakov, who for ever after is said to have felt he behaved very badly towards Tatyana Nikolayevna, persuaded his wife in April 1924 that they should get divorced: 'You know, it just suits me to say that I am a bachelor. But don't worry, everything's the same as before; the divorce will simply be a formality.' And indeed, for a while the couple continued to live together in Bolshaya Sadovaya Street. But during the summer of that year he arranged that they should move out of the noisy fifth-floor apartment into another, quieter apartment in the same block. Later Tatyana Nikolayevna was to realize that he had done this in order not to leave her in unpleasant surroundings; for meanwhile, it turned out, he was actively looking for somewhere to live with Lyubov Yevgenyevna. Late in November he suddenly announced that he was leaving for good, and moved in with Lyubov Yevgenyevna. Their marriage was officially registered some time later, on 30 April 1925. Tatyana Nikolayevna, who had few resources except a certain skill at hat-making, was left to fend pretty much for herself, although Bulgakov occasionally gave her some financial assistance. Apparently he felt so conscience-stricken about her that when he became gravely ill in 1940, he especially asked to see her in order to ask her forgiveness; but by that time Tatyana Nikolayevna was living in Siberia and could not be reached.

This rather more unattractive side of Bulgakov is revealed in the portions of his diaries that emerged from the KGB's archives and were published for the first time in 1989–90. What has survived is evidently not the entire text of the original: the copy made by the OGPU's typists appears to comprise a selection of those passages where Bulgakov specifically commented on political topics and current affairs. As an observer of the political scene, Bulgakov turns out to have been quite acute about the direction in which things were moving both inside Russia and in Europe: his comments, as early as 1923, on the way Europe seems to be sliding towards a division between a Communist and a Fascist camp show some prescience. Bulgakov deplores the fact that Curzon is able to humiliate the new Soviet government in 1923 by presenting them with an ultimatum concerning certain outstanding grievances; and he notes with concern the developments in the politics of the Orthodox Church, with the Patriarch Tikhon apparently capitulating to the faction known as the Living Church, which sought compromises with the Bolsheviks. Bulgakov also records with a certain malicious glee the rivalries within the Bolshevik leadership – although his prediction of the fall of Trotsky was to turn out to be a little premature. It is notable that Bulgakov, like many of his contemporaries, always tended to look upon Trotsky, the Commissar for the Red Army, as the driving force behind the Bolsheviks, rather than Lenin.

In these diaries Bulgakov is very frank, a foolishness which taught him a painful lesson when the diaries were confiscated, and which he never indulged in again; amongst other things, they contain traces of a condescension towards Jews which has caused some dismay amongst his present-day admirers. He is also candid when it comes to speaking about himself and his relationship with Lyubov Yevgenyevna, whom he describes as his 'wife' for some months before the official registration of their marriage. There is an unattractive irritation with himself that he should be so physically infatuated with her, and there is a hint of his doubts about the strength of her commitment to him, which seem to have led on occasion to his making scenes. Other memoirists have also hinted that he was capable of being very irascible. The diaries reveal, too, Bulgakov's obsessive preoccupation with his health, which may be attributable to the fact that as a doctor he knew that there was always a danger he might succumb to the same disease as his father. He describes an attack of rheumatism in his knees as well as the recurrence of a swelling behind his ear, which had to be operated on more than once before he could be reassured that it was not a malignant growth. In addition, we can trace in the pages of the diaries the indications of a nervous susceptibility which would lead in due course, when his life really became difficult, to bouts of terror at being left alone and a fear of walking alone on the street. Overall, the image of Bulgakov that emerges from his diaries is not quite that of the cultivated man of letters he was to project in later years. In the early 1920s he writes as though he were much younger than his thirty-odd years; perhaps because he is starting out on a new career, he writes with some of the brash self-consciousness of a youth showing off about his dashing lifestyle and excessive drinking. What comes through most strongly, though, is his now obsessive ambition to achieve great success as a writer.

At the beginning of 1925, the portents were good: *The White Guard* was coming out in the journal *Rossiya*, the collection *Diaboliada* was in the pipeline, and Bulgakov was about to formalize his new marriage. And it was at this point, on 3 April 1925, that he received a letter that was to mark the beginning of a new phase in his life, a cryptic invitation to him to drop in at the Moscow Arts Theatre to discuss a matter that might prove of interest. This letter (page 62), which he would later make the starting-point of his *Theatrical Novel*, was to launch his career as one of Moscow's most popular dramatists.

23 October 1921. From Moscow to Kiev
To his sister Nadezhda

My dear Nadya,

How are you? I haven't written to you until now, because I was very tired. I kept putting off writing letters. How is your health? And how is Andrey? [. . .]

The jesting tone of my letter can be explained by the desire to drown out the horror that I feel at the thought of the coming winter. Still, the Lord God will not fail me. Maybe we'll die, but maybe we won't. I have masses of work, but it doesn't mean much yet in actual fact. But maybe things will get better. I am concentrating all my energies, and am indeed achieving some tiny results.

I'll write in more detail in the next letter. I really am very tired. You run around like a dog, and live on nothing but potatoes. [. . .]

I send you and Andrey a big kiss.

Tasya too.

Your loving Mikhail.

P.S. Verses

On Bolshaya Sadovaya Street
Stands a great block of apartments.
In the block live our brothers,
The organized proletariat.
 And I was engulfed by the proletariat,
 Just like, if you'll pardon the expression, an atom.
It's a shame that certain amenities are lacking,
The w . . . r-cl . . . t doesn't work, for example.
 The hand-basin is also cracking –
 During the day it's dry, at night it overflows on to
             the floor.
We eat what we can:
Potatoes and saccharin.
The electric light is of a strange brand –
First it's flickering, then bright for no reason at all.
Just now, by the way, it's been burning for several days
              non-stop.
And the proletariat is very glad.

Through the left wall a woman's voice strikes up with
'A poor seagull . . . '
While through the right wall they're playing the bala-
laika . . .

9 November 1921. From Moscow to Kiev
To his sister Nadezhda

Dear Nadya,

I will write briefly since I am in a great hurry. Nothing,
absolutely nothing could compare with the effect produced by
your two letters of 3 November. I immediately passed on to
Boris your request about stocking up with potatoes. I had no
intention of letting Andrey be taken off the housing register;
on the contrary, I specifically stated that he lived here as well
as us.

I still retain a small shadow of hope that before deciding on
the horrors of moving back here, you will weigh up the state of
Andrey's health.

Take a careful look at him. I say this to you as a doctor.

Greetings to all. Tasya and I kiss you and Andrey.

Mikhail.

17 November 1921. From Moscow to Kiev
To his mother

Dear Mama,

How are you, how is your health? Please write as soon as you
can find a free moment. Any news from the family is a pleasure,
especially in the drudgery of my life at present.

I very much regret that in a short letter I cannot communicate
to you a detailed picture of what Moscow is like at the moment.
Briefly, I can say that a furious battle is going on for survival
and to adapt to the new conditions of life. Having arrived six
weeks ago in Moscow with just what I could carry, I have,
it seems to me, achieved the maximum that it was possible to
achieve in that time. I have a job. True, that is far from being
the most important thing. You have to know how to get paid as
well. And, can you imagine, I have achieved that as well. True,

only on a tiny scale as yet. But all the same, Taska and I are already more or less managing to eat this month, we've stocked up with potatoes, she's got her shoes mended, we've begun to buy firewood, and so on.

You have to work not just normally, but frenetically. From morning to night every day without a break. All Soviet institutions are being turned inside out and people are getting the chop. My organization is also to be axed, and is evidently living out its last days. So that very soon I will be without a job. But these are trifles. I have already undertaken steps so as not to be left behind and to move across to private-sector work in good time. You have probably already heard that it's possible to survive in Moscow only through private enterprise or through trading. And my, so to speak, government post was worthwhile only inasmuch as I was able to be paid about one million for it last month. In government jobs they pay you stingily and in arrears, which is why it is impossible to go on living just with one such job any more.

I am making attempts to get work in the flax industry. Apart from that, yesterday I received an invitation on conditions that have as yet to be clarified to join a new industrial newspaper. It's a real commercial enterprise, and they're trying me out. Yesterday and today I was, so to speak, being tested. Tomorrow they should let me have an advance of half a million. That will mean that they like my work, and it's possible that they will then let me take charge of their news items. And so, the flax, the industrial newspaper and whatever freelance work turns up, that's what lies ahead. The course I marked out while I was in Kiev for finding work and pursuing my speciality [as a writer] turns out to have been the right one. It would be impossible to work with any other speciality. At best it would mean going hungry.

The end of November and December will be difficult, at the moment when I move over to private enterprise. But I am counting on the enormous number of my acquaintances, and now quite justifiably on the energy that I have had willy-nilly to display. I have a huge number of acquaintances in journalism, in the theatre and simply in business. That means a great deal in present-day Moscow, which is making the transition to a new kind of life such as it has not witnessed for a long time: savage competition, bustle, the need to show initiative and so on. It is impossible to live outside that life, you would simply perish. I have no wish to be among the number of those who perish.

Taska is looking for a job as a sales assistant, which is very difficult since the whole of Moscow is still naked and barefoot and is trading ephemerally; for the most part they're using their own strengths and resources, and employing just their own people. Poor Taska is having to exert all her strength to grind rye using an axe-head, and to prepare meals out of all sorts of rubbish. But she's doing very well! In other words we're both engaged in a desperate struggle. The most important thing is to have a roof over our heads. Andrey's room has been my salvation. With Nadya's arrival, that question will become ominously complicated, of course. But I am not thinking about that as yet, because my day is already full of heavy cares as it is.

In Moscow they count only in hundreds of thousands or in millions. Black bread is 4,600 roubles a pound, white is 14,000. And the prices are rising and rising! The shops are full of goods, but what can you buy! The theatres are full, but yesterday as I was passing by the Bolshoy on business (I can no longer imagine how it would be possible to go anywhere not on business!) the touts were selling tickets for 75, 100 and 150 thousand roubles! In Moscow there is everything: shoes, cloth, meat, caviare, preserves, delicacies, everything! Cafés are opening, they're sprouting like mushrooms. And everywhere hundreds of thousands of roubles, hundreds! Hundreds!! There is the buzzing of a wave of speculation.

I dream of just one thing: of surviving the winter, of not succumbing in December, which will be the hardest month, I reckon. Taska's support is invaluable to me: given the enormous distances that I have to run around (literally) over the whole of Moscow, she saves me a great deal of energy and strength by feeding me and leaving for me to do only those things that she can really not do herself: chopping wood in the evening and fetching potatoes in the morning.

We both go around Moscow in our light coats. For that reason I somehow walk about sideways on (I don't know why, my left side feels the draught more). I dream of getting Tatyana warm footwear. She hasn't got a thing except her shoes.

But maybe we'll survive! Just so long as we have a room and health!

I don't know whether you are interested to have such a detailed description of Moscow, and whether it is sufficiently comprehensible to you in Kiev?

I am writing all this with the aim of showing you in what conditions I have had to realize my *idée fixe*. And that consists in re-establishing the norm within three years – an apartment, clothes, food and books. Whether I will succeed remains to be seen.

I won't tell you, because you won't believe it, how thrifty Taska and I have become. We cherish each and every log.

Such is the school of life.

At night I am writing *The Notes of a Country Doctor* [*A Country Doctor's Notebook*] in snatches. It may be that something solid will come out of it. I am also working over *The Ailment* [the story *Morphine*]. But there's no time, no time! *That's what I find painful!*

For Nadya

A request: please tell Nadya (I don't have the strength to write to her separately, I'm falling asleep!) that I need all the material for a historical drama – everything concerning Nicholas II and Rasputin in 1916 and 1917 (the murder and the seizure of power). Newspapers, a description of the palace, memoirs, and *above all Purishkevich's* Diary – *that's crucial!* A description of their clothes, portraits, memoirs etc. She'll understand!

I cherish the idea of creating a grandiose drama in five acts by the end of 1922. I have a few sketches and plans already. The thought is terribly alluring. [. . .]

Of course with this all-consuming work, I will never be able to write anything sensible, but at least the dream and the work on it are precious. If the *Diary* comes into her hands just briefly, then I would ask her *immediately* and straight away to copy out word for word everything concerning the murder and the gramophone, the conspiracy between Felix and Purishkevich, Purishkevich's reports to Nicholas, the personality of Nikolay Mikhaylovich, and to send it to me in letters (I suppose that's all right? If she marks it 'Material for a drama'?). Maybe it's awkward of me to ask her to take on such a burden, but she will understand. The Rumyantsev Library doesn't have sets of newspapers for 1917!! I'd be very grateful. [. . .]

I send you a big kiss, dear Mama.

Tasya too. We send kisses to everybody.

Mikhail.

P.S. My most agreeable memory in recent days has been – can you guess?

How I slept on the divan in your room and drank tea with French rolls. I would give a great deal to spend even two days just lying down like that, drinking my fill of tea and not thinking about anything. I'm so dreadfully tired.

I send a big kiss to Ivan Pavlovich.

To Kostya: it's time he wrote me a letter!

1 December 1921. From Moscow to Kiev
To his sister Nadezhda

My dear Nadya,

Why don't you write?! At one time I was subjected to an onslaught by the crew from our dear house committee. 'But Andrey Mikhaylovich [Zemsky] isn't here 365 days in the year. He should be taken off the register. And we don't know where you've sprung from either . . . ' etc. etc.

Without in any way declaring war I exercised diplomatic tolerance, putting up with their insolent and familiar tones as much as was appropriate. [. . .] They've evidently left off for the moment. I insisted that Andrey should not be taken off the register. So for the moment all is as it was. [. . .]

I am in charge of news items for the *Trade and Industry Herald*, and if I go crazy, that will be the reason. Can you imagine what is involved in publishing a private newspaper?! [. . .] I am going completely mad. And the printing-paper!! And what if we don't get enough advertising? And the news items!! And the censorship!!! I spend the whole day on hot coals. [. . .]

Don't be surprised by the wild untidiness of this letter. It's not on purpose, but because I am literally tired to death. I've given it all up as a bad job. I can't even think about any writing. I am happy only when Taska treats me to some hot tea. She and I are eating immeasurably better than at the beginning. I wanted to write you a long letter with a description of Moscow, but this is what came out . . .

I send you a kiss.

Mikhail.

Kiss Andrey for me.

Please give Kostya the enclosed letter.

15 December 1921. From Moscow to Kiev
To his sister Nadezhda

Dear Nadya,

This deathly silence from Kiev is beginning to worry me. Why don't you write?

I am overwhelmed with work at the *Herald*. Taska and I are now eating perfectly reasonably. If the *Herald* keeps flourishing, then I hope that we shall survive. I earn three million a month. It's just miserable that it doesn't come with guaranteed rations.

I'll write briefly (it's half-past two in the morning). Would you write and report to me the prices in the Kiev market (white flour and rye flour by the pood [a measure of about 36 lb.], bread by the pound, butter by the pound, sunflower oil, meat by the pound (different kinds?), pork, milk (by the jug or some other measure), lump sugar and granulated by the pound and so on). And check the source. Indicate what date the prices relate to. So, for example: the market prices in Kiev on such-and-such a date: meat (lb.) etc. [. . .]

If you don't want to take this on, maybe Andrey would? I'll be waiting for an answer.

Why don't you write? I send you a kiss.

Mikhail.

30 December 1921. From Moscow to Kiev
To his sister Nadezhda

Dear Nadya,

Please write and tell me what is going on. I haven't heard a whisper from you. The editorial board of the *Herald* has sent you an invitation to become their correspondent. Send in reports a couple of times a week on the prices in the market. [. . .] Maybe you could look for a representative who would sell the *Herald* in Kiev? If you succeed, let me know.

I wish you all a happy New Year.

Mikhail.

10 January 1922. From Moscow to Kiev
To his sister Nadezhda

Dear Nadya,

Today I received your letter of 1 Jan. with a note dated 2 Jan. You shouldn't even need to ask about the cost of the newspapers and of sending them! Send them immediately. It goes without saying that the moment the first batch of them arrives we will transfer an advance to you (and will continue to cover the costs!). [. . .]

I do understand that you need money, but there was nothing I could do about getting any sent until I'd had a reply from you!! I'll put the pressure on now.

I'm in a hurry. I kiss you and Andrey.

Your Mikhail. [. . .]

P.S. Could you possibly let me know straight away what newspapers are being published in Kiev (are there any private ones?). In my next letter I'll send you a sketch, 'Moscow's Doing Business'. Maybe you could get it taken somewhere? It might be interesting for Kiev now that we have the New Economic Policy.

13 January 1922. From Moscow to Kiev
To his sister Nadezhda

Dear Nadya,

Today the *Herald* received your report of the prices in the market for 31 December, and I immediately insisted that the editor should get 50 thousand transferred to you. That's been done. And at the same time as your report came in a terrible blow fell, the significance of which you will instantly appreciate, and which I am writing to you about in confidence. The editor has told me that under the pressure of external circumstances the *Herald* is going bust. The ed. says there is still some hope, but I know for certain that it won't survive the seventh issue. Finita! [. . .]

You will appreciate how I must feel today as I disappear up the chimney together with the *Herald*.

Crushed, in a word.

Otherwise I would describe to you how all night long on Christmas Eve and through Christmas Day water poured through the ceiling of my room.

I send kisses to everyone.

Mikhail.

From Bulgakov's diary
25 January 1922

I've been neglecting my diary, which is a pity, since a lot of interesting things have been happening. [. . .] I am still without a job. My wife and I are eating very badly, which is why I don't feel like writing. Black bread costs 20 thousand a pound.

26 January 1922

I have joined an itinerant group of actors; we're going to perform in the suburbs. They pay 125 a performance, which is appallingly little. And of course there will be no time to write because of these performances. It's a vicious circle. My wife and I are half-starving.

2 February 1922. From Kiev to Moscow
From his sister Nadezhda (telegram)

Mama has passed away. Nadya.

From Bulgakov's diary
9 February 1922

This is the blackest period of my life. My wife and I are starving. I have had to accept a little flour, vegetable oil and some potatoes from my uncle. [. . .] I have run all over Moscow, but there are no jobs. My felt boots have fallen apart.

15 February 1922

Veresayev is very ugly, and he looks like a middle-aged Jew (he's very well preserved). He has very narrow eyes with heavy, drooping eyelids, and he's bald. He has a low voice. I liked him very much. [. . .] Veresayev is close to the students, who insist that the burning issues of the day should be addressed, and demand truthful solutions. He doesn't say much, but when he does, it comes out in a clever and cultured fashion.

24 March 1922. From Moscow to Kiev
To his sister Nadezhda

My dear Nadya,

[. . .] I cannot tell you how much I was cheered by the news of Vanya's health. [. . .]

Apart from the Scientific and Technical Committee I am working for a new big newspaper (an official one). With the two jobs I earn only 197 roubles a month (40 million according to the People's Commissariat of Finance rate), i.e. half of what Tasya and I need to live on (if you can call my existence over the last two years living). She, of course, isn't working, but does the cooking on a small iron stove. [. . .]

I won't begin to describe life in Moscow. It is so much like something from a fairy-tale that it would take eight extra pages to tell you about it. Otherwise it would be impossible for you to understand. And then I don't know whether you are interested? Anyway, I will mention two or three details, plucking them out at random.

The most characteristic things that have struck me are that 1) a man who is not properly clothed is lost; 2) the number of trams is increasing while, according to the rumours, shops and theatres (except for 'grotesque' shows) are closing down and private publishing houses are going bust. It is impossible to tell you about prices, since the currency is falling at a dizzying rate, and sometimes prices have changed from one morning to the same evening. For example, in the morning vegetable oil costs 600, and by the evening it's 650. Today I bought myself a pair of yellow English boots in the market for four and a quarter million. I was in a terrible hurry to get them, since they will cost 10 within a week.★

Everything else, as I've said, is indescribable. The housing problem is extraordinary. It's fortunate for me that that fifth-floor nightmare where I have struggled to live over the last half-year is cheap (about 700 thousand). [. . .]

They turned the heating off a week ago.

I am literally overwhelmed with work. I don't have time to write or to study French properly. I am putting together a library for myself (the second-hand booksellers, ignorant and impudent bastards, are more expensive than the shops). [. . .]

Please write. I send you a kiss.

Mikhail.

★ Just now, as I was about to seal the letter, I discovered that the boots are not English but American, and that the soles are made of cardboard. My God, I am so fed up with all this!

24 March 1922. From Moscow
To his sister Vera

Dear Vera,

On many occasions I have tried to sit down and write to you but, can you believe, I am so tired after all my drudgery that sometimes in the evenings I don't have the strength to squeeze a line out of myself. Last autumn I received a letter from you and replied to it straight away. Evidently it didn't reach you. The young man who came here (he saw only Tasya and didn't find me in) said that you were cross with me for being silent. Now I want to pick up my correspondence with the family again, and I hope you will write to me.

First of all: did you receive the news of Mama's death? (She died of typhus on 1 February 1922.) Varya sent you a telegram from Kiev. [. . .]

The most dreadful problem in Moscow is that of housing. I am living in the room Andrey Zemsky left behind. The room is terrible, the neighbours too. 10 Bolshaya Sadovaya Street,

Flat # 50

Flat 50. I don't feel secure there, and it was an awful lot of bother to get it. I won't write about the prices in Moscow, they're unbelievable. [. . .] I have a great many acquaintances in Moscow in the worlds of journalism and the theatre, but I don't see people very frequently since I am consumed by my work and dash about Moscow purely and simply on journalistic business. [. . .]

I'm very anxious to know how you are living. You're not going hungry?

Everyone has gathered at Ivan Pavlovich's (Lyolya, Kostya, Varya and Lena), and Andrey and Nadya are at Vasily Pavlovich's.

I miss the family.

Vanya and Kolya are well, so I am told.

I will expect a letter from you describing your life and your plans.

I send you a kiss.

Your Mikhail.

18 April 1922. From Moscow to Kiev
To his sister Nadezhda

Dear Nadya,

I am sorry that I didn't have time to send you greetings for Easter. My life is such drudgery that I literally don't have a minute. I just had two days to catch my breath over the holiday. And now my nightmare has begun again. [. . .]

The rent is going up. One and a half million for April. The heating was turned off in March. All the book-bindings are covered in mould. [. . .]

I am making efforts to find a room. But it's hopeless. They demand enormous sums just for telling you where to find one. [. . .]

Prices. There's no point in telling you: they change by hundreds of thousands each day. Before the holiday white flour cost 18 million a pood. White bread was 375 thousand a pound, and butter was one million 200 thousand a pound. [. . .]

I send you a kiss.

Mikhail.

45

6 October 1922. Moscow
To fellow-writers

M. A. Bulgakov is working on the compilation of a complete bibliographical dictionary of modern Russian writers, with their literary profiles. The comprehensiveness of the dictionary will depend to a significant degree on the extent to which authors themselves will respond and provide lively and useful information about themselves. The author requests all Russian writers in all the towns of Russia and abroad to send autobiographical material to the following address: Moscow, 10 Bolshaya Sadovaya Street, Flat 50.

29 December 1922. Moscow
From Ye. Krichevskaya (editor of *On the Eve*)

P. Sadyker has been to see me and told me that he saw you and Katayev, and that he came to an agreement with you about a permanent post which would provide you with a regular income. I could only welcome such a decision.

23 January 1923. From Moscow to Kiev
To his sister Vera

Dear Vera,

Thank you all for your telegram and greetings. I was very delighted to hear that you were in Kiev. Unfortunately it wasn't possible to tell from the telegram whether you had come back for good or just for a time. My dream is that all our family should settle down at long last in secure nests in Moscow and in Kiev.

I feel that you and Lyolya, together and amicably, should be able to make lives for yourselves in the same spot where Mama did. I may be wrong, but it seems to me that it would be better for Ivan Pavlovich too if someone were to remain with him from the family which is so closely linked and so indebted to him. I keep thinking sadly about Kolya and Vanya, and about the fact that none of us now has any means of helping them. I think of Mama's death with great sorrow, and of the fact that it means that there is now no one left in Kiev with Ivan Pavlovich. My only wish is that your coming should not bring discord into the

46

family but, on the contrary, should bind the Kievans even more closely together. That's why I was so delighted when I read the words 'loving family'. That's the most important thing for all of us. Truly, only one spark of goodwill, and you would all settle down wonderfully together. I can judge by myself: after all the difficult trials of these last years I prize peace and quiet above all! I would so like to be amongst my family. But there's nothing to be done about that. Here in Moscow, in conditions that are immeasurably more difficult than where you are, I am determined to get my life running normally.

And that means that my hopes for Kiev rest with you, Varya and Lyolya. I have talked about it a lot with Lyolya. All that we have gone through has had an effect on her as on everyone else, and like me she wants there to be peace and harmony in Kiev.

My great plea to you is that you should live on amicable terms with one another in memory of Mama.

I am working very hard and am dropping with exhaustion. I may succeed in making a brief visit to Kiev in the spring, and I will hope to find you there and to see Ivan Pavlovich. If you do settle down in Kiev, consult with Ivan Pavlovich and Varvara to see whether it's not possible to do something to preserve Mama's plot of land at Bucha. I would be dreadfully sorry if it went.

Please give Ivan Pavlovich warmest greetings from me and Tasya.

Your brother Mikhail.

21 February 1923. From Berlin to Moscow
From P. Sadyker (at *On the Eve*)

Much respected Mikhail Vasilyevich [sic],

Now that we have published our first books, it is becoming possible for us to publish new books rapidly. During my stay in Moscow you offered me your *Cuff-notes* for publication, but at the time I was unable to take any decision since I did not know how our publishing house was placed. I would now like to ask you to offer us publication rights. Unfortunately, we cannot offer Moscow royalties. The maximum that we can pay is seven to eight dollars per printer's sheet.

Spring 1923. Moscow
To his sister Nadezhda

Dear Nadya,

Big kisses to you, Andrey and the infant. Thank you for the pie. I am very sorry that you didn't come. I would have treated you to a rum baba. I'm really in a ghastly state, I'm ill and everyone has abandoned me. I haven't shown myself because I am urgently finishing off the first part of a novel; it's called *The Yellow Banner* [*The White Guard*]. And soon I will come and see you. [. . .]

Your Mikhail.

From Bulgakov's diary
24 May 1923

It's a long time since I have sat down to my diary. On 21 April I left Moscow for Kiev and stayed there until 10 May. I had an operation in Kiev on a swelling behind my left ear. I didn't manage to get to the Caucasus as I had intended. I got back to Moscow on 12 May. [. . .]

Altogether we seem to be on the eve of great events. Today there were rumours in the papers that English naval ships were to be dispatched to the White Sea and the Black Sea, and there was news that Curzon refuses to hear of any compromises and has demanded that Krasin (who dashed off to London in an aeroplane straight after the ultimatum) should carry out the terms of the ultimatum to the letter.

Life in Moscow is bustling, especially in comparison with Kiev. This manifests itself principally in the fact that a sea of beer is being drunk in Moscow. And I am drinking a lot of it too. Altogether I've begun to let myself go recently. Count Aleksey Tolstoy has arrived from Berlin, and is leading a dissolute life and behaving rather impudently. He drinks a lot.

I've become quite unsettled, and I haven't written anything for six weeks.

11 July 1923

The longest gap in my diary. And what has been happening meanwhile has been of enormous importance. That sensational

48

conflict with England ended quietly, peacefully and shame-
fully. The Government made the most humiliating concessions.
[. . .]

The day before yesterday on walls and fences there appeared
an appeal from the Patriarch, beginning with the words 'We, by
the grace of God, Patriarch of Moscow and of all Russia . . . '.
Its message: that he is a friend to Soviet power, condemns the
White Guard, but also condemns the Living Church. There will
be no reforms in the Church except for a new orthography and
style. There's an unbelievable row going on now in the Church;
the Living Church is furious, because they wanted to get rid of
Patriarch Tikhon altogether. [. . .]

It's a horrid, cold and rainy summer.

White bread costs 14 million a pound.

25 July 1923

As before, life is chaotic, rushed and nightmarish. Unfortunately I am spending a lot of money on drink. [. . .] Because
of my work for *The Hooter*, which takes up the best part of the
day, I have scarcely made any progress on my novel.

Moscow is extremely lively, and there is more and more traffic.

27 August 1923

I sat next to Katayev. [Aleksey] Tolstoy was speaking about
literature, and mentioned me and Katayev as contemporary
writers. My book [*Cuff-notes*] has still not come.

28 August 1923. From Krolevets to Moscow
From the writer Yury Slyozkin

Dear Mikhail,

I am writing to you from the blissfully run-down little town of
Krolevets, where I have come from Chernigov to spend the rest
of the summer. This is authentic countryside, with innumerable
orchards, vegetable gardens, ravines, dusty hawthorn trees and
delightful little houses painted in bright colours. I am in a state of
bliss here: in the mornings I write, then I sunbathe, go for strolls,
read and eat until I'm bursting. Everything is cheap and of good
quality, and tasty; I was already collapsing under all the berries,
and now I'm guzzling apples – all different kinds, colours and
flavours. And they cost two roubles 50 kopeks for ten! I'm not

even missing Moscow, although it's high time . . .

I'll probably stir myself at the beginning of the month. What's happening at *On the Eve*? [. . .] Any news of our Berlin books? When are they finally going to come out? And what's new in literature, anyway?

In Chernigov and in Krolevets I gave lectures about Moscow, in which I mentioned you and Katayev as the most talented of the young writers working for *On the Eve*.

And what of your novel? I have high hopes of it. Have you finished *Diaboliada*? I'm looking forward to hearing it when I get back. [. . .]

I kiss Tanyusha's little hands; tell her – in fact I'll tell her myself – what's in my heart . . . there is no need of witnesses.

I send you a kiss.

Your Yury Slyozkin.

31 August 1923. From Moscow to Krolevets
To the writer Yury Slyozkin

Dear Yury,

I am hurrying to reply to you so that the letter will find you still in Krolevets. I am envious of you. In Moscow I've become completely worn out. [. . .]

The publication of our books is causing me considerable irritation; they still haven't appeared. Finally Potekhin told me that he was expecting them any day now. According to rumours they are ready. (The first to come out will be yours and mine.) It'll be interesting to see whether they do let them come out. I am extremely concerned about mine. It didn't occur to them, of course, to send me any proofs.

I've finished *Diaboliada*, but it's scarcely likely to get through anywhere. Lezhnev [at *Rossiya*] has refused to take it.

I've finished the novel, but it hasn't been typed yet, it's lying in a big heap while I have a good think about it. Here and there I am making corrections. [. . .]

I don't think there will be time for me to send our books to you in Krolevets. Probably by the time I get hold of them you will already be in Moscow.

It's difficult to tell you much that's new in a short letter. In any case, things are clearly livening up, rather than declining, in the world of literature and publishing.

Come back soon! There are lots of interesting things to talk about.

Tanya sends greetings to you and Lina. And I send Lina a separate supergreeting.

They're drinking an inordinate quantity of beer in Moscow at the moment.

I send you a kiss.

Your M. Bulgakov.

From Bulgakov's diary
2 September 1923

Today Katayev and I visited Aleksey Tolstoy at his dacha. He was very friendly today. The only thing I don't like is the incorrigible manner he and his wife have of talking to young writers in an offhand way. But his truly considerable talent makes up for everything else. [. . .]

In the midst of my spleen and my yearning for the past, and despite these ridiculous cramped circumstances I find myself in, in this vile room in this foul apartment-block, I sometimes experience, as at this moment, bursts of confidence and strength. And I become aware of the thought darting up in me that it is true, I am immeasurably more powerful a writer than any of those I know. But in conditions such as the ones I have presently to endure I may have to kowtow to them.

3 September 1923

After the terrible summer some wonderful weather has set in. For several days now there has been bright sunshine and it has been warm. Each day I go off to work at this *Hooter* of mine, and waste the day there absolutely irretrievably.

Life has worked out in such a way that I have little money but I am living, as always, beyond my modest means. You eat and drink well and plentifully, but then there's no money to buy anything else. I can't get through a single day without that damned pigswill – beer.

18 September 1923

I'm not feeling well today. I am short of money. The other day

I received news of Kolya [his brother Nikolay] – a letter from him; he is ill with anaemia and feels depressed and miserable. I wrote to *On the Eve* in Berlin to get them to send him 50 francs. I hope those swine will do it. [. . .]

Until I have my own apartment I will not be a human being, but half of one.

30 September (17 September according to the old [pre-Revolutionary] calendar) 1923

Probably because I am a conservative . . . 'to the core', I was going to write, but that's a cliché: well, in a word, a conservative . . . I am always drawn to my diary on the old saints' days. What a pity that I no longer remember the precise date in September when I arrived in Moscow two years ago. Two years. Has much changed in that time? Of course, a great deal has. But all the same, this anniversary finds me in the same room, and just the same person inside.

Apart from anything else, I am unwell . . .

First, politics, which are just as vile and unnatural as ever. There's still a lot of unrest in Germany. The mark, however, has begun to go up again, [. . .] but there is an internecine struggle going on in Bulgaria. They're fighting the Communists! [. . .] As far as I am concerned there is not the slightest doubt that these minor Slav states are just as backward as Russia, and so represent a splendid breeding-ground for Communism. Our newspapers are blowing events up in every possible way, although who knows, maybe the world really is splitting into two parts – Communism and Fascism.

No one knows what will happen. [. . .]

If I discount the real and imaginary fears in my life, then I must admit that there is only one major flaw in my life at the moment – the lack of an apartment.

As a literary figure I am making my way slowly, but I am making progress, of that I am convinced. The only problem is that I can never be clear and confident that I really have written something well.

5 October 1923

In Germany, instead of the expected Communist revolution, they have ended up with overt and sweeping Fascism.

18 October 1923

Today I went to see the doctor to get advice about the pains in my leg. He made me very miserable by saying that he'd found I was really in a bad way. I will have to take my treatment seriously. The really dreadful thing is that I am afraid to take to my bed, since I am being undermined in the delightful organ [*The Hooter*] for which I work, and they might show me the door without any pity. [. . .] A French roll costs 17 million, while a pound of white bread costs 65 million. Ten eggs yesterday cost 200. [. . .]

I haven't heard a word about *Cuff-notes*. That's evidently the end of that.

19 October 1923

I am waiting for a reply from Nedra about *Diaboliada*.

On the whole, I have enough for food and trifles, but there's nothing for clothes. And if it weren't for being ill, I would face the future fearlessly. So let's trust in God and live, that's the best way, and the only way.

26 October 1923

I am unwell, and that's unpleasant, because I may be forced to take to my bed. [. . .] On my way back from *The Hooter* I dropped in at Nedra to see P. N. Zaytsev. They are going to take my story *Diaboliada*, but they won't give more than 50 roubles a printer's sheet. And there'll be no money at all before next week. It's an idiotic story, not fit for anything. But Veresayev (who is one of the editors at Nedra) liked it very much.

In moments of ill-health and loneliness I succumb to melancholy and envious thoughts. I bitterly regret that I abandoned medicine and condemned myself to an uncertain existence. But God is my witness that my love of literature was the only reason for doing it.

Literature is a difficult business at present. For me, with my opinions, [. . .] it is difficult to get published and just to live. Given all that, my ill-health has come at a bad time as well.

But I mustn't be dejected. I've just been looking through *The Last of the Mohicans*, which I recently purchased for my library. What fascination there is in sentimental old Fenimore Cooper. His David, who is constantly singing snatches of the Psalms, was the one who turned my thoughts towards God.

Maybe He's not needed by the bold and the brave, but for such as myself it is easier to live with the thought of Him. My illness is a complex and a lingering one, and I am completely run down. It could hinder me from working, which is why I fear it; and that's why I place my hopes in God. [. . .]

We are a barbaric and unhappy people. [. . .]

My premonitions with regard to people never let me down. Never. A crowd of exceptional swine has begun to group itself around *On the Eve*. And I can congratulate myself on being one of their number. Oh, I shall have a very hard time of it later on, when it comes to scraping the accumulated mud off my name. But there is one thing I can say to myself with a clear conscience. Iron necessity forced me to publish my things with them. If it hadn't been for *On the Eve*, then neither *Cuff-notes*, nor much else in which I have been able to express at least something truthful in literature, would have seen the light of day. You would have to be an exceptional hero to keep total silence for four years, to keep silent with no hope that you will ever be able to open your mouth in the future. I, unfortunately, am not a hero. [. . .]

There is no letter from Kolya. I have neglected my correspondence with Kiev irretrievably.

27 October 1923

I've just been looking [. . .] at a suite of boudoir furniture, which is going for a very low price – 60 roubles. Tasya and I decided to buy it, if they are prepared to defer payment until next week. This will be clarified tomorrow, although I'm taking a risk; they should pay me for *Diaboliada* at Nedra next week.

Late October 1923. Moscow
To his sister Nadya

Dear Nadya,

I have sold a story, *Diaboliada*, to the Nedra publishing house, and the doctors have found that both my knee-joints are affected; furthermore, I have bought a suite of furniture covered in silk which is quite decent. It's already standing in my room.

What will happen now I don't know; my illness (rheumatism) is depressing me very much. But if I don't snuff it like a dog – I'd very much like not to die just now – then I'm going to buy a carpet. [. . .]

I send a kiss to little Chizhka.

Your deceased brother Mikhail.

From Bulgakov's diary
29 October 1923

The heating went on for the first time today. I spent the entire evening sealing the windows. This first day of heating was marked by the fact that the notorious Annushka left the kitchen window wide open all night. I positively don't know what to do with the swine who inhabit this [communal] apartment. Because of my illness my nerves have really gone to pieces, and these sorts of things drive me to distraction.

6 November 1923

I am reading Gorky's masterly work *My Universities*. I have been thinking a great deal, and one way and another have come to recognize that I must stop playing around. What's more, literature has become my life. I am never going to go back to any form of medicine now. I don't much like Gorky as a person, but what a giant, what a powerful writer he is, and what awesome and important things he has to say about the writer. [. . .] I am frightened by the fact that I am thirty-two, by the years I have squandered on medicine, by my illness and weakness. I have this idiotic swelling behind my ear, which has already been operated on twice. [. . .]

I am going to study from now on. I can't believe that the voice that keeps troubling me at the moment is anything but prophetic. It must be. There is nothing else for me to be. I can be only one thing – a writer. I must observe, and I must study, and keep my own counsel.

8 January 1924

In the newspapers today there is a bulletin about the health of L. D. Trotsky. It begins with the words 'L. D. Trotsky became ill on 5 November last year . . . ' and ends ' . . . leave, and is

relieved of all his duties for a period of not less than two months.'
I need make no comment on this historic bulletin.

And so, on 8 January 1924, Trotsky was given the push. God
alone knows what will happen to Russia. God help her!

22 January 1924

Just now (at 5.30 in the evening) Syomka told me that Lenin
has died. According to him, there was an official announcement
about it.

25 February 1924

This evening I received from Pyotr Nikanorovich [Zaytsev]
a brand-new copy of the Nedra almanac. In it is my story
Diaboliada. [. . .] And so, for the first time, I have been
published not in the pages of newspapers or in slender journals,
but in a book, an almanac. Yes . . . And how much torment it
has cost me!

15 April 1924

In Moscow there have been numerous arrests of people with
'distinguished family names'. And again sentences of internal
exile. David Kiselgof [later Tasya's second husband] was here
today. As usual he was full of fantastic rumours. He says that
a manifesto from [the Grand Duke] Nikolay Nikolayevich is
supposedly going around in Moscow. The devil take all the
Romanovs! They're the last thing we need now!

25 May 1924. Moscow
To Pyotr Zaytsev (at the Nedra publishing house)

Dear Pyotr Nikanorovich,

I am leaving *Cuff-notes* for you, and beg you most earnestly
to decide its fate as quickly as possible. [. . .]

I would be very glad if you did take *Cuff-notes*. Personally I
am very fond of it.

It would be a very good thing if Nikolay Semyonovich
[Angarsky] were to invite people to a reading *soon*. I would
read it myself, and its fate would be decided at once.

For myself I wish nothing, except death. That's the parlous
state my affairs are in!

Your M. Bulgakov.

P.S. I will telephone you and drop in today and tomorrow.

31 May 1924. Moscow
To Pyotr Zaytsev (at the Nedra publishing house)
Dear Pyotr Nikanorovich,

As always, it never rains but it pours: I'm in bed with appendicitis. [. . .] I won't take up the offer of a job, but as soon as I have the money I'm going to leave for the south.

Can you tell me what's happening about my *Cuff-notes*?

Your M. Bulgakov.

From Bulgakov's diary
21 July 1924

This evening, as usual, I was at Lyubov Yevgenyevna's [she was soon to become Bulgakov's second wife]; I went away into the rain feeling sad and somehow homeless.

Ilf and Yury Olyesha have just arrived from Samara. There are two trams in Samara. On one of them it says 'Revolution Square – Prison', and on the other it says 'Square of the Soviets – Prison'. Something like that. In other words, all roads lead to Rome! [. . .]

Anyway, it is interesting chatting to Olyesha; he is sarcastic and witty.

25 July 1924

During the day I telephoned Lezhnev [at *Rossiya*] and discovered that there was no point at this stage in negotiating with Kagansky about publishing *The White Guard* as a separate volume, since he has no money at present. This is a new shock. [. . .] I am sure that I shall end up with *The White Guard* on my hands. In other words, the devil knows what's going on. Late, at around twelve, I went to see Lyubov Yevgenyevna.

6 August 1924

It will be interesting to see how long the 'Union of Socialist Republics' can survive in these circumstances [after the collapse of Anglo-Soviet negotiations].

9 August 1924

They've introduced buses in Moscow. [. . .] For the moment there are just a few of them. They're very attractive, massive but elegant at the same time; they're painted brown, and the window-frames (they have glassed-in windows) are yellow. They have just one deck, but they're enormous.

26 August 1924

I went to Professor Martynov's clinic about the foul swelling behind my ear. He says he doesn't believe it is malignant, and said I should have some X-rays.

26 September 1924

I've just come back from the Bolshoy Theatre; Lyubov Yevgenyevna and I went to *Aida*. [. . .] All day long I've been trying to get money for a room with Lyubov Yevgenyevna.

18 October 1924

I'm having considerable difficulties with my grotesque story [*The Fateful Eggs*]. Angarsky [from Nedra] has [identified] about twenty passages that will have to be changed because of censorship considerations. I wonder whether it will get through the censors?

20–21 December 1924

The hopes of the White émigrés and the counter-revolutionaries inside the country that the disputes over Trotskyism and Leninism would lead to bloody conflicts or a coup inside the Party have of course, as I predicted, come to nothing. All that's happened is that Trotsky has been swallowed up. [. . .]

Moscow is full of mud, but on the other hand there are more and more lights. Two processes have come strangely to coexist here: life is getting under way, and at the same time it is suffering from complete gangrene. In the centre of Moscow, starting at the Lubyanka, the Waterway Organization has drilled out the earth for an experimental Metropolitan underground system. That is new life. But the Metropolitan won't be built, because there's no money for it. That's gangrene.

They're working out a new traffic scheme. That is life. But there is no traffic, because there are no trams; and it's laughable, but there are only eight buses for the whole of Moscow.

Housing, families, scholarship, work, standards of living and practical ideas – these are all suffering from gangrene. Nothing moves. Everything has been devoured by Soviet officialdom, which is a gaping maw. Every step or movement made by a Soviet citizen becomes a torment which consumes hours, days,

and sometimes months. There are some shops open. That is
life. But they go bust, and that's gangrene. And it's the same
in everything else.

The state of literature is dreadful.

23 December 1924

Today is the 23rd according to the new calendar, so tomorrow
is Christmas Eve. They were selling green fir-trees outside Christ
Church. I left home very late today, at about two, partly because
my wife [i.e. Lyubov Yevgenyevna, to whom he was not yet
officially married] and I slept in very late as usual. We were
woken at half-past twelve by Vasilevsky [Lyubov Yevgenyevna's
former husband], who'd arrived from Petersburg. Once again I
was forced to let the two of them go off together on their affairs.
[. . .] I didn't get hold of any money anywhere today, and so
came home feeling sour and sullen. I was very annoyed when I
thought about their journey together [. . .] and a terrible rage
came over me when I got home [. . .]. Under no circumstances
must I talk about politics.

26 December 1924

I couldn't restrain myself [at a literary evening at Angarsky's]
from getting involved several times in the conversation: I made
a speech about the fact that it was difficult to work at present,
and attacking censorship and so on, things I oughtn't to have
said. Lyashko, a proletarian writer, who instinctively felt an irre-
sistible antipathy towards me, made objections with ill-concealed
irritation: 'I don't understand what this "truth" is that comrade
Bulgakov is talking about.' [. . .] When I talked about the fact
that the present age was an age of swine, he replied with hatred,
'You're just talking rubbish.' [. . .]

But more than by all these Lyashkos, I am bothered by the
question, am I a writer or not?

27–28 December 1924

I am writing at night because almost every night my wife and
I don't get to sleep until three or four in the morning – we've
got into this rather idiotic habit. We get up very late, at twelve,
or sometimes at two or four in the afternoon. [. . .]

Moscow is a splendid city. Today I didn't see my only true
and tender love, the Kremlin. [. . .] I happened to see on a

news-stand on Kuznetsky Bridge Street the fourth number of *Rossiya*. In it was the first part of my *White Guard*, or rather not the first part, but the first third. I couldn't resist buying another copy at a second news-stand. [. . .] The novel seems partly weak and partly very powerful to me. I can't make sense of my own impressions any more. Above all my attention was drawn to the dedication ['This book is dedicated to Lyubov Yevgenyevna Belozerskaya']. Well, that's just how things worked out: there she is, my wife. [. . .] I have noticed that she waddles slightly when she walks. Given the way my ideas are developing, it's terribly stupid, but it appears that I am in love with her. One thought concerns me. Would she have adapted so cosily to just anybody, or was it specially for me? [. . .] Not for my diary, and not for publication: my wife overwhelms me sensually. That's good, and desperate, and sweet, and at the same time hopelessly complicated: just at the moment, as it happens, I am poorly and for me she . . . Today I saw her getting changed before we went out to Nikitina's, and watched greedily. [. . .] . . . the witch has got me bogged down like a cannon in a swamp . . . [. . .] But I can't imagine myself on my own, without her. Obviously I've got used to her.

2–3 January 1925

As I was walking past the Kremlin and had reached the tower on the corner, I looked up, paused, and began to look at the Kremlin, and I had just begun to think to myself, 'How long, oh Lord?', when a grey figure with a briefcase popped up from behind me and looked me over. Then he attached himself to me. I let him go ahead, and we walked for about a quarter of an hour together. When he spat from the parapet, I did the same. I managed to get away near the Alexander II monument.

3 January 1925

I'm in a dreadful state: I'm falling more and more in love with my wife. It's so infuriating: for ten years I've refused to have anything to do with . . . Women are just women. And now I am demeaning myself to the extent even of slight jealousy. Somehow she's very dear to me and sweet. And fat.

4 January 1925

Today [my story] *Bohemia* came out in *Krasnaya Niva* [*The*

Red Cornfield], Number 1. This was my first appearance in the boggy cesspit of specifically Soviet journals. I read it through today, and liked it very much.

5 January 1925

'How will it all end?' asked one of my acquaintances today. Questions like these are asked mechanically and dumbly, and hopelessly, and with indifference, and just for the sake of it. At that precise moment in his apartment, in the room across the corridor, some Communists were getting drunk. There was some sharp stench in the corridor, and one of the Communists, so my acquaintance informed me, was sleeping, drunk as a pig. He was invited to join them and couldn't refuse. He would go into their room with a polite and ingratiating smile, because they summoned him constantly. He kept coming back to me and cursing them in a whisper. Yes, all this will end somehow, I do believe that. [. . .]

Today at *The Hooter* I sensed with horror for the first time that I can't write sketches any more. I'm physically incapable of it. I am committing an outrage on myself and on my physiology.

16 January 1925

The day before yesterday I attended a reading given by Andrey Bely. [. . .] He was recounting his recollections of Valery Bryusov. All this produced an intolerable impression on me; it's all symbolist rubbish. [. . .] I left without waiting for the end. After the Bryusov there was supposed to be an extract from Bely's new novel. *Merci*.

14 February 1925. Moscow
From Boris Leontyev (at the Nedra publishing house)

Please bring the manuscript of *The Heart of a Dog* with you to read.

20 February 1925. Moscow
From Boris Leontyev (at the Nedra publishing house)

Dear M. A.,

Hurry up, please do everything you can to let us have your story *The Heart of a Dog*. Nikolay Semyonovich [Angarsky] may be going abroad in about two or three weeks' time, and we won't have time to get the thing through the Censorship Committee. And it will scarcely be possible to pull it off without him. If you don't wish the book to be shelved until the autumn, hurry, hurry.

3 April 1925. Moscow
From Boris Vershilov (at the Moscow Arts Theatre)

Most esteemed Mikhail Afanasyevich!

I would very much like to make your acquaintance and talk over a number of matters with you which are of interest to me and which may perhaps whet your curiosity.

If you are free, I would be glad to receive you tomorrow evening (4 April) in the Studio's premises . . .

With greetings.

B. I. Vershilov.

3

1925–1930

The mysterious note that Bulgakov received in April 1925 was an invitation from Boris Vershilov, a director at the Moscow Arts Theatre, to go and discuss with him the possibility of adapting the novel *The White Guard* for the stage. Vershilov and his colleagues at the Arts Theatre had not, of course, even read the complete text of the novel, since it had only begun to appear in the journal *Rossiya* in December 1924 and Bulgakov was still partly revising the text. But the idea fitted in very well with Bulgakov's own plans, since he himself had already begun in January 1925 to sketch out a stage adaptation of the novel; as he worked, he must have been recalling his 1921 play about his family, *The Turbin Brothers*, which he had burned in 1923. This invitation, at last, was the real fulfilment of the dreams he had been cherishing for so long. In an early chapter of his savagely satirical *Theatrical Novel*, written some ten years later when his experiences with the Moscow Arts Theatre and its Directors, Konstantin Stanislavsky and Vladimir Nemirovich-Danchenko, had turned sour and bitter, he recalls his open-mouthed entrancement when he first arrived at the Arts Theatre: ' . . . we found ourselves in a small auditorium which could seat about three hundred spectators. Two lamps burned faintly in the chandelier hanging from the ceiling, the curtain was open, and the stage gaped before me. The stage was solemn, mysterious and empty. Darkness filled its edges, but in the centre, faintly gleaming, was the figure of a golden horse, prancing on its hind legs. [. . .] "This is my world . . . " I whispered, not realizing that I had begun to speak out loud.' The emblem of the horse here is immediately recognizable as a parody of the Moscow Arts Theatre's emblem, Chekhov's seagull, which figures on its curtain. And indeed Bulgakov was, as one of the in-house directors was later to put it, the Moscow Arts Theatre's Chekhov for the Soviet period, the author most identified with the Theatre during the late 1920s and early 1930s, when he wrote a whole series of plays specifically for them. The relationship between Bulgakov and the Moscow Arts Theatre was not, however, to follow a smooth course after this initial euphoric meeting.

The writing of the play of *The White Guard* occupied Bulgakov throughout the spring and summer of 1925, part of which he spent on holiday with Lyubov Yevgenyevna in the Crimea at the invitation of the poet Maksimilian Voloshin, who held open house for leading literary figures of the day – this invitation, too, was a mark that Bulgakov had at last arrived on the literary scene. The task of adapting such a long novel was not, however, an easy one, and despite all Bulgakov's previous experience as a playwright in Vladikavkaz, he ended up in September 1925 with a cumbersome five-act drama which could not possibly, in the Theatre's opinion, be performed in a single evening. In October 1925 Bulgakov wrote to Vasily Luzhsky at the Theatre in a state of high indignation at the criticisms made of his text, adopting a surprisingly combative tone for an author who had only just been offered the chance of a first major breakthrough. But on this occasion the Theatre managed to soothe Bulgakov's ruffled feelings, and by the end of January 1926 he had rewritten the text and trimmed it to four acts. This second version of the play *The White Guard* (published only in 1983, by Lesley Milne) was duly rehearsed for the next six months, until June 1926. But when the dress rehearsal was held, the Chief Repertory Committee, the Soviet licensing organization for the theatre, made the first of its many baneful interventions in the fate of Bulgakov's works. They declared that '*The White Guard* is from beginning to end an apologia for the White Guard and [. . .]

is completely unacceptable; it cannot be staged in the form adopted by the Theatre.' Under protest, as can be seen from his letter to the Theatre of 4 June 1926 (page 79), Bulgakov was compelled to make drastic alterations. These included cutting the play down to three acts; omitting a powerful scene where the Ukrainian nationalists under Petlyura torture a Jew among others; transforming the ending, so that the youngest Turbin, Nikolka, should be seen to be moving towards the Bolshevik position, and so that the play should close with the swelling song of the Internationale; and changing the play's title to avoid the provocative use of the word 'White' altogether – which was how the anodyne *Days of the Turbins* came to be chosen instead.

This row with the Chief Repertory Committee was not the only unpleasantness to mar the summer of 1926. Bulgakov was also having problems with another theatre, the Vakhtangov, over the staging of his second Moscow play, *Zoyka's Apartment*, written during the latter part of 1925. A greater contrast with his *Days of the Turbins* could scarcely be imagined. Instead of the noble sentiments and the realistic setting of Kiev, Bulgakov here portrays in a lurid light the underworld of Moscow during the NEP period. The play is set in a dressmaker's which at night functions as a brothel, and concerns a group of characters involved in theft, fraud, drug-dealing and, finally, murder. Bulgakov's letters to the play's director Aleksey Popov, the first of which was sent from the dacha outside Moscow where he was holidaying in July 1926, show him to be in a semi-hysterical state over the Theatre's request that this play too be cut down to three acts, and reveal a somewhat paranoid suspicion on his part that the Theatre is intending to delay the production.

Perhaps one of the reasons behind his jumpy nerves was that his flat had recently been subjected to a search by the OGPU, during which his diaries and the manuscript of *The Heart of a Dog* were confiscated. Marietta Chudakova has suggested that this search on 7 May 1926 was carried out in connection with a case being mounted against Isay Lezhnev, the editor of the journal *Rossiya*. This journal, after publishing two-thirds of the novel *The White Guard*, was closed down by the authorities at the end of 1925, with Lezhnev retaining the last part of the novel in his hands. Bulgakov had little to fear from the case against Lezhnev, with whom he was in any case himself in dispute over this manuscript of *The White Guard*, but he must have been shattered by the intrusion of the police state into his life and the confiscation of diaries so private – and so revealing – that even his wife Lyubov Yevgenyevna did not know that he was writing them.

There had already been other indications in the preceding year or so of the shakiness of his position in the eyes of the Soviet authorities. The *Diaboliada* collection had been confiscated shortly after its publication by Nedra in the summer of 1925, although a reprint was then permitted in April 1926. Nedra had decided not to publish *The Fateful Eggs* as a separate volume after it had appeared in one of their almanacs, and Bulgakov's hopes that it might be translated and published in other countries were dashed when D. Umansky, the official who had agreed to promote the text abroad, had a change of heart on political grounds. This was followed by the news from Nedra that *The Heart of a Dog* had also been deemed unacceptable for publication by the influential Party figure L. B. Kamenev. Bulgakov was still at least hoping that a complete edition of the novel *The White Guard* might get published, although negotiations he entered into with two separate publishing houses eventually came to nothing.

It was against this background that Bulgakov's *The Days of the Turbins* was finally premièred in the Moscow Arts Theatre on 5 October 1926, rapidly followed by *Zoyka's Apartment* at the Vakhtangov Theatre on 28 October. *The Days of the Turbins* was, despite having been so hacked about, an immediate and sensational success with the public. It was the first play since the Revolution to portray the Whites as anything other than bloodthirsty oppressors, and there are reports that people in the audience groaned and fainted with emotion at Bulgakov's sympathetic depiction of the plight in which they and so many of their loved ones had found themselves between 1917 and 1921. The reactions of the critics, on the other hand, were harsh, since for them it confirmed that Stanislavsky's Moscow Arts Theatre remained a forum for reactionary works. Orlinsky was one of many critics to wage an unremitting campaign over the following years against what he sneeringly called 'Bulgakovism', and most of the Communist establishment dominating the literary press attacked Bulgakov on ideological grounds with vicious articles and reviews. But the play was an enormous box-office success, and this gulf between real popularity and critical opprobrium was to characterize Bulgakov's position for the rest of his life. The Chief Repertory Committee, meanwhile, confined itself to restricting the play for performance in the Moscow Arts Theatre alone: throughout its remarkable run virtually no other Soviet theatre was ever allowed to stage it, so that Bulgakov was deprived both of a wider audience and of what would have been a much-needed steady source of income.

Bulgakov's undiminished creative energy at this time was such that, well before the premières of *The Days of the Turbins* and *Zoyka's Apartment* in October 1926, he had already signed a contract for a third play, which was to be staged at the Kamerny Theatre under the direction of Aleksandr Tairov. This play – which was finally delivered to Tairov rather late, in March 1927 – was *The Crimson Island*, which was based on an idea he had earlier used for a story published in the newspaper *On the Eve*; one of Bulgakov's characteristic traits is indeed this facility for the adaptation and transposition of works, whether his own or someone else's, from one genre to another. *The Crimson Island* is a burlesque, using characters from Jules Verne to retell the story of the Revolution as a squabble between the natives of an island, which is initially exploited with some success by foreign colonialist aristocrats. The structure of the work is that of a play within a play, with the frame setting being that of a Moscow theatre; and Bulgakov uses this frame to mock the crude and ludicrously arbitrary decisions of the Soviet censors with regard to the banning or permitting of works on the basis of their political message. In particular, the absurd censor Savva Lukich was apparently made up in performance to resemble another of Bulgakov's most virulent critics, Vladimir Blyum.

As soon as *The Crimson Island* had been delivered, Bulgakov embarked on the writing of his fourth Moscow play, *Flight*. During the summer of 1927 he was also moving house with

Lyubov Yevgenyevna; after living in a series of apartments, they now moved into one on Bolshaya Pirogovskaya Street, a few hundred yards from the golden domes of Moscow's Novo-Devichy Convent. Here they spent the remainder of their married life together, although Bulgakov would soon come to complain of the darkness of the apartment and of the noise from the neighbouring tram-park.

The new play, *Flight*, was another commission from the Moscow Arts Theatre, although the well-known director Meyerkhold wrote to Bulgakov – whom he didn't know – in an attempt to poach the play for his own theatre. *Flight*, completed in March 1928, is probably Bulgakov's most accomplished work for the theatre. Drawing on Lyubov Yevgenyevna's tales of life in emigration, it extends its portrayal of the Whites beyond the Revolutionary fighting shown in *The White Guard* to a depiction of the Whites as fleeing refugees and as indigent émigrés in Constantinople and Paris. As so often with Bulgakov's writing, the play is finely poised between tragedy and farce; but what distinguishes it from his earlier work is the daring of its construction, as a sequence of eight dreams. These include extraordinary set pieces such as the station platform festooned with corpses hanging from the lamp-posts, supposed traitors condemned to death by the melancholy and crazed White General Khludov; and the absurd cockroach races (the word for 'race' in Russian is the same as that for 'flight') set up as a distraction and a source of income by Russian émigrés in Constantinople. The play apprehensively explores themes of guilt and retribution originally touched on in Bulgakov's autobiographical prose of the Civil War period. These preoccupations stem from some apparent failure on the author's part to prevent violence or murder, and are also connected with a sense of having failed to look after his younger brothers properly. Bulgakov's concern with guilt and cowardice is further developed in a number of his later works, and became central to *The Master and Margarita*.

By the summer of 1928, the continuing campaigns against Bulgakov in the press had finally begun to have serious and damaging consequences. In February 1928 Bulgakov had submitted an application for permission to travel abroad, partly in order to bring to book a certain Zakhar Kagansky, who was doing his best to seize control of Bulgakov's royalties abroad, and also to visit Paris and see his brother. He was brusquely refused permission to travel by the Moscow City Council. On returning from visits to Leningrad in April 1928, where he saw his friend the writer Yevgeny Zamyatin, and to the Caucasus in May, Bulgakov learned that *Flight* was not going to be licensed for performance; and that decisions had been taken by the Chief Repertory Committee to take off *The Days of the Turbins* as soon as a production of any other play was ready to be staged, and to take off *Zoyka's Apartment* straight away. During the summer, Bulgakov's hopes kept being raised that these decisions would be rescinded in time for the forthcoming season, and in August he travelled to Odessa to discuss the possibility of staging *Flight* in a theatre there. In September he received the news – rather startling in the circumstances – that *The Crimson Island*, which the Repertory Committee had been considering for a whole year and a half, was going to be approved for performance. Early in October, *Flight* too was suddenly given permission after all, but almost as suddenly the decision was once again reversed, this time owing to impassioned speeches made to the Repertory Committee by two more of Bulgakov's most implacable opponents, the critic Leopold Averbakh and the playwright Vladimir Kirshon. In December *The Crimson Island* was given an in-house première, but the Kamerny Theatre's own Artistic Council expressed grave reservations about it. As 1929 began, the successes Bulgakov had achieved since 1925 were clearly under threat.

The final touch to the wreck of all Bulgakov's plays was given by Stalin himself, in the first of what was to be a number of direct interventions in his affairs on Stalin's part. In a letter written on 2 February 1929, in response to some questions put to him by the playwright Bill-Belotserkovsky, Stalin declared, '*Flight* is one manifestation of an endeavour to stimulate pity, if not sympathy, for certain sections amongst the most contemptible anti-Soviet émigrés; so that means it is an attempt to justify, or semi-justify, the White cause. In its present form *Flight* is an anti-Soviet phenomenon. All the same,

I would have nothing against the staging of *Flight* if Bulgakov were to add to the eight dreams one or two more, in which he would depict the inner social springs of the Civil War in the USSR, so that the spectator should be able to understand that all these Serafimas [a reference to the heroine of *Flight*] and various aspiring university lecturers, all "honourable" in their own ways, ended up being chucked out of Russia not because of some whim of the Bolsheviks, but because they were living off the people (despite being "honourable"); and that the Bolsheviks, in driving out these "honourable" supporters of exploitation, were carrying out the will of the workers and the peasants, and for that reason were acting absolutely correctly.'

In the same letter, Stalin described *The Crimson Island* as hack-work. But he went on to write of *The Days of the Turbins* as a work demonstrating the overwhelming strength of Bolshevism. This bizarre interpretation suggests that Stalin had swallowed the rather crude final rewriting of the play which Bulgakov had undertaken in order that it should reach the stage, and that he read the play – as a bullying temperament was perhaps likely to do – as proof that in overcoming the Whites the Bolsheviks had defeated a tough enemy, one worthy of respect. Whatever we think of this interpretation, the fact remains that Stalin was evidently very fond of the play: the Arts Theatre's records indicate that he went to see it no fewer than fifteen times. Bulgakov himself appears to have believed that Stalin held him in greater respect for having spoken out honestly in the play than he would have if he had pretended to be more pro-Bolshevik. This assumption on Bulgakov's part explains a great deal about why and how he decided to address Stalin in the letters he wrote to him, starting in 1929. Stalin's enjoyment of *The Days of the Turbins* may also have been a significant factor in Bulgakov's being saved from arrest in periods such as 1929–30, when many of his friends and acquaintances in the world of art and literature, like his brother-in-law Andrey Zemsky, were sent on various pretexts into two- or three-year sentences of internal exile or prison.

For all Stalin's apparent appreciation of *The Days of the Turbins*, the actual effect of his February 1929 letter was to put an end to all the productions of Bulgakov's works in Moscow: *The Crimson Island* did run until the summer, but *The Days of the Turbins* was soon taken off, and *Flight* was abandoned. Together with the earlier taking off of *Zoyka's Apartment*, these developments completed the elimination of Bulgakov from the Soviet stage. He was left with only two small bright spots on the horizon to relieve his despair. The first was that on 28 February 1929 he made the acquaintance of Yelena Sergeyevna Shilovskaya, the wife of a highly-placed military man. Bulgakov's marriage to Lyubov Yevgenyevna had not brought him all the happiness he sought, and he was certainly swept off his feet by the remarkably attractive Yelena Sergeyevna. She was to be the real love of his life, and during the spring and summer of 1929 he plunged headlong into an affair with her. The second talisman for the future was that during that spring Bulgakov returned to a prose text he had done some work on the previous year (he had even got as far as offering one chapter of it to Nedra for publication, although it was not accepted). These were the beginnings of the great novel he would work on intermittently for the rest of his life, *The Master and Margarita*.

In July 1929, though, he summoned up his courage and wrote an outspoken letter addressed to members of the Soviet Government (Stalin, Kalinin and Svidersky) and to the writer Maksim Gorky, calling attention to his plight and describing the frustration of all his efforts to get published or staged over the past ten years (page 93). His conclusion, as he suggests, is that the only option is for him to be expelled together with his wife (he is still thinking in terms of Lyubov Yevgenyevna) from the Soviet Union. Bulgakov's public statements in letters such as these tend slightly – and, in the circumstances, understandably – to the melodramatic; but they are fascinating documents which reflect his perhaps naïve hopes that by speaking unambiguously it would be possible to enter into a rational dialogue with the arbiters of Soviet culture. The key to success in these matters, as everyone knew, was the mediation of Maksim Gorky, the grand old man of Soviet letters whose visits back to the Soviet Union from emigration in 1928 and 1929 had been a major propaganda coup for the Bolsheviks. Bulgakov knew from Veresayev that

Gorky held him in some esteem, and his letters to Gorky following up both his July letter and his reiteration, in September, of his basic request (to Yenukidze, a member of the Central Committee) are to be understood in this light. But on this occasion all his requests and complaints met with no response from the authorities.

None the less, undeterred and displaying remarkable resilience, in October 1929 Bulgakov began work on yet another new play, the first draft of which he completed by early December. This was something completely different again from the four previous Moscow plays: no longer a modern subject, and no longer set in Russia, but instead, a biographical play about Molière. Bulgakov immersed himself in the historical sources and read numerous French and Russian biographical accounts of Molière. He then condensed all his material into a depiction of Molière's life which, rather than conforming at all to a conventional biography, gives an imaginative impression of the pressures under which Molière had to work. It was not surprising, in view of his recent experiences, that Bulgakov highlighted two particular difficulties Molière had to contend with. The first was the pressure of public opinion, which latched on to the rumours about Molière's supposedly incestuous relationship to his wife Armande. The second was the relationship between the writer and the ruler, between Molière and Louis XIV, Bulgakov's portrayal of which was naturally read by his contemporaries as suggesting analogies to the modern world.

Once more, Bulgakov took his play to the Moscow Arts Theatre in the hope that it would be staged, and once more his hopes were dashed. On 18 March 1930 the Repertory Committee informed him that the play would not be licensed for performance. This provoked him later that month to write his most important letter to the Soviet Government, which is the last document in this chapter (page 103). In it, he recounts the vilification to which he has been subjected in the Soviet press, and infers that there is genuinely no place for him in Soviet culture. He insists quite openly on the need for freedom of the press and for the existence of satire, and acknowledges that his class background and convictions are at odds with the requirements of Soviet society; once again he concludes that the only humane solution would be for him to be allowed to leave the country with his wife. If that is not possible, and if he is to escape penury, he challenges the Government to find him a job. And this time, Bulgakov did receive an answer.

19 April 1925. From Zagreb to Moscow
From his brother Nikolay (postcard)

Christ is risen, my dear Misha! May you be happy and healthy!

This depicts the Institute of Experimental Pathology and Pharmacology where I am presently living and working.

10 May 1925. From Moscow to Koktebel (in the Crimea)
To the poet Maksimilian Voloshin

Most esteemed Maksimilian Aleksandrovich,

N. S. Angarsky has passed on to me your invitation to Koktebel. I am extremely grateful to you; would you be so kind as to drop me a line to say whether my wife and I might have a room for two in July-August? It would be very pleasant to visit you. Please accept my greetings.

M. Bulgakov.

21 May 1925. Moscow
From Boris Leontyev (at the Nedra publishing house)

Dear Mikhail Afanasyevich,

I am sending you *Cuff-notes* and *The Heart of a Dog*. Do what you like with them. Sarychev at the Censorship Committee declared that there was no point in even tidying up *The Heart of a Dog*. 'It's an entirely unacceptable piece' or something similar.

26 May 1925. Moscow
From Boris Vershilov (a director at the Moscow Arts Theatre)

How are things going as regards the play, our *White Guard*? I am still spellbound by your novel and I am longing to start work on your text. By my reckoning the first act of 'our' play ought to be finished by now?

28 May 1925. From Koktebel (in the Crimea) to Moscow
From the poet Maksimilian Voloshin

Dear Mikhail Afanasyevich,

I will be delighted to see you at Koktebel, whenever you can come, and you shall have a room for two.

I beg you to bring with you all your works (published or otherwise).

7 June 1925. Moscow
From Isay Lezhnev (at the journal *Rossiya*)
Dear Mikhail Afanasyevich!
You've entirely forgotten us at *Rossiya*. It's high time you handed in the material for Number 6 for typesetting; we need to typeset the end of *The White Guard*, and you still haven't delivered the manuscript. I must earnestly request you not to let this business drag on.

Summer 1925. From Koktebel (in the Crimea) to Moscow
To Pavel Markov (at the Moscow Arts Theatre)
I am working on my play, *The White Guard*. It will be ready by the beginning of August.

31 August 1925. Moscow
From Ilya Sudakov (a director at the Moscow Arts Theatre)
At three o'clock tomorrow (Sunday) you must read the play to K. S. Stanislavsky at his flat at 6 Leontyevsky Lane.

Early autumn 1925. Moscow
From Boris Leontyev (at the Nedra publishing house)
It's a very important and unpleasant matter: some sort of scandal has arisen in the upper regions concerning *Diaboliada*. Some sort of attack, as yet unclear, on us. Right now they're confiscating the book from us.

11 September 1925. Moscow
From Boris Leontyev (at the Nedra publishing house)
Your story *The Heart of a Dog* has been returned to us by L. B. Kamenev. At Nikolay Semyonovich [Angarsky]'s request he read it through and gave his opinion on it: 'It's an acerbic broadside about the present age, and there can be absolutely no question of publishing it . . . '
Of course one cannot put the blame simply on two or three

particularly sharp pages; they would scarcely alter the opinion of a man like Kamenev. Nevertheless, it seems to us that your earlier refusal to submit an amended text played a regrettable part in all this.

28 September 1925. Moscow
From the writer Vikenty Veresayev

Mikhail Afanasyevich!

If ever things are a bit tight, please turn to me for help. I would be delighted if you would do so in the same straightforward way as I am now proposing it! Please understand that I am by no means doing this as a personal favour to you, but because of my wish to protect, at least in some small way, that major artistic talent that you represent.

In view of the persecution to which you are currently being subjected, I thought that it would be agreeable for you to know that Gorky (I had a letter from him this summer) sets great store by your work and admires you.

5 October 1925. Moscow
From Ilya Sudakov (a director at the Moscow Arts Theatre)

Deeply esteemed Mikhail Afanasyevich!

1) The directors for *The White Guard* have been chosen (B. I. Vershilov and me). 2) We have decided how to distribute the parts, and they should be confirmed tomorrow. [. . .] Could I ask you to meet me and B. I. Vershilov at 3.30 tomorrow in the Theatre? I would like to reread the novel *The White Guard*. Would you be so kind as to bring a copy with you, if you have one? Rehearsals of *The White Guard* will start as soon as the parts have been typed. The production will be in March, on the Arts Theatre's Main Stage.

With respectful greetings,

Your I. Sudakov.

15 October 1925. Moscow
To Vasily Luzhsky (at the Moscow Arts Theatre)

Deeply esteemed Vasily Vasilyevich!

Yesterday's meeting, at which I had the honour to be present, demonstrated to me that the situation with regard to my play is complicated. Questions were raised about putting it on on the Second Stage, about next season and, finally, about a radical reshaping of the play amounting in effect to the creation of a new play.

While I am happy to agree to certain improvements as work proceeds on it under its directors, at the same time I do not feel I have the strength to write the play over again.

The harsh and profound criticism of my play at yesterday's meeting was bound to make me feel seriously disappointed with my play (I welcome criticism), but it did not convince me that the play ought to be put on on the Second Stage.

And, finally, the question of the season can be resolved in only one way as far as I am concerned: this season, not next.

For this reason, deeply esteemed Vasily Vasilyevich, I would ask you urgently to place before the Board of Directors for consideration and a categorical reply the following question:

Is the Arts Theatre prepared unconditionally to include the following points in the contract for the play?

1. Production only on the Main Stage.

2. This season (March 1926).

3. Changes, but not a radical reshaping of the outline of the play.

If these conditions were to prove unacceptable to the Theatre, then I would beg leave to consider a negative reply a sign that the play *The White Guard* is free for me to dispose of as I choose.

Yours respectfully,

M. Bulgakov.

26 October 1925. Moscow
To the Arbitration Tribunal of the All-Russian Union of Writers

Declaration

Since the closing down of the publishing house that produces the journal *Rossiya*, Isay Grigoryevich Lezhnev, editor of the journal *Rossiya*, has retained the final part of my novel *The*

White Guard without having any rights to it, and refuses to give it back to me.

I request that the Arbitration Tribunal investigate the question of the printing of *The White Guard* by Lezhnev, and that it protect my interests.

Mikhail Afanasyevich Bulgakov.

10 November 1925. From Vienna to Moscow
From D. Umansky

I read through your story [*The Fateful Eggs*] again after my arrival in Vienna; its contents could be interpreted in a sense unfavourable to the USSR, and I have changed my mind. In my opinion it is not worth publishing it in any foreign language outside the USSR! Satire deserves to be handled with the utmost care! Don't you agree?

6 December 1925. Moscow
To the writer Vikenty Veresayev

Dear Vikenty Vikentyevich!

I came to visit you to congratulate you without any ceremony. Yesterday, as I was intending to send you a formal letter, I started to reread you, and ended up not writing the letter; but as the night went on I became more and more convinced of the great significance of all that you have written in your long career.

More than once during the last astonishing years I have taken your books off the shelf and been convinced that they are full of life. It is not given to us to know the span of men's lives, but I believe with the utmost sincerity that I will hold your next book in my hands and that it will move me as much as your *Notes of a Doctor* moved me many years ago, as I crossed the threshold and began to make the difficult climb upwards.

That will be a true joy and a sign that our Russian Literature lives on – and with it, my love.

I kiss you warmly,

Mikhail Bulgakov.

1926. Moscow
Autobiographical notes for his friend Pavel Popov

One of my characteristics is that I need to listen to music. In fact I could say that I worship good music. It's very conducive to creative work. I am very fond of Wagner. Best of all I like a symphony orchestra with trumpets. There was no music at all when Petlyura's forces or the Bolsheviks entered Kiev.

. . . My favourite writer is Gogol; in my opinion no one can compare with him. I read *Dead Souls* at the age of nine, and thought of it as an adventure story. [. . .]

Dreams are of exceptional importance for me. Nowadays I have only melancholy dreams. [. . .]

The image of a lamp with a green shade is a very important image for me. It derives from my childhood impressions of the image of my father, writing at a desk.

4 April 1926. From Koktebel (in the Crimea) to Moscow
From the poet Maksimilian Voloshin

Dear Mikhail Afanasyevich,

Do not forget the existence of Koktebel and the Voloshin household, and that they always await you. [. . .] Let me request you in advance to bring with you the end of *The White Guard*, of which I know only Parts 1 and 2, and the continuation of *The Fateful Eggs*. Need I say that we are very much hoping that you and Lyubov Yevgenyevna will come, and that we are very fond of you.

Our winter passed quietly and happily. I painted nothing but watercolours and wrote no poems at all. By going on a diet I lost 20 lb. Now our springtime mode of existence has surged into life, and our first guests have arrived.

4 June 1926. Moscow
To the Council and Board of Directors of the Moscow Arts Theatre

I hereby have the honour to inform you that I am not prepared to accept the excision of the Petlyura scene from my play *The White Guard*.

My reason: that the Petlyura scene is organically linked with the rest of the play.

I am equally not prepared to agree that the play should be called *Before the End*, even if it is going to be renamed.

I am also not prepared to accept that a four-act play should be turned into a three-act one.

I am willing to discuss a different title for the play *The White Guard* with the Council of the Theatre.

If the Theatre is not prepared to accept the points laid out in this letter, then I request that the play *The White Guard* be taken off.

Mikhail Bulgakov.

24 June 1926. Moscow
To the Chairman of the Council of People's Commissars

On 7 May this year representatives of the OGPU carried out a search of my flat (warrant 2287, file 45), during the course of which were confiscated, after they had been duly noted in the record, the following manuscripts which have an enormous intimate value for me:

The story *The Heart of a Dog* (two copies) and my diary (three notebooks).

I earnestly request that these be returned to me.

16 July 1926. From Zubrilovka (Saratov Province)
From Aleksey Popov (a director at the Vakhtangov Theatre)

Greetings, dear Author!

This is your wicked enemy, the director you detest, writing to you. [. . .] Yesterday I received a letter from Kuza [at the Vakhtangov] in which he told me about your conversation with him and the plans for rewriting *Zoyka's Apartment*, and asked me to send you my opinion, *which I am now doing*.

I implore you, in the best interests of this matter, in the interests of the success of the production and of the play, to cut it down to three acts. [. . .]

I would be glad if, 'gritting your teeth', you would reply to me at the following address by 5 August: Zubrilovka Village, Saratov Province, A. D. Popov.

26 July 1926. From Kryukovo (near Moscow) to Zubrilovka (Saratov Province)

To Aleksey Popov (a director at the Vakhtangov Theatre)

Greetings, dear director!

I received your letter of 16 July yesterday in Kryukovo – outside Moscow.

There is evidently some misunderstanding: I imagined that I had sold the Studio a *play*, and the Studio imagines that I have sold it an outline, which it can develop however it sees fit.

Tell me, please, you're a director, how can a four-act play be turned into a three-act one? [. . .]

To put it briefly, *Zoyka* is a four-act play. It is im-poss-ib-le to turn it into a three-act play.

I am not going to write a new three-act play. First, I am ill, secondly, I am exhausted, and, thirdly, the people who watched the rehearsals were quite right when they told me, 'Don't listen to them,' (the Council, forgive me!) 'it's they who are to blame for everything.'

Fourthly: I imagined it would be like this: I write plays, the Studio puts them on. But it doesn't put them on! Oh, no! The Studio's not concerned with productions! It's busy with a mass of other matters: it's drawing up plans for rewrites. Evidently I'll have to put it on myself! But I don't have a theatre! (*Unfortunately!*) [. . .]

So will you finally let me know: is the Vakhtangov going to put *Zoyka* on or not? Or are we going to be rewriting it until 1928? [. . .]

I hope you won't feel aggrieved at this rather muddled letter.

In a few days' time I will begin to hand the new *Zoyka* in to the Studio typist. If I don't snuff it. If it comes out worse than the first, then all of you will be to blame for it! (*And above all the Council!*)

I am writing to you without any gritting of the teeth. You've put a lot of work into this. And so have I.

Greetings!

Your M. Bulgakov. [. . .]

I am in Moscow frequently. I come in from the dacha.

3 August 1926. From Zubrilovka (Saratov Province) to Moscow
From Aleksey Popov (a director at the Vakhtangov Theatre)

Greetings, esteemed Mikhail Afanasyevich!

I received your long letter and regret very much that exhaustion, irritability, and particularly *your mistrust of the theatre* to whom you have entrusted your play, are hindering efficient and fruitful work. The result of this mistrust is that you see malicious intent on the part of the Council where it is in fact working intensively on the play and is involving you in that work. In your mistrust and indignation you go so far as to doubt whether we *want* to put your play on. What is this nonsense?! Mikhail Afanasyevich! And what has 1928 to do with anything?! The play has been in preparation for two and a half months and will be ready in our usual period of three and a half to four months, and you know that perfectly well.

11 August 1926. From Moscow to Zubrilovka (Saratov Province)
To Aleksey Popov (a director at the Vakhtangov Theatre)

Esteemed Aleksey Popov!

Yes, exhaustion is right. In May a number of surprises not directly connected with the theatre were sprung on me, and in May too we had to rush *The White Guard* through in the Moscow Arts Theatre Studio (a preview for the authorities!); in June endless fiddly little bits of work, because not one of my plays has provided me with any income as yet; and in July the corrections to *Zoyka*. In August, everything all at once. But it's not a question of 'mistrust'. What would be the point of that? [. . .] There's just one thing: you look upon my characters somewhat differently from the way I do, and you want to make them work together slightly differently as well. But only slightly! And we can quite easily come to some agreement about it! [. . .]

I hope that we are threatened neither by discussions, nor by war, nor by confusion. No less than the Studio I wish for a successful outcome, not for a disaster!

And as proof of that, here is a summary of what I am working on at the moment. [. . .] For all my *willingness* to squeeze the events into three acts, I cannot understand how to do it. Please understand that the formula of the play is that it is in four sections. [. . .] Maybe you will succeed in putting the third and fourth acts on as two scenes (of one act); but why are you so keen that it should be three acts?

19 August 1926. Moscow
To the writer Vikenty Veresayev

[. . .] When do you intend to come back? How is your health? Are you working on Pushkin? How is the sea? I would be delighted to receive replies to these questions. I always think of you warmly.

As I rush back and forth between Moscow and a dacha outside Moscow (where I play tennis in the rare interludes when it is not raining), I have achieved a persistent and noticeable worsening of my health. My numerous acquaintances cheer me up when I meet them by telling me how unwell I look, and by enquiring tenderly and sympathetically why I am in Moscow, or else they start insisting that . . . I shall be rich in the autumn!! (A reference to the theatre.)

They have drummed this latter idea into my head so effectively that I have begun to cherish the notion that I might pay my debts off this autumn!!

In rare moments of lucidity, however, I recognize that any thought of being rich is folly.

And so, I wish you a good holiday.

Yours devotedly,

M. Bulgakov.

17 November 1926. Moscow
From Vasily Kuza (at the Vakhtangov Theatre)

This time it seems as though our torments are over; the Repertory Committee has hailed the show [*Zoyka's Apartment*] and called it interesting and socially useful. They made just two alterations; I'll tell you about them when I see you tomorrow.

18 November 1926. Moscow
To the writer Vikenty Veresayev

Dear Vikenty Vikentyevich!

Enclosed are two tickets for your wife and you for *The Days of the Turbins*. Furthermore I enclose the first 50 roubles in payment of my debt to you. Only yesterday did my royalties begin to trickle in (huge sums have been taken by my main creditors, and first amongst these was the Theatre). That is the sole reason for my delay in paying you back.

I send you my deepest thanks; meanwhile I am setting off to the OGPU (I have been called in again [presumably in connection with the Lezhnev case]).

With sincere devotion, yours,

M. Bulgakov.

7 February 1927. Moscow
Speech at a public discussion of *The Days of the Turbins* and other recent productions in Moscow, held at the Meyerkhold Theatre

The previous speaker stated that NEP-men go to *The Days of the Turbins* in order to have a little weep, and to *Zoyka's Apartment* to have a good laugh. I don't wish to enter into a discussion or to take up your attention for long in order to try to convince Comrade Orlinsky of anything, but for several months now – or, to be precise, since 5 October 1926, a memorable day for me because it was the day of the première of *The Days of the Turbins* – this man, this figure, has been making me want to say a couple of things. [. . .]

Whenever he says or writes something about my play he says something that isn't true. For example, today he mistakenly stated that 'the author and the Theatre panicked and changed the name of the play'. As far as the author is concerned, that is untrue. I can't entirely speak for the Theatre, of course, and I don't know whether they were in a panic [. . .]. But I didn't change the title in a panic. [. . .] I know quite definitely that the author insisted that the first and basic title of the play – *The White Guard* – should be preserved. [. . .] That's the first thing. There is another very important detail [. . .], and this detail concerns the lack of batmen, workers and peasants in the play. [. . .] About the batmen. I, the author of the play *The Days of the Turbins*, having been in Kiev during the time of the Hetman [Ukrainian leader] and of Petlyura, and having seen the White Guards in Kiev from the inside, from behind those cream curtains, can confirm that at that time in Kiev, at the time when the events of my play take place, you couldn't have got a batman for his weight in gold [*laughter and applause*]. [. . .]

I can well imagine two scenes with a batman: the first one as I would have written it, the other as Orlinsky would have written it. In mine it would have gone like this: 'Vasily, put on the samovar,' says Aleksey Turbin. 'Yes sir,' replies the batman, and then he would disappear for the rest of the play. Orlinsky wants a different batman. But let me assure you that a good man such as Aleksey Turbin would not have dreamed of thrashing his batman or throwing him out on his ear – which is what Orlinsky is actually interested in. [. . .]

I have nothing against the play being criticized as much as you please, but I would like information about it to be accurate. And I would maintain that the critic Orlinsky has absolutely no knowledge of the 1918 period described in my novel and my play.

24 February 1927. Moscow
To his sister Nadezhda
Dear Nadya,

Here are two tickets for you and one (second row of the circle) for Marusya.

M.

They're all for tomorrow.

3 March 1927. Moscow
From a secretary at the Kamerny Theatre
You promised Aleksandr Yakovlevich [Tairov] that you would send the play [*The Crimson Island*] yesterday. Accordingly he arranged with the Repertory Committee that he would deliver the play to them today. Alas! He has nothing to deliver. And

meanwhile this is a very good moment and there is a good atmosphere which Aleksandr Yakovlevich, of course, very much wants to take advantage of. I beg you to send copies of the play back with the messenger . . . We musn't let this moment pass, since the entire composition of the Committee is changing in a few days' time and it will be much more difficult to get the play through then . . .

4 March 1927. Moscow
From a secretary at the Kamerny Theatre

I acknowledge receipt of two copies of *The Crimson Island* on behalf of the Kamerny Theatre.

26 May 1927. From Tiflis to Moscow
From Vsevolod Meyerkhold (Director of the Meyerkhold Theatre)

Deeply esteemed Sir!

Unfortunately I do not know your first name or patronymic.

I would like to ask you to give me your play for next season. Smyshlayev has told me that you already have a new play, and that you would not be opposed to the idea of its being put on in the theatre I run.

Please write to me in Rostov-on-Don, where I shall be for the whole of June. [. . .]

Greetings,

V. Meyerkhold.

24 June 1927. From Rostov-on-Don to Moscow
From Vsevolod Meyerkhold (Director of the Meyerkhold Theatre)

Much esteemed Mikhail Afanasyevich!

Thank you very much for responding to my letter.

Ah, how disappointing that you don't have a play for me!

But what you can do?

We must meet in the autumn. I shall ask you to promise that we will talk on the telephone – 3 04 11 – (I would ask you to ring me), and we will arrange a time and a day to meet. [. . .]

With greetings,

V.Meyerkhold.

December 1927. From Moscow to Paris
To Vladimir Binshtok (a Soviet copyright agent)

I have received word from abroad that a certain Kagansky, together with others whose names I do not know, is claiming that he has my permission to handle my novel *The White Guard* and my play *The Days of the Turbins*.

This is to certify that I have given no such permission to Kagansky, nor to anyone else.

14 December 1927. From Zagreb to Moscow
From his brother Nikolay

Good and glorious Misha,

I am well aware that you have helped most warmly to support me, just as you used to help Vanya [their brother Ivan]. It is difficult for me at the moment to express the strength of my feelings for you, but please believe that they are strong and sincere. Vanya and I are always writing to each other about you, and about what we hear and read about you, and rejoice with you. [. . .]

Work well, and may you have health and happiness. We send warm kisses to you and to your wife Lyuba. Thank you.

Kolya.

21 February 1928. Moscow
Additional notes to an application for permission to travel abroad

Purpose of foreign travel

I am travelling in order to call to account Zakhar Leontyevich Kagansky, who has declared abroad that he has supposedly acquired from me the rights for *The Days of the Turbins*, and on this basis has published the play in German, retaining for himself the 'rights' to the play in America, etc. [. . .]

I am going to Paris to negotiate with the Théâtre des Mathurins about a production of *The Days of the Turbins*, and to negotiate with the Société des Auteurs [et Compositeurs] Dramatiques, of which I have become a member.

I request that you allow me out with my wife, who will serve as my interpreter. It would be very difficult for me to conduct my business without her (I do not speak German).

In Paris it is my intention to study the city and to think over the production plan for *Flight*, which has been taken on at the Moscow Arts Theatre (Act IV of *Flight* is set in Paris).

The trip will under no circumstances take more than two months, after which it is imperative that I be back in Moscow for the production of *Flight*.

I hope that I will not be refused permission to travel on this important business, which I have here honestly described.

M. Bulgakov. [. . .]

P.S. If permission to travel were to be refused I would be placed in an extremely difficult position as regards my further work as a dramatist.

8 March 1928. Moscow
From the Administrative Department of Moscow City Council

This is to declare that the Administrative Department of Moscow City Council refuses to grant you permission to travel abroad.

12 March 1928. From Moscow to Leningrad
To Lyudmila and Yevgeny Zamyatin (the writer)

Dear Lyudmila Nikolayevna and Yevgeny Ivanovich!

Moscow greeted me rather sourly, and straight away I fell ill. [. . .] As I departed from your enchanting city in melancholy spirits I left behind me on some coat-hook, either yours or Nikolay Ernestovich [Radlov]'s, my scarf (two colours – lilac and black). Please send it on to me! Give everyone greetings from me! I hope you have a merry holiday,

Your M. Bulgakov. [. . .]

P.S. Moscow is very disagreeable.

20 July 1928. From Moscow to America
To Herbert Biberman (a theatrical agent) (written in English)

Dear Mr Biberman,

Your kind letter is at hand.

I have to inform you owing to misuses occured [sic] with the producing and publishing of my piece 'The days of the Tourbinys' on the European Continent, I had to transfer all my rights, by means of a special agreement, to the Fisher's Publishing Firm [Fischer Verlag], which since is representing my interests abroad.

Therefore I beg you to direct to the Fisher's Firm all the money due for the producing or the publishing of that piece of mine.

Heraby [sic] I enclose a copy of my agreement with Fishere [sic].

I am, dear Mr Biberman,

Yours truly,

M. Bulgakoff.

18–19 August 1928. From Konotop; near Kiev; and Odessa to Moscow
To his wife Lyubov Yevgenyevna

Dear Topson,

The journey is going well and I'm glad to be seeing the Ukraine. Only I'm ravenously hungry on this train. I am feeding myself on tea and on the views. I'm alone in my compartment and very pleased that it's possible to write. Greetings to the household, including the cats. I hope that by my return the second one will no longer be there (sell him into slavery).

Tush, tush, tush . . .

Your M. [. . .]

I'm beginning to believe in my star: the weather's turned bad!

Your M.

Tush, tush, tush!

How a man is drawn to the land where he was born.

13 September 1928. From Leningrad to Moscow
From the writer Yevgeny Zamyatin

Congratulations on *The Crimson Island*!

Dear old man,

Allow me to remind you of your promise to give me an article, 'The Première', for the Theatre Union almanac. When are we to expect it? It's high time.

Please don't imitate our mutual friend Bulgakov, who simply shelves his letters, but be honourable and answer instead. [. . .]

Yours, Yevg. Zamyatin.

27 September 1928. From Moscow to Leningrad
To the writer Yevgeny Zamyatin

Dear Yevgeny Ivanovich!

This time I've delayed replying to your letter precisely because I wanted to reply as quickly as possible.

To the seven pages of 'The Première' that were lying motionless in my right-hand drawer I added another thirteen over the last two weeks. And then yesterday I took all twenty of those closely written sheets, corrected all the mistakes on them first, and then burned them in the stove which you have sat next to more than once.

And it's a good thing that I came to my senses in time.

Given the people all around me who are still alive, there can be no question of putting this opus into print.

It's a good thing I didn't send it. Forgive me for not having kept my promise, but I am quite confident when I say that you wouldn't have printed it in any case.

So there won't be any 'Première'!

And altogether there's an end, evidently, to my foray into the sphere of *belles-lettres*.

Which isn't as bad as the fact that I have been neglecting my business correspondence. I'm simply a wreck.

After your congratulations a feeling of (reverential) horror was added to the love I bear for you.

You congratulated me two weeks before *The Crimson Island* was permitted.

Which means you're a prophet.

As for the permission, well, I don't know what to say. I wrote *Flight* and handed it in.

But it's *The Crimson Island* that's been passed.

It's mystical.

Who? What? Why? For what purpose?

The thickest of fogs has enveloped my brain.

I hope you won't deprive me of your prayers. [. . .]

Ah, Leningrad, entrancing city!

Your M. Bulgakov.

8 October 1928. From Moscow to Berlin
To the publishers Ladyzhnikov

The present letter is to authorize Ladyzhnikov Publishers to translate my play *Zoyka's Apartment* into German, to include the play amongst their plays, and to protect my interests as an author on the conditions set out in Ladyzhnikov Publishers' letter to me of 3 October 1928.

I would like to inform you that I have not granted any rights to the play either to Mr Livshits or to Mr Kagansky.

25 April 1929. From Moscow to Zagreb
To his brother Nikolay

Dear Kolya,

Today I learned that your move to Paris is already decided upon. I am very glad of it, and sincerely wish that your destiny there will be a happy one. I would ask you to let me know as soon as you set off, and to send me your address *the moment* you reach Paris. It is possible that I will be able to provide you with material assistance.

I have already asked you not to get indignant with me because my letters are so rare. Our long and terrible separation has changed nothing; I haven't forgotten you and Vanya, nor will I forget you. [. . .]

M.

3 May 1929. From Zagreb to Moscow
From his brother Nikolay

Dear Misha,

[. . .] My departure was planned for the end of May, but will probably take place only in the last few days of June, since I am kept here by the gynaecology clinic and forensic medicine – my last work and examinations. In addition, I am waiting for the French government's permission to enter the country and work there as a foreigner. [. . .] I am deeply grateful to you for all that you have done for me (and believe me, you have done a lot!), for always being ready to help me with advice and action. But I earnestly request you not to undertake anything until I should ask you for something. Believe me, as well as my deep and sincere gratitude, the knowledge that the help given to me entails deprivation and a constraint on the needs of someone else is something that causes me constant worry.

15 July 1929. From Leningrad to Moscow
From the writer Yevgeny Zamyatin

Dear comrade instructor,

I quite understand that every reminder of the city where you were obliged 10 (ten) times to eat humble pie at the billiard table is not particularly pleasant to you. Believe me, only extreme necessity constrains me to subject you to this unpleasantness.

As you know, I have given up writing plays. But I would urgently like to offer the Moscow theatres one good American play [*The Front Page*]. And for that I need to know which theatrical folk are in Moscow at the moment. [. . .]

Your Yevg. Zam. (alias Faux Pas).

19 July 1929. From Moscow to Leningrad
To the writer Yevgeny Zamyatin

Dear Yevgeny Ivanovich!

As far as eating humble pie at the billiard table is concerned, there exists a well-known phrase: 'My turn today, but tomorrow it's yours, mate!' [. . .]

Yours until the grave (which is not too far off).

M. Bulgakov.

23 July 1929. From Moscow to Zagreb
To his brother Nikolay

Dear Kolya,

Congratulations on graduating from university!

My wish for you is that you should remain at heart just as I remember you many years ago.

Although, dear Doctor, you know better than anyone what to wish for yourself. I am sure that yours will be a bright life after all your trials. [. . .]

Your M. Bulgakov.

July 1929. Moscow
To Stalin, Kalinin, Svidersky and Gorky

To Y. V. Stalin, General Secretary of the Party,
M. I. Kalinin, Chairman of the Central Executive Committee,
A. I. Svidersky, Head of the Chief Committee on Art,
and to Aleksey Maksimovich Gorky,
from the writer
Mikhail Afanasyevich Bulgakov
(Moscow)

Declaration

This year ten years will have passed since I began to pursue a literary career in the USSR. Of those ten years I have devoted the last four to drama, during which time I have written four plays. Three of these (*The Days of the Turbins, Zoyka's Apartment* and *The Crimson Island*) have been put on by State theatres in Moscow, while the fourth, *Flight*, was taken on by the Moscow Arts Theatre for production but was banned during the course of work on it.

Recently I have been informed of the banning of *The Days of the Turbins* and *The Crimson Island*. *Zoyka's Apartment* was taken off after 200 performances last season by order of the authorities. So that at the beginning of this season all my plays have ended up being banned, including *The Days of the Turbins* which had run for about 300 performances. [. . .]

Previous to this my story *Cuff-notes* had a ban imposed on it. My collection of satirical stories *Diaboliada* is not permitted to be reprinted, while a collection of sketches has been banned as well, as have all public readings of my story *The Adventures of Chichikov*. My novel *The White Guard* had its publication in the journal *Rossiya* interrupted, since the journal itself was banned.

As my works have come out Soviet critics have paid me more and more attention, although not one of my works, whether fiction or drama, has ever received any approving review anywhere. On the contrary, the more my fame in the USSR and abroad has grown, the more the press reviews have become savage, until in the end they have simply turned into frenzies of abuse.

All my works have received grotesque and unfavourable reviews, and my name has been slandered not only in the periodical press, but even in such publications as the *Great Soviet Encyclopaedia* and the *Literary Encyclopaedia*.

Powerless to defend myself, I put in an application for permission to go abroad, even just for a short period. I was refused that permission . . .

My works *The Days of the Turbins* and *Zoyka's Apartment* have been stolen and taken abroad. In the city of Riga one publishing house 'completed' my novel *The White Guard* and issued under my name a book with an illiterate ending. My royalties abroad have begun to be misappropriated.

At that point my wife Lyubov Yevgenyevna Bulgakova put in a second application for permission to travel abroad on her own to sort out my affairs, while I proposed to remain behind as a hostage.

We were refused permission.

I have several times applied for the OGPU to return my manuscripts, and have either received refusals or received no answer at all to my applications.

I requested permission to send my play *Flight* abroad in order to protect it from being misappropriated abroad.

I was refused permission.

At the end of this tenth year my strength is broken. Since I no longer have the strength to survive, since I am persecuted and know that it is impossible that I shall ever be published or staged within the USSR again, and since I am close to suffering a nervous breakdown, I am turning to you to request you to intercede with the Government of the USSR to ask them to EXPEL ME FROM THE USSR TOGETHER WITH MY WIFE L. Ye. BULGAKOVA, who joins me in this request.

M. Bulgakov.

10 August 1929. From Paris to Moscow
From his brother Nikolay

Dear Misha,

I send you heartfelt greetings from the top of the Eiffel Tower. I have arrived safely and am beginning to get the feel of the place. [. . .]

Nikolay.

24 August 1929. From Moscow to Paris
To his brother Nikolay

Dear Kolya!

Thank you very much for having been to visit Vladimir Lvovich [Binshtok]. Would you please keep the royalties you received from him in Paris until my next letter, in which, as appropriate, I will write and tell you what to do with the money.

I am extremely grateful to you for your readiness to help me in my literary affairs. I would have expected nothing else.

As for the point that I am stingy when it comes to letters – well, what can you do?

And now, dear brother, I must inform you that I am in a bad way.

All my plays have been banned from the stage in the USSR, and they will not print a single line of my prose. During 1929 my annihilation as a writer has been effected. I have made one final effort and submitted an application to the Government of the USSR, in which I have asked that my wife and I be allowed to go abroad for whatever period they decide.

In my heart I have no hope. One ominous indication is that they would not let Lyubov Yevgenyevna out alone, despite the fact that I was to stay behind (this was a few months ago).

Dark rumours are already creeping around my name like a snake, to the effect that I am doomed in every sense of the word.

If my application is turned down, then I will just have to assume that the game is over, and that it's time to put away the cards and snuff out the candles.

I shall have to sit in Moscow and not write, because not only can they not bear to see my works, they can't even bear to see my name with equanimity.

Without being pusillanimous, I should tell you, brother, that my ruin is just a question of time unless, of course, a miracle occurs. But miracles tend to happen infrequently.

I would ask you most earnestly to write and tell me whether you have understood this letter, but absolutely without writing to me *any words of consolation or sympathy*, in order not to worry my wife.

So there's a more generous letter for you.

The dreadful thing is that this spring I felt so weary that I succumbed to indifference. After all, there is a limit.

I am glad that you have got settled and I believe that you will make a career as a scientist. Write and tell Ivan that I remember him. Get him to write me at least a few lines. Your letters are a great consolation to me, and I imagine that, having read this letter, you will write to me often. Describe Paris to me (it goes without saying that I mean just its exterior life).

And so I will take up your kind offer, and in my next letter I will ask you to carry out a few more errands. I won't overburden you.

Well then, I send you a kiss, dear Nikol –
                    your M. Bulgakov.

P.S. Please reply *immediately* to this letter. [. . .]

Vladimir Lvovich wrote and said that you were 'terribly nice', and that was pleasant for me. Do you mean to say he didn't give you a copy of my book? I forgot to ask him to do that.

3 September 1929. Moscow
To Avel Yenukidze (Secretary of the Central Executive Committee of the USSR)

– In view of the fact that the absolute unacceptability of my works to the Soviet public is quite apparent,

– in view of the fact that the complete banning of my works which has been effected in the USSR condemns me to ruin,

– in view of the fact that my annihilation as a writer has already brought about a catastrophe for me in material terms (I can provide documentary evidence of my lack of savings, of the fact that it is impossible for me to pay my taxes and indeed to live, starting from next month),

– given my immense exhaustion,

– and the fruitlessness of all my endeavours,

I appeal to the highest body in the Union – the Central Executive Committee of the USSR, and I request that I be permitted, together with my wife Lyubov Yevgenyevna Bulgakova, to go abroad for whatever period the Government of the Union feels it necessary to stipulate.

MIKHAIL AFANASYEVICH BULGAKOV
(author of the plays *The Days of the Turbins*, *Flight* and others).

3 September 1929. Moscow
To the writer Aleksey (Maksim) Gorky

Much esteemed Aleksey Maksimovich!

I have submitted a request to the Government of the USSR to be permitted to leave the USSR with my wife for whatever period they see fit to stipulate.

I would like to ask you, Aleksey Maksimovich, to support my petition. I wanted to set out everything that's been happening to me in a detailed letter, but my exhaustion and sense of hopelessness are too great. I can't write anything.

Everything's been banned, and I am ruined, persecuted, and completely alone.

Why keep a writer in a country where his works cannot exist? I ask for a humane resolution – that they should let me go.

Yours respectfully,

M. Bulgakov.

28 September 1929. Moscow
To the writer Aleksey (Maksim) Gorky

Much esteemed Aleksey Maksimovich!

Yevgeny Ivanovich Zamyatin has informed me that you received my letter, but that you would like to have a copy of it.

I don't possess a copy of it, but the letter's content was approximately the following:

'Through A. I. Svidersky I submitted an application to the Government of the USSR, in which I asked them to take note of my intolerable situation and to permit me together with my wife Lyubov Yevgenyevna Bulgakova to go abroad on holiday for whatever period the Government sees fit to stipulate.

'I wanted to write to you in detail about what was happening to me, but my excessive weariness no longer even lets me work.

'One thing I can say: why keep a writer in the USSR whose works cannot exist in the USSR? In order to condemn him to ruin?

'I request a humane resolution – that they should let me go. I earnestly ask you to intercede on my behalf.

'I would ask you not to deny me the courtesy of letting me know that you have received this letter.'

I would now like to add the following to that letter:

– all my plays have been banned,

– not a line of mine is being printed anywhere,

– I have no work ready, and not a kopek of royalties is coming in from any source,

– not a single institution, not a single individual will reply to my applications,

– and, briefly, everything that I have written during ten years of work in the USSR has been destroyed. All that is left is for the last remaining thing to be destroyed – me. I request that a humane resolution should be pronounced – that they should let me go!

Yours with respect,

M. Bulgakov.

14 October 1929. Moscow
From the Moscow Arts Theatre

Citizen M. A. Bulgakov,

In view of the banning by the Chief Repertory Committee of the production of the play *Flight*, the Board of Directors of the Moscow Arts Theatre requests you, according to point 6 of the contract signed by you, to return the advance you received for this play, a sum of 1,000 roubles.

28 December 1929. From Moscow to Paris
To his brother Nikolay

Dear Kolya,

I have had no news from you, and this makes me think that something has happened to you.

I would ask you please to reply to this letter with a telegram – to tell me whether you are well, your address, and urgently (if it is possible by telegraph) to transfer to me the royalties you received from Binshtok.

Your Mikhail.

P.S. I am in a painful situation.

16 January 1930. From Moscow to Paris
To his brother Nikolay

Dear Kolya,

I received your letter of 6 January in good time. [. . .] I am sorry to be so late in thanking you. I beg you not to get angry at the gaps in our correspondence. Please write more often. Please don't fall silent. My recent silence has been caused by a deterioration in my situation [. . .].

Let me tell you about me:

All my literary works have perished, as have my literary plans. I am condemned to silence and, quite possibly, to complete starvation. In unbelievably difficult circumstances in the second half of 1929 I wrote a play about Molière. It has been recognized as the most powerful of my five plays by the best specialists in Moscow. But all the indications are that it will not be allowed on stage. My torments with it have already been going on for six weeks, despite the fact that it's all about Molière and the seventeenth century . . . and despite the fact that I haven't touched upon the modern world in it at all.

If this play perishes then I have no means of saving myself – I am already *enduring a calamity* now. I have no protection or assistance. Quite soberly I am telling you that my ship is going down, and that the water is already coming over the bridge. I must drown with courage. Please read what I am saying attentively.

If there is any possibility at all of sending my royalties (through the bank? a cheque? I don't know how), I would request you to send them: *I don't have a single kopek.* I hope, of course, that you would send it through official channels, so as not to provoke any unpleasantnesses for us. [. . .]

I await news from you with impatience.

I wish you happiness in life!

Your Mikhail.

27 January 1930. From Paris to Moscow
From his brother Nikolay

I cannot send what you have asked me by telegraph, since it is unfortunately impossible; they don't accept any transfers to the USSR by post. I am investigating other possibilities . . .

19 February 1930. From Moscow to Paris
To his brother Nikolay

Dear Kolya!

On 17 February I received a notification from the Bank for Foreign Trade in Moscow that a transfer of 40 dollars had arrived in my name, and yesterday (18 February) I received the money itself.

It goes without saying that I declined to take the dollars in kind but received 77 roubles 66 kopeks according to the State Bank's rate of exchange (one rouble 94 kopeks to the dollar).

I am very grateful to you for all your pains, and very touched [. . .].

I send you a kiss and much gratitude,

Your Mikhail.

21 February 1930. From Moscow to Paris
To his brother Nikolay

Dear Kolya,

You ask whether I am interested in your work? I am extremely interested! I received your abstract of *Bacterium prodigiosum*. I am glad and proud that in the most difficult circumstances you have managed to make your own way. I remember you as a young man, I have always loved you, and now I am firmly convinced that you will become a scholar.

I am interested not only in this work, but also in what you will do in the future, and you will give me great pleasure by sending me everything that you publish. Believe me that none of your friends and relatives will be more attentive to every line you write than me.

Many of my acquaintances have questioned me about our family, and it has always consoled me that I was able to talk about your great abilities.

The one thought that pains me is that it seems we shall never in our lives have the opportunity to see each other again. My fate has been tangled and fearsome. Now it is leading me towards silence, and for a writer that is tantamount to death.

I have a question for you in return: are you interested in my literary work? Write and tell me. If you are even slightly interested, then listen to what I have to tell you as attentively as you can (although my experience and intuition, I think, suggest to me after a careful reading of your letters that there is interest and attention there).

I have endeavoured to carry out my tasks as a writer as best I can in the most unbelievably difficult conditions. At present my work has been halted. I constitute a complex (as I imagine) piece of apparatus, the production of which is simply not needed in the USSR. This has been all too clearly demonstrated to me, and they are demonstrating it to me once again in connection with my play about Molière.

At night I painfully rack my brains to think up some means of salvation. But I can't see anything. Who else, I begin to think, can I write an official letter to? . . .

Now to more immediate things:

Be a good fellow, and please put up with this nuisance for a while longer (I don't imagine that I will burden you for much longer!). Would you send me some more money, again through the bank, against the royalties that Vladimir Lvovich gave you? These sums, even if they are very paltry, are vital to me. I don't know how much he gave you. But don't send it all, and instead do this: I badly need tea, coffee, socks, and stockings for my wife. If it's not too difficult, send me a parcel with tea, coffee, two pairs of socks and two pairs of ladies' stockings (number 9) (definitely not silk). I don't know how much it will cost. Preferably like this: first and foremost the parcel, and if there is any left over, then 10 dollars or so through the bank, and keep the rest yourself for any expenses of mine. If my calculations are wrong, then just the parcel.

If by any chance Vanya should be in difficulties, then send me the parcel, and send him some of my money. You work it out, please!

On 15 March my first payment to the Inspector of Finances is due (income tax for the last year). I must suppose that, unless some sort of miracle takes place, then there will be nothing left at all in my small and completely damp flat (incidentally, I have been suffering from rheumatism for several years). My goods and chattels don't concern me much: well, chairs and cups, to hell with them! But I am fearful for my books! My library is not up to much, but all the same, without books I've had it! When I am working I work very seriously – I have to read a lot.

Everything from the words 'On 15 March' onwards is not intended to be taken seriously – I'm not complaining or asking for help in the matter, I'm just telling you in order to divert myself.

Reconcile yourself to the idea that my letters to you will become frequent (although I repeat that this won't last long, probably). I'm not much of a master when it comes to letters: you struggle and struggle, the words won't come off the pen, and I can't express my thoughts properly . . .

I am very much looking forward to getting news from you. Be cheerful and bold, and don't forget your brother Mikhail. If you have a moment, think about Mikhail Bulgakov.

I send you a kiss,

Mikhail.

18 March 1930. Moscow
From the Chief Repertory Committee
I am writing on the instructions of the Chairman of the Chief Repertory Committee to inform you that your play *A Cabal of Hypocrites* [*Molière*] has not been licensed for performance.

25 March 1930. From Moscow to Paris
To his brother Nikolay
Dear Kolya,
There is no news from you, which is very sad. I wrote you a letter asking you to send me a parcel (socks and coffee).
Don't send it. They say that the duty has gone up considerably.
Instead I would earnestly ask you to purchase and send immediately (the person is gravely ill) the medical preparations listed in the attached note to the following address:
Nadezhda Yevgenyevna Tarnovskaya,
Flat 34, 98 Karl Liebknecht Street, Leningrad.
I would be very obliged to you,
Your Mikhail.

28 March 1930. Moscow
To the Soviet Government
The following letter is addressed to the Soviet Government:
I.
After the banning of all my works, I began to hear voices among many citizens of my acquaintance, all giving me one and the same piece of advice: that I should write a 'Communist play' (I am quoting them in inverted commas), and that quite apart from that I should address to the Government of the USSR a penitential letter, which would contain a renunciation of my previous opinions, as expressed in my literary works, and assurances that henceforth I was going to work as a fellow-travelling writer loyal to the idea of Communism.
The aim: to escape persecution, destitution, and death as the inevitable finale.
I did not follow that advice. I would scarcely have succeeded

in appearing in a favourable light in the eyes of the Government of the USSR by writing a mendacious letter, which would have represented a sordid and indeed naïve political somersault. I did not even make any attempt to write a Communist play, being quite confident that I could not succeed in writing such a play.

My growing desire to put an end to my torments as a writer obliges me to address a truthful letter to the Government of the USSR.

2.

When I carried out an analysis of my albums of cuttings, I discovered that there had been 301 references to me in the Soviet press during my ten years of work in the field of literature. Of these, three were complimentary, and 298 were hostile and abusive.

These 298 reflect, as in a mirror, my life as a writer.

Aleksey Turbin, the hero of my play *The Days of the Turbins*, was described in verse in print as a 'SON OF A BITCH', while the author of the play was presented as someone 'suffering from DOG-LIKE SENILITY'. I was referred to as a 'literary SCAVENGER', picking over scraps after 'a good dozen guests HAVE THROWN UP'.

They wrote:

' . . . MISHKA Bulgakov, my friend, WHO IS ALSO, IF YOU WILL PARDON THE EXPRESSION, A WRITER, POKES AROUND IN RUBBISH-TIPS . . . I am asking you, brother, why you've got such an UGLY MUG . . . I am a delicate type, just BASH HIM OVER THE HEAD WITH A BASIN . . . As common citizens we have no more need of the Turbins than a DOG NEEDS A BRASSIÈRE . . . THAT SON OF A BITCH just swans in, THAT TURBIN, LET'S MAKE SURE HE GETS NO TAKINGS NOR ANY SUCCESS . . . ' (*The Life of Art*, Number 44, 1927).

They've written about 'Bulgakov, who has remained what he always was, ONE OF THE NOUVEAU BOURGEOIS BREED, spraying vitriolic but impotent spittle over the working class and its Communist ideals' (*Komsomol Pravda*, 14 November 1926).

They have stated that I enjoy the 'ATMOSPHERE OF A DOG'S WEDDING around some red-headed wife of a friend [a reference to Yelena in *The Days of the Turbins*]' (A. Lunacharsky, *Izvestiya*, 8 October 1926), and that my play *The Days of the Turbins* 'STINKS' (stenographic record of an agitprop meeting in May 1927), and so on, and so forth . . .

Let me hasten to state that I am quoting not in order to complain about the critics or to engage in any sort of polemics. My aim is far more serious.

I can prove with documents in my hands that the entire press of the USSR, together with all the institutions to whom control of the repertory has been entrusted, throughout all the years of my literary career, has unanimously and with EXTRAORDINARY FURY demonstrated that the works of Mikhail Bulgakov cannot exist in the USSR.

And I declare that the Soviet press is ABSOLUTELY CORRECT.

3.

My burlesque *The Crimson Island* may serve as the starting-point for this letter.

All the critics in the USSR without exception greeted this play by declaring that it was 'untalented, toothless and quite wretched', and that it represented 'a lampoon on the Revolution'.

There was perfect unanimity, until it was suddenly and quite unexpectedly broken.

In Number 12 of the *Repertory Bulletin* for 1928 there appeared a review by P. Novitsky, in which it was stated that *The Crimson Island* was an 'interesting and witty parody' in which 'there rises up the malevolent spirit of the Grand Inquisitor, who crushes artistic creativity and cultivates SERVILE, OBSEQUIOUSLY ABSURD DRAMATIC CLICHÉS which destroy the personality of actor and author alike', and that in *The Crimson Island* the issue at stake is 'the dark and malevolent force that cultivates HELOTS, TOADIES AND EULOGISTS . . . '

It was said that 'if such a dark force does exist, then the

INDIGNATION AND MALICIOUS WIT OF THIS DRAMA-
TIST, WHO IS ACCLAIMED BY THE BOURGEOISIE,
ARE FULLY JUSTIFIED'.

One might ask, where does the truth lie in all this?

What is *The Crimson Island* when it comes down to it – 'a
wretched, untalented play' or 'a witty burlesque'?

The truth is to be found in Novitsky's review. I would not
presume to judge how witty my play is, but I admit that in the
play there does indeed rise up a malevolent spirit, and that it
is the spirit of the Chief Repertory Committee. It is they who
nurture helots, eulogists and cowed 'lackeys'. It is they who are
strangling creative thought. They are destroying Soviet drama,
and they will succeed in destroying it.

I did not express these views in whispers, in corners. I set
them out in a dramatic burlesque and staged that burlesque in
the theatre. The Soviet press, rushing to the defence of the Chief
Repertory Committee, wrote that *The Crimson Island* was a lampoon on the Revolution. That's ridiculous nonsense. There are a
number of reasons why there is no lampoon on the Revolution
in my play, of which, owing to lack of space, I shall mention only
one: owing to the extraordinary grandiosity of the Revolution, it
would be IMPOSSIBLE to write a lampoon on it. A pamphlet
is not a lampoon, and the Chief Repertory Committee is not the
Revolution.

But when the German press writes that *The Crimson Island* 'is
the first call in the USSR for freedom of the press' (*The Young
Guard*, Number 1, 1929), it is writing the truth. I admit it. To
struggle against censorship, whatever its nature, and whatever
the power under which it exists, is my duty as a writer, as are
calls for freedom of the press. I am a passionate supporter of
that freedom, and I consider that if any writer were to imagine
that he could prove he didn't need that freedom, then he would
be like a fish affirming in public that it didn't need water.

4.

That is one of the characteristics of my creative work, and
that alone is sufficient to make it impossible for my works to
exist in the USSR. But all the other characteristics that emerge
in my satirical stories are connected with that first point: the

black and mystical hues (I am a MYSTICAL WRITER) in which I have depicted the innumerable horrors of our everyday existence; the poison in which my language is soaked; my deep scepticism about the Revolutionary process that is taking place in my backward country, and the way in which I set against it my beloved Great Evolution; and, most important of all, my depiction of those dreadful traits of my people which, long before the Revolution, caused the most profound pain to my teacher M. Ye. Saltykov-Shchedrin.

It need scarcely be pointed out that it has never occurred to the Soviet press to take note of all this, preoccupied as it was with making unconvincing statements to the effect that there was 'SLANDER' in the satire of M. Bulgakov.

Only once, at the beginning of my notoriety, was it noted with a hint of haughty astonishment that:

'M. Bulgakov WISHES to become the satirist of our age' (*The Book-Pedlar*, Number 6, 1925).

Alas, the verb 'wishes' is incorrectly used here in the present tense. It ought to be translated into a pluperfect: M. Bulgakov HAD BECOME A SATIRIST, and he did so precisely at the very moment when no true satire (of the kind that penetrates into forbidden zones) was even thinkable any more in the USSR.

It did not fall to me to have the honour of expressing this criminal thought in print. It is expressed with perfect clarity in an article by V. Blyum (*Literaturnaya Gazeta*, Number 6), and the purport of this article can be brilliantly and precisely condensed into a single formulation:

ANYONE WHO WRITES SATIRE IN THE USSR IS QUESTIONING THE SOVIET SYSTEM.

Am I thinkable in the USSR?

5.

And, finally, my other characteristic traits are to be found in those ruined plays of mine, *The Days of the Turbins* and *Flight*, and in the novel *The White Guard*: my stubborn depiction of the Russian intelligentsia as the best social stratum in our country. In particular, my depiction, in the traditions of *War and Peace*, of an aristocratic family of the intelligentsia, which because of the will of immutable fate is cast during the Civil War years into the camp of the White Guard. This sort of depiction is entirely natural for a writer who has ties of blood with the intelligentsia.

But in the USSR this kind of depiction results in the author, together with his fictional heroes, earning a reputation – despite all his great efforts to stand in a dispassionate position with regard to the Reds and the Whites – as a member of the White Guard and an enemy; and once he has achieved this reputation, as anyone can understand, he can consider himself a finished man in the USSR.

6.

My literary portrait is complete, and it is a political portrait as well. I cannot say what depth of criminality may be sought in it, but I would make this one request: that nothing more should be sought beyond it. It has been executed with absolute honesty.

7.

At present I have been wiped out.

This annihilation was greeted by Soviet public opinion with great joy and was deemed an 'ACHIEVEMENT'.

R. Pikel, noting my annihilation (*Izvestiya*, 15 September 1929), expressed the following liberal thought:

'We do not thereby intend to say that the name of Bulgakov has been struck off the list of Soviet dramatists.'

And in order to reassure a writer who was already lying with a knife in his back, he added that 'they were talking only about his past dramatic works'. However, real life, in the shape of the Chief Repertory Committee, then proved that there was no foundation whatsoever for Pikel's liberalism.

On 18 March 1930 I received from the Chief Repertory Committee a document which informed me laconically that my new play *A Cabal of Hypocrites* (*Molière*), not one of my past works, WAS NOT TO BE LICENSED FOR PERFORMANCE.

Let me say briefly: that under those two lines of an official document now lie buried all my work in the libraries, my fantastic dreams, and a play which had received from competent theatrical specialists innumerable testimonials to the effect that it was a brilliant play.

R. Pikel is deluded. It is not only my past works that have perished, but also my present and all my future works. And I personally, with my own hands, threw into the stove a draft of a novel about the devil, the draft of a comedy, and the beginning of a second novel entitled *The Theatre*.

All my things are past rescuing.

8.

I would request the Soviet Government to take into account the fact that I am not someone who is active in politics, but a literary man, and that I have devoted everything I have produced to the Soviet stage.

I would like to draw your attention to the following two remarks about me in the Soviet press.

Both of them come from implacable enemies of my works, for which reason they are extremely valuable.

In 1925 it was written that:

'A writer is emerging WHO DOESN'T ATTEMPT TO DISGUISE HIMSELF EVEN IN THE COLOURS OF A FELLOW-TRAVELLER' (L. Averbakh, *Izvestiya*, 20 September 1925).

And in 1929:

'His talent is as evident as is the socially reactionary nature of his creative work' (R. Pikel, *Izvestiya*, 15 September 1929).

I would like you to take into account the fact that for me, not being allowed to write is tantamount to being buried alive.

9.

I REQUEST THAT THE SOVIET GOVERNMENT GIVE ORDERS FOR ME TO LEAVE THE TERRITORY OF THE USSR AS SOON AS POSSIBLE, TOGETHER WITH MY WIFE LYUBOV YEVGENYEVNA BULGAKOVA.

10.

I appeal to the humanity of the Soviet authorities and request that they magnanimously allow me, a writer who cannot be of any use at home in his own fatherland, to leave for freedom.

11.

And if on the other hand even what I have written is unconvincing, and I am to be condemned to lifelong silence in the USSR, then I would request the Soviet Government to give me a job for which I am qualified and to second me to some theatre to work as a director on their staff.

I particularly and precisely and emphatically request that ORDERS SHOULD BE GIVEN AND I SHOULD BE SEC-ONDED, because all my own endeavours to find work in the only field in which I can be useful to the USSR as an exception-ally well-qualified specialist have resulted in a complete fiasco. My name has been rendered so odious that proposals on my part that I should apply for a job have been met with ALARM, regardless of the fact that in Moscow there is a huge number of actors and directors, together with theatre managements, who are perfectly aware of my virtuoso knowledge of the stage.

I would like to offer the USSR the services of an entirely honourable specialist director and actor, without a trace of the saboteur, who will undertake conscientiously to stage any play, beginning with Shakespeare and coming right up to plays of the present day.

I request that I be appointed an assistant director to the Moscow Arts Theatre – to that best of schools, which is headed by such masters as K. S. Stanislavsky and V. I. Nemirovich-Danchenko.

If I am not to be appointed a director, then I request that I be appointed a regular extra. And if I cannot be an extra, then I request to be given a job as a stage-hand.

And if even that is impossible, then I request the Soviet Government to take whatever action concerning me it considers necessary, but at least to take some sort of action, because at the moment what is staring me in the face, as the author of five plays and as someone who is famous both in the USSR and abroad, is destitution, the street and death.

M. Bulgakov.

4

1930–1932

Yelena Sergeyevna has left us her recollections of what Bulgakov told her when he rushed round to see her on the evening of 18 April 1930, some three weeks after he had sent his letter to the Soviet Government. 'He lay down after his lunch, as always, to have a sleep, but the telephone immediately rang, and Lyuba called him, saying that someone was wanting to speak to him from the Central Committee. M. A. didn't believe it, and decided it was someone playing a trick on him (people did that sort of thing at the time), and all tousled and grumpy picked up the receiver and heard, "Mikhail Afanasyevich Bulgakov?" "Yes, yes!" "Comrade Stalin will speak to you now." "What? Stalin? Stalin?" And immediately afterwards heard a voice speaking with a pronounced Georgian accent.'

In the course of their conversation three important points were touched upon. Stalin's first question was whether Bulgakov really wanted to go abroad; Bulgakov, somewhat stunned and unprepared, replied, 'I have thought a great deal recently about the question of whether a Russian writer can live outside his homeland. And it seems to me he can't.' We will never know what would have happened if Bulgakov had declared at that moment that he really did want to leave the country, and clearly he must have been aware that there was a considerable risk that Stalin, instead of granting the request, might order his arrest for his anti-Soviet sentiments. Be that as it may, Bulgakov's statement that he would prefer to stay in Russia evidently drew a favourable response from Stalin, who next asked him where he would like to work – what about the Moscow Arts Theatre? Bulgakov explained that he had asked about that and had been refused, at which Stalin suggested that he should try applying again: in other words, the dictator was indicating that at a word from him everything would be different. Thirdly, Stalin proposed that he and Bulgakov should meet sometime and have a talk. Bulgakov's immediate response was enthusiastic, revealing a possibly naïve, but very human, belief – or at least hope – that perhaps his torments were all the result of some misunderstanding; perhaps the General Secretary didn't really know what was going on, and would alter things if only they could be explained properly to him. Certainly the fact that this conversation, which Bulgakov felt had been promised him, never came to pass was something that Bulgakov ever after construed as a rejection. It was a sore point to which he returned again and again, and it was one of the things that poisoned his life over the following ten years.

With hindsight Bulgakov's attitude towards Stalin appears to have been politically naïve and even morally dubious. As we have seen, Bulgakov had no illusions whatsoever about the harm being done to literature and drama in the Soviet Union by the dogmatism and narrow-mindedness of the Communist censorship, and his own experience was of a persecution so persistent and insidious that it amounted to the silencing of his artistic voice. As in the case of many of his contemporaries, however, his attitude to Stalin as an individual was a slightly different matter. This was largely because Stalin excelled at playing a kind of cat-and-mouse game with leading cultural figures, which meant that they became drawn into a kind of horrified, yet fascinated, relationship with him.

Maybe Stalin was simply satisfying his vanity by taking such a personal and individual interest in the careers of certain Moscow intellectuals, but the fact was that his very specific interventions often came to signify the difference between death, at one extreme, and success and access to an audience, at the other. Nadezhda Mandelstam in her book *Hope Against*

Hope, for example, describes two instances four years later, in 1934, when Stalin initiated telephone conversations that left indelible impressions on his interlocutors. The first, a relatively trivial example, concerned Isay Lezhnev, the former editor of *Rossiya* who had refused to return Bulgakov's manuscript of *The White Guard* to him and had then been arrested in 1926; it was in connection with his trial that Bulgakov's apartment was searched by the OGPU. By 1934 Lezhnev was currying favour with the Party authorities, and Stalin telephoned in person to tell him that he would be given permission to publish a certain book; the unfortunate Lezhnev was out at the time, and subsequently spent an entire week waiting by the telephone, desperately hoping that Stalin would ring back. The other such incident recounted by Nadezhda Mandelstam concerned her husband, the poet Osip Mandelstam, who had been arrested in May 1934. Stalin telephoned the poet Boris Pasternak out of the blue to tell him that Mandelstam's case had been reviewed and that everything would be all right; Pasternak, completely flustered, concluded his conversation by saying that he would like to have a talk with Stalin. 'About what?' 'About life and death,' Pasternak replied, at which point Stalin hung up. Pasternak tried to ring back, but the operator refused to put him through; and he too, like Bulgakov, was ever after to regret that he had not said the right things, and that a further conversation never took place. Stalin does appear to have held some of the more intractable artists of his age – Shostakovich, Prokofiev, Akhmatova, Pasternak and Bulgakov – in a curious kind of respect. Provided that, unlike the poet Mandelstam, they refrained from explicitly personal attacks on him, Stalin was content to tolerate their survival, just so long as he could keep tugging at the strings to remind them who was really in control.

Whatever we make of the relationship between Stalin and Bulgakov, the fact remains that Stalin's telephone call, which was immediately followed by the Moscow Arts Theatre's taking Bulgakov on on its staff as an assistant director, at last resolved the desperate situation he had found himself in after the banning of the five plays he had created since 1925. Subsequently Yelena Sergeyevna would frequently point out that by this intervention

Stalin may possibly have saved Bulgakov from suicide and hence, if nothing else, given him ten more years of life.

In May 1930 Bulgakov began his official employment with the Moscow Arts Theatre with work on a stage version of Gogol's novel *Dead Souls*. His role was supposed to be that of assistant director, but as soon as he saw the text of the adaptation the Theatre was proposing to use, he set about producing one of his own. As usual, his text was considerably altered by the Theatre – in this case by the joint Director of the Theatre with Stanislavsky, Vladimir Ivanovich Nemirovich-Danchenko – and the adaptation ended up a far safer and more conventional play than the one Bulgakov had originally envisaged. He had proposed to include as one of the characters Gogol himself, writing his satire of squalid Russian provincial life from the refined setting of Rome, but this entire framework was rejected. As so often in the Arts Theatre, the production was an agonizingly long time in rehearsal, as Bulgakov complained in a 1932 letter to Pavel Popov (page 143) in which he looks back over the history of the play; but when it did come out it was a success, and the revised version of Bulgakov's adaptation was used by the Arts Theatre for many decades afterwards.

In April 1930, immediately after Stalin's telephone call, Bulgakov was also appointed to a theatre called TRAM (the Young Workers' Theatre), and during July 1930 he travelled with them down to the Crimea, a journey comically described in his letters to his wife Lyuba. Once he was there, Bulgakov started sending telegrams to Yelena Sergeyevna to try to persuade her to join him, and when she didn't reply immediately he demanded that Lyuba find out whether she was ill. These exchanges suggest, as some of Lyubov Yevgenyevna's friends were to confirm in later interviews, that she was largely aware of the relationship between Bulgakov and Yelena Sergeyevna, and that this was no longer a painful subject for her – by then she was apparently pursuing her own separate life. Yelena Sergeyevna nevertheless apologetically refused in the end to join him.

The year 1930 became a relatively happy one for Bulgakov, with great joy in love and increased confidence about his work

overshadowed only by anxieties about money. In 1931, however, difficulties began to mount up again. First of all, there
came the very painful decision made by Yelena Sergeyevna
that they should stop seeing each other. Her husband Yevgeny
Aleksandrovich Shilovsky, learning of their affair, insisted that
it should come to an end; and Yelena Sergeyevna, anxious for
the welfare of their two sons, Yevgeny (Zhenya) and Sergey
(Seryozha), agreed to his conditions that she would neither see
Bulgakov nor even talk to him over the telephone. From 25
February 1931 until sometime in June 1932 they did not speak
to each other, and Bulgakov was cast into deep depression and
loneliness. His letters of the period suggest that he no longer
felt very close to Lyubov Yevgenyevna, and he describes himself
living more or less alone with his dog Bouton (named after
Molière's servant in his own play).

By the end of May 1931, feeling that he had carried out
honourably the terms of his understanding with Stalin, Bulgakov
decided to write him a further letter (page 125), this time with
the request that he be allowed to go abroad with Lyubov
Yevgenyevna from 1 July to 1 October. He opened his letter
with quotations from Gogol, justifying his desire to visit foreign
countries by the assertion that his love for Russia would only
increase as a result, just as Gogol had travelled to Italy in order
to write *Dead Souls*. This time, however, there was no reply
from Stalin, and Bulgakov's depression deepened. His letters
to his friends the writer Veresayev and the dramatist Natalya
Venkstern exude a melancholy which was to characterize many of
his letters written during the following years. During the summer
of 1931 he completed one of his weaker plays, *Adam and Eve*, a
science-fiction piece on the dangers of the war that seemed to
be threatening, which had been commissioned by the Krasny
Theatre in Leningrad. But in the autumn the play was rejected
both by the Krasny Theatre and by the Vakhtangov Theatre in
Moscow.

In the late summer of 1931 Bulgakov accepted a commission
from a different Leningrad theatre to do an adaptation for the
stage of another great nineteenth-century classic, Tolstoy's *War
and Peace*. This commission, which Bulgakov can scarcely have

taken on with much enthusiasm, was at least greeted with interest by one of his friends, the literary scholar Pavel Popov. Popov had been friendly with Bulgakov in Moscow during the 1920s, but Bulgakov had heard nothing of him since his arrest in 1929. In the autumn of 1931 he suddenly received a letter from Popov telling him that he had been permitted to live in Leningrad with his wife Anna Ilyinichna, who was Lev Tolstoy's granddaughter. When he heard about the project on *War and Peace*, Popov offered to ask his wife, who was doing some work on the drafts of the novel, to provide Bulgakov with material for his stage adaptation. Pavel Popov was to become a very important friend for Bulgakov, especially over the next few years, and the letters Bulgakov wrote to him during this time assume the nature of a kind of diary and record of his literary career. Popov, who was devoted to Bulgakov and a great admirer of his work, cherished the ambition of one day writing his biography; and for the rest of Bulgakov's life the two men corresponded on a fairly regular basis, providing us with invaluable insights into Bulgakov's state of mind.

This re-establishing of contact with Pavel Popov came on the eve of Bulgakov's losing contact with another of his friends, the writer Yevgeny Zamyatin. Zamyatin – author of the anti-Utopian novel *We* (1920), which would later influence George Orwell in the writing of *1984* – was in some respects very different from Bulgakov. Where Zamyatin was concerned that the increasing dogmatism in Soviet culture threatened to stifle innovation and experimentation in the future, for example, Bulgakov was always more worried about the damage Soviet cultural policy was doing to the heritage and traditions of the past. Zamyatin lived in Leningrad, which meant that the two writers didn't see each other very frequently. Yet for some years they had been close friends, and the jocular intimacy of their letters is unlike the rather formal style Bulgakov usually tended to adopt in his correspondence. After virulent attacks on him in the Soviet press, Zamyatin too had addressed a letter to Stalin asking to be allowed to leave the USSR; and, thanks to the intercession of Gorky, he actually did obtain permission to leave. In the late autumn of 1931 Bulgakov was making arrangements to see Zamyatin and his wife before their departure. This must have been a bitter experience for Bulgakov, serving only to reinforce his sense that he had been singled out arbitrarily to be prevented from ever seeing the rest of the world, an ambition that by now had turned into an obsession.

Gorky may not have been able to persuade the Soviet Government to let Bulgakov travel in 1929, but he was at least able to help Bulgakov in one respect in the autumn of 1931, by putting in a good word for the play about Molière, the banning of which in March 1930 had provoked Bulgakov's first letter to the Soviet Government. During the summer of 1931, Bulgakov made a number of alterations to the text of the Molière play, toning down in particular some hints of the supernatural; and the result was that on 3 October it was finally licensed for performance – at first only in Moscow and Leningrad, but with the proviso that it could be performed elsewhere in due course. At last, Bulgakov's spirits began to rise; and this more positive mood is reflected in his spontaneously complimentary letter to Stanislavsky at the Arts Theatre, written on the last day of 1931 (page 135), in which he expresses his delight at the way Stanislavsky has succeeded in bringing *Dead Souls* to life during rehearsals.

Then in the middle of January 1932 came a really astonishing piece of news; that the Government had requested that the Moscow Arts Theatre revive *The Days of the Turbins*, banned since 1929. The explanation that eventually emerged was that Stalin had come to watch another play at the Arts Theatre and had asked why *The Turbins* was no longer being performed; Nemirovich-Danchenko had found some tactful way of explaining that it had been taken off as a result of Stalin's own negative assessment of Bulgakov's works in 1929, and a telephone call was received in the Theatre the very next day asking how soon the play could be put back on. Bulgakov nearly collapsed at the news, and when his friend Fedya Mikhalsky from the Arts Theatre rushed round to see him, he found him with his feet in a basin of hot water and with cold compresses on his head and heart! Thenceforth, *The Days of the Turbins* was to remain constantly in the Theatre's repertory, providing Bulgakov with virtually his only regular income.

The bitter experience of the previous three years had, however, taught Bulgakov just how fragile all such successes could prove. And indeed, he had only just – with great relief – sent his completed adaptation of *War and Peace* off to Leningrad in February, and begun to recover from his excitement over *The Days of the Turbins*, when a new blow landed on him from an entirely unexpected quarter, from Leningrad, where the Bolshoy Dramatic Theatre had already signed a contract for the Molière play. Suddenly Bulgakov received word that they were cancelling the production, a decision he found utterly baffling. For once, as he told Popov, he could not blame the authorities, who had indeed licensed the play for performance. Over the following weeks he was to learn, to his furious indignation, that the blow had been dealt him by a single individual, a rival playwright, the Communist writer Vsevolod Vishnevsky. The influential Vishnevsky had merely written an article in the local newspaper deploring the Theatre's choice of Bulgakov's play and calling on them to put on something more 'relevant' to the interests of the workers, and the Theatre had cancelled the production on the spot. Bulgakov was shattered by this calamity, and his letters of March and April 1932 show him wrestling in anguish with the question of how he could have acted differently in the past so as to avoid the frustrations that now meet him at every turn. He talks of having committed 'five fatal mistakes' in his life, a cryptic remark which is difficult to decipher: we may speculate that these 'mistakes' include his failure to emigrate in 1921; his failure to speak out during his conversation with Stalin in 1930 and demand to be allowed to leave; and, perhaps, the fact that he had allowed Yelena Sergeyevna to abandon him.

The spring of 1932 dragged on, with the usual depressing letters arriving from his brother Nikolay in France about attempts by various dubious characters to misappropriate his royalties abroad. Although he was still living with Lyubov Yevgenyevna, their marriage was clearly at an end. Bulgakov was desperate to move out of his apartment on Pirogovskaya Street and gain some sort of foothold in a new apartment-block being built for writers, but this was going to be impossible unless he could raise the money for a deposit, and his financial position remained very difficult. But at last his personal affairs took a vital turn for the better. In June 1932 Yelena Sergeyevna brought their separation to an end by asking him to see her, and although after their meeting she went away for the summer to think over what they should do, Bulgakov was filled with new hope. Perhaps fired by this fresh optimism, Bulgakov signed a contract in July 1932 with the publishers of a series called 'Lives of the Great' for a prose biography of Molière. Although the production of his play about Molière had been cancelled in Leningrad, and the Arts Theatre was dragging its feet over it in Moscow, Bulgakov returned to the topic of Molière with enthusiasm and energy. He plunged into historical research, reading a great many studies of Molière, the early biography of him by Grimarest, and historians of the period such as Eugène Despois. That summer he found himself for the first time in three years writing a work to which he felt genuinely committed.

In the early autumn, when Yelena Sergeyevna returned to Moscow, there were still some painful discussions to be endured; not just with her husband Yevgeny Aleksandrovich Shilovsky, but also with her elder son Yevgeny, who was to remain with his father. But in September 1932 Yelena Sergeyevna's marriage was finally dissolved; on 3 October Bulgakov got his divorce from Lyubov Yevgenyevna (for whom they found a separate room – even if it was in the immediately adjoining apartment); and on the next day, 4 October 1932, Bulgakov and Yelena Sergeyevna were married. After spending a couple of weeks in Leningrad they returned to Moscow to start their life together in the Pirogovskaya Street apartment, with Yelena Sergeyevna's six-year-old son Seryozhka, and for Bulgakov a period of genuine personal happiness began which was to do much to compensate for the professional frustrations and political terrors of the decade.

10 May 1930. Moscow
To the Board of Directors of the Moscow Arts Theatre

I request that the Board of Directors of the Moscow Arts Theatre should take me on as a member of staff in the position of director.

M. Bulgakov.

15–17 July 1930. From near Kursk; near Simferopol; and Miskhor to Moscow
To his wife Lyubov Yevgenyevna

15 July 1930. Morning. Near Kursk

Well, Lyubanya, you can be glad for me, I've got away! You're missing me, of course? [. . .] It looks as though I will know my address once we get to Sevastopol. Sweetie, drop in at the tailor's. Open all correspondence. Yours.

The exuberant energy of the TRAM [Young Workers' Theatre] lot swept them through the train, and they brought back the news that there was a place in a first-class carriage. In Serpukhov I paid the difference and moved. In the buffet at Serpukhov there was not a single drop of any kind of liquid. Can you imagine the TRAM people with a guitar, no pillows, no teapots, no water, lying on slatted wooden bunks? By morning they'll be a heap of little corpses, I suppose. I have set up house on the top bunk. I feast my eyes with disgust on the landscapes. The sun. Geese.

16 July 1930. Near Simferopol. Morning

Dear Lyubanya! There's bright sunshine here. The Crimea is just as nasty a part of the world as ever. The TRAM people are as perky as cucumbers. In the buffets at the station there are a few things to be had, but for the most part they're pretty empty. In the south the womenfolk bring cucumbers, cherries, eggs, white loaves, onions and milk out to the trains. The train is running late. [. . .] I send you a kiss! How's Bouton [his dog]?

Please, my angel, could you go and see Bychkov the tailor and tell him to hold on to my suit for the moment. I'll try it when I get back. If there's a telegram from the theatre in Leningrad send me a telegram.

M.

17 July 1930. Crimea. Miskhor. Pension Magnolia
Dear Lyubinka, I've settled in well. The weather is inde-
scribably beautiful. I'm really sorry that none of my friends is
here, and that I'm with a lot of folk I don't know.* You have
to make your own arrangements about food, it seems there's
absolutely nothing to be had. Our vouchers for the pension are
quite reasonable. It's a shame that I couldn't bring you (my
conscience is gnawing at me that I'm in the sun on my own).
I'm about to go to Yalta in a motor-launch, I want to have a
look at what's there. Greetings to all. I send you a kiss.

Mak.

* But the TRAM people are nice.

July 1930. From Miskhor to Moscow
To Yelena Sergeyevna Shilovskaya (subsequently Bulgakov's wife) (telegrams)

[1] Certain your department could urgently acquire with
weighty document Moscow travel agency vouchers south coast
Crimea Sevastopol.

[2] Imagine department will find place some pension Miskhor-
Yalta coast. How's health? Greetings your family. Telegraph
Crimea Miskhor Pension Magnolia. Bulgakov.

22 July 1930. From Miskhor
To his friend the playwright Natalya Venkstern

Dearest Natalya Alekseyevna!
There's intense heat in the Crimea. The sea – is as it always
is . . . The tedium is not just green, but something monstrous,
the sort of thing you see only in dreams. I'm intending to come
back in the first few days of August.

28 July 1930. From Miskhor to Moscow
To his wife Lyubov Yevgenyevna (telegram)

Why no letters from Lyusetta [Yelena Sergeyevna]? Must
be ill.

July 1930. From Moscow to Miskhor
From Yelena Sergeyevna (telegrams)

[1] Hello dear friend Mishenka. I think of you often and you are very dear to my heart. Get better and have a good rest. I would like to see you happy and cheerful and dreadfully attractive. Your Madeleine Cowardy the Unreliable.

[2] Dearest Mishenka terribly glad your return soon beg you don't torment me Puzanovsky.

31 July 1930. From Zagreb (where he had returned for the summer) to Moscow
From his brother Nikolay

Dear Misha,

I am writing this letter lying in the Ear, Nose and Throat Clinic at Zagreb University. On 29 July I had two operations performed on my nose and throat. [. . .] Your silence, of course, depresses me deeply, especially since several of my letters in a row have remained unanswered. I have some news of you from elsewhere – e. g. about your appointment at the Moscow Arts Theatre – but in the absence of any letters from you I can't attach much significance to anything. [. . .]

Nikol.

6 August 1930. Moscow
To Konstantin Stanislavsky (joint Director of the Moscow Arts Theatre)

Much esteemed Konstantin Sergeyevich,

Now that I have returned from the Crimea, where I was recovering from nervous ailments after these last two very difficult years, I am writing to you a few simple and unofficial lines:

The banning of all my plays compelled me to address a letter to the Government of the USSR, in which I asked either to be allowed out of the country, if it was now really impossible for me to work as a playwright, or to be offered the opportunity to work as a director in some theatre in the USSR.

There is only one theatre that is the best. And you know it well.

And in my letter to the Government I wrote, 'I request to be allowed to join the best school, headed by those masters K. S. Stanislavsky and V. I. Nemirovich-Danchenko.' Note was taken of my letter, and I was given the opportunity to submit an application to the Arts Theatre and to join their staff.

After my pain and grief at the destruction of my plays, I began to feel better when – after a long pause, and already in a new capacity – I crossed the threshold of the theatre that you have created for the glory of the nation.

Dear Konstantin Sergeyevich, please accept your new director with a light heart. Believe me, he loves your Arts Theatre. [. . .]

Respectfully yours,

Mikhail Bulgakov.

7 August 1930. From Moscow to Zagreb
To his brother Nikolay

Dear Nikol,

Yesterday I received your letter from Zagreb dated 31 August 1930. [. . .] *Before that I hadn't received any of your letters.* My last letter to you contained a request for medicines. I didn't get any reply to it or to the preceding one. [. . .]

1) The Moscow Arts Theatre: the information about my appointment there is accurate. I've been appointed a director [. . .].

2) I badly need money. And this is why: I have been allocated a salary of 150 roubles a month at the Arts Theatre, but I don't actually get that because I have to hand it over to clear the last quarter of my income tax for last year. I'm left with just a few roubles a month. Apart from that, I get 300 roubles a month from a theatre called TRAM (the Young Workers' Theatre). I joined it at approximately the same time as I joined the Moscow Arts Theatre.

But the financial wounds I have suffered over the last year are so painful and so irreparable that the 300 TRAM roubles are simply swallowed up in the abyss of my debts (it's just like a sticky cobweb).

I am not writing this to bore you or to complain. Even in

Moscow some sons of bitches have been spreading a rumour that I earn 500 roubles a month in each theatre. For several years now people have been spinning fantasies around my name in Moscow and abroad. For the most part spiteful ones.

But you, of course, will realize that you can obtain trustworthy information about me only from my letters, however sparse they may be.

And so: if you have any of my money, and if there is any possibility whatsoever of transferring it to the USSR, then transfer it *without wasting a moment*. [. . .]

Get well soon. I hope that your operation will have an entirely favourable outcome. I'm glad that you're absorbed in your scholarly work. Be brilliant in your research, bold and cheerful, and always have hope. Lyuba sends greetings.

Your Mikhail.

4 September 1930. Moscow
From Konstantin Stanislavsky (joint Director of the Moscow Arts Theatre)

Dear, good Mikhail Afanasyevich!

You cannot imagine how glad I am that you have joined our theatre! I have only had the opportunity to work with you on a few rehearsals of *The Days of the Turbins* and even then I sensed in you a theatre director (and maybe even an actor?!).

Molière and many others combined these professions with literature! With all my heart I welcome you. I sincerely believe in your success, and would very much like to start working with you as soon as possible.

29 December 1930. Moscow
To the Board of Directors of the Moscow Arts Theatre

I am carving out time between the rehearsals of *Dead Souls* and my work in the evenings for TRAM in order to create the role of the Leader (or Reader) [a narrator figure for *Dead Souls*] – and every day and at every moment I am obliged to tear myself away from it in order to rush around the town looking for money. I consider it my duty to inform the Board of Directors that I am at the end of my tether.

18 March 1931. Moscow
To Konstantin Stanislavsky (joint Director of the Moscow Arts Theatre)
Dear and much esteemed Konstantin Sergeyevich!

I have left TRAM, since it was impossible for me to cope with the work for them.

I am turning to you with the request that I be taken on as an actor as well as a director at the Moscow Arts Theatre.

Early 1931. Moscow
To Yosif Stalin (draft)
[. . .] Much esteemed Yosif Vissarionovich!

About eighteen months have passed since I fell silent as a writer. And now, since I am feeling gravely ill, I would like to ask you to become my first reader [a reference to Tsar Nicholas I's role as personal censor to the poet Pushkin] . . .

30 May 1931. Moscow
To Yosif Stalin
Much esteemed Yosif Vissarionovich!

'More and more the desire grew in me to become a modern writer. But at the same time I saw that, in depicting the contemporary scene, it was impossible to attain that highly attuned and tranquil state that is essential to the execution of a great and harmonious work.

'The present is too animated, it is too stirring, it is too stimulating: *a writer's pen shifts imperceptibly over into satire.*

' . . . it has always seemed to me that some great self-sacrifice awaited me in my life, and that precisely in order to serve my fatherland *I would have to develop myself somewhere far away from it.*

' . . . I knew only that I was travelling not at all in order to delight in foreign lands, but rather in order to endure, exactly as if I had foreseen that I would recognize the value of Russia only outside Russia, and that I would attain love for her only when I was far away.'

N. Gogol

I earnestly request you to intercede on my behalf with the

Government of the USSR so that I may be sent on leave abroad for the period 1 July to 1 October 1931.

I would like it to be known that after eighteen months of silence I have been irrepressibly fired with new creative projects and that these projects are powerful and of broad scope; and I would ask that the Government grant me the opportunity to carry them out.

Since the end of 1930 I have been suffering from a grave form of neurasthenia, with attacks of fearfulness and chest pains, and at the present moment I am very low.

I have my projects, but no physical strength, and I have absolutely none of the conditions necessary for me to carry out my work.

The cause of my illness is absolutely clear to me.

In the broad field of Russian literature in the USSR I have been the one and only literary wolf. I was advised to dye my fur. An absurd piece of advice. Whether a wolf dyes his fur or has it clipped, he will still look nothing like a poodle.

I have been treated like a wolf. For several years I have been pursued according to all the rules of wolf-baiting in a fenced-in yard.

I feel no anger, but I am very weary, and at the end of 1929 I collapsed. After all, even a beast can become weary.

At that point the beast declared that he was no longer a wolf, nor a writer. That he was renouncing his profession. That he was falling silent. And that, to be frank, was pusillanimous.

There is no such thing as a writer who falls silent. If he falls silent, it means he was never a true writer.

For if a true writer were to fall silent, then he would perish.

The cause of my illness is the persecution that I have endured for many years, followed by silence.

Over the last year I have done the following:

– despite great difficulties, I transformed Gogol's *Dead Souls* into a play,

– I worked on the rehearsals of this play in the capacity of a director at the Moscow Arts Theatre,

– I worked in the capacity of an actor, taking the parts of actors who were off sick during those rehearsals,

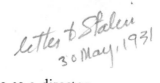

– I was appointed by the Moscow Arts Theatre as a director for all the campaigns and Revolutionary festivals of the year,

– I worked in the Young Workers' Theatre (TRAM), switching from daytime work at the Arts Theatre to evening work at TRAM,

– I left TRAM on 15 March 1931, when I felt that my brain was refusing to function, and that I was not bringing TRAM any benefit,

– I agreed to undertake a production for the Health Education Theatre (and will complete it by July).

And at night I began to write.

But I overtaxed my strength.

I am run down.

At present my impressions are all monochrome, my plans are draped in black, and I am poisoned by melancholy and by habitual irony.

During the years when I have been working as a writer, every citizen, whether he belongs to the Party or not, has drummed into me and continues to drum into me that from the very moment when I wrote and published my first line through until the end of my life, I will never see any other countries.

If that is the case, then my horizons are limited, and I am deprived of the highest schooling for a writer, I have lost the opportunity to decide for myself questions of enormous significance. What has been inculcated in me is the psychology of a prisoner.

How am I to sing of my country, the USSR?

I weighed everything up before writing to you. I need to see the world, and once I have seen it, to return. That's the key point.

I would like to inform you, Yosif Vissarionovich, that leading figures in the arts who have travelled abroad have solemnly warned me that I should never be able to stay there.

I have been warned that, in the event of the Government's opening the door for me, I would have to be particularly careful so as not somehow to slam the door behind me accidentally and cut off my way back, thereby bringing upon myself a disaster that would be even worse than the banning of my plays.

The common view of all those who have taken a serious interest in my work is that I would be unthinkable in any land other than my own – the USSR – since I have been deriving all my strength as a writer from the USSR for the past eleven years.

I am sensitive to such warnings, the most weighty of which have come from my wife, who has been abroad. At the time when I was asking to be exiled she announced to me that she would not wish to remain abroad, and that I would perish there from misery in under a year.

(I myself have never been abroad in my life. The information in the *Great Soviet Encyclopaedia* to the effect that I have been abroad is incorrect.)

'This kind of Bulgakov is not the sort we need in the Soviet theatre,' wrote one critic in admonitory fashion when I was banned.

I don't know whether I am needed in the Soviet theatre, but I know I need the Soviet theatre as much as I need air to breathe.

I request the Government of the USSR to let me out until the autumn and to permit my wife Lyubov Yevgenyevna Bulgakova to accompany me. I make the latter request because I am seriously ill. I have to be accompanied by someone close to me. I suffer from attacks of terror when I am on my own.

If any further explanations are needed to supplement this letter, I will provide them for whoever would like to summon me.

But as I conclude this letter I want to tell you, Yosif Vissarionovich, that my dream as a writer would be to be summoned to see you in person.

Please believe me when I say that this is not because I see it as being the most advantageous development for me, but because your conversation with me over the telephone in April 1930 left a deep mark in my memory.

You said, 'Perhaps you really do need to go abroad . . . ?'

I have not been indulged with many such conversations. Moved by that phrase, I have been working in good faith as a director in the theatres of the USSR for the last year.

M. Bulgakov.

29 June 1931. From Moscow
To the writer Vikenty Veresayev

I have already become afraid to telephone or write or call on decent people: I realize myself that I have disappeared from the scene in an unseemly way.

But I trust that you will believe me when I say that the theatre has completely swallowed me up. I'm simply not here. Principally *Dead Souls*. Quite apart from the adaptation and the corrections to it, which are clearly going to go on for ever, there is directing, and on top of that acting (by the way, I'm signing up as an actor as well in the autumn – what do you think of that?). [. . .]

All this has ended badly: I have become ill, Vikenty Vikentyevich. I won't enumerate the symptoms, I will just say that I have stopped answering any official letters. And a venomous thought often comes to me: have I not in fact run my course? The scientific name for this is neurasthenia, if I am not mistaken.

1 July 1931. From Moscow to Zubtsov (on the Volga)
To his friend the playwright Natalya Venkstern

It all depends on my work. If all goes well I will try to get away to Zubtsov sometime in July (perhaps after the 10th). [. . .] My plan is to sit alone in the wing of the house and write, while at the same time I shall enjoy elevated literary conversation with you. Apart from writing I will lead a simple life: dressing-gown, slippers, sleeping and eating.

When I get there I will tell you a great many things which are intended specially for you. [. . .] I shall sit there like Diogenes in his barrel.

22–28 July 1931. From Moscow
To the writer Vikenty Veresayev

When I came back today after spending twelve days swimming and writing in Zubtsov, your letter of 17 July was waiting for me, and I was delighted by it. [. . .]

Why indeed do we see each other so rarely? In that dark year [1929] when I was crushed, and the cards suggested only one thing – that I should put an end to it all and shoot myself –

you came and lifted my spirits. It was the tender wisdom of a writer! [. . .]

There are different ways of being busy. Mine is unnatural. It is a blend of the darkest disquiet, which I suffer from because of trivialities that I shouldn't be busying myself with, of complete hopelessness, of neurasthenic fears and of helpless endeavours. My wing has been broken.

I have neglected seeing people and writing letters. [. . .] I can't even compose five lines of a letter. I am afraid to write! I burn the beginnings of letters in the stove. [. . .]

Vikenty Vikentyevich! Please read what comes next attentively. Give me some advice.

I suffer from one tormenting unhappiness. And that is that my conversation with the General Secretary never took place. What that means for me is horror, and the darkness of the grave. I have a frantic desire to see other countries, if only briefly. I get out of bed with this thought every morning and I go to sleep with it.

For a year I have been racking my brains, trying to work out what happened. After all, I wasn't hallucinating, was I, when I heard his words? After all, he did utter the phrase 'Perhaps you really do need to go abroad. . . ?'

He did say it! What went wrong? After all, he did want to see me? . . . [. . .]

There are two theories going around Moscow. According to the first (and it has numerous advocates), I am under the closest, most unremitting surveillance, and therefore my every line, thought, phrase and step is being weighed up. It's a flattering theory, but alas, it has one major flaw. So that in reply to my question, 'But why, in that case, if it's all so interesting and important, will they not let me write?', the narrow-minded inhabitants of Moscow came to the following conclusion: 'But that's the whole point. You write God knows what, and that's why you have to be purified by fire in a crucible of hardship and trouble, so that when you have been cleansed, praises will start to flow from your pen.'

But that completely turns the formulation that 'being determines consciousness' on its head, since it's impossible to imagine even physically that a man whose existence consisted of hardship and trouble would suddenly burst out in praises. For that reason I'm opposed to that theory.

There is another theory. It has virtually no advocates, but at least I belong to their number.

According to this theory, there's nothing there at all! No enemies, no crucible, no surveillance, no desire for praise [. . .] – nothing. No one is interested, no one needs it, so what are we talking about? A citizen's plays were put on, and then, well, they were taken off, so what's the problem? Why should this citizen, some Sidor or Pyotr or Ivan, start writing to the Central Executive Committee or the Ministry for Education and goodness knows where else with applications and requests, and about going abroad too?! And what will be the reward for his pains? He'll get nothing. Neither good nor bad. There will simply be no reply. And that's perfectly right and reasonable! For if you were to start replying to every Sidor, you'd end up with a right Tower of Babel.

So there's a theory for you, Vikenty Vikentyevich! Only that one doesn't work either. Because right in the middle of my despair, interrupting it, fortunately, the General Secretary did telephone me a year or so ago. And you can trust my judgement: he conducted the conversation powerfully, clearly, in a statesmanlike fashion and with elegance. Hope flared up in this writer's heart: only one step remained – that I should see him and discover my fate. [. . .]

But then a thick veil descended. More than a year passed. And to write another letter, of course, was impossible.

And nevertheless I did write a letter this spring and sent it off. Composing it was an agonizing labour. When it's the General Secretary, only one thing is possible – the truth, and it must be serious. But you just try and say everything in a letter. You'd have to write forty pages. That truth could be better expressed in telegraphic form:

'I am being destroyed by nervous exhaustion. *Let me have a change of scene* for three months. I will come back!'

And that's all. And the reply could be telegraphic too: 'Send him off tomorrow.'

At the thought of such a reply my worn-out heart began to

thud, I seemed to see light. I imagined the floods of sunshine over Paris! I wrote the letter. I quoted Gogol, and I attempted to communicate the things that pierce me to the heart.

But the floods of light faded away. There was no reply. And now, sombre feelings. One person tried to console me: 'It never reached him.' That cannot be. Another, a practical soul with no floods or fantasies, subjected my letter to professional scrutiny. And came away completely dissatisfied.

'Who's going to believe that you are so ill your wife has to accompany you? Who's going to believe that you will come back? Who's going to believe that?'

And so on.

Since I was a child I have detested those words 'Who's going to believe that?' It's a phrase that has its home somewhere where I don't live, where I can't exist. I could ask a dozen such questions: 'And who's going to believe that Gogol is my mentor? And who's going to believe that I have great projects? And who's going to believe that I am a writer?' And so on and so forth.

I have nothing good to look forward to now. But still one thought torments me. And so, the time has come for me to think about more important things. But before making any decisions about important and fearful things, I would like to be granted, if not leave to travel, then at least some information. Can I have information?

I must finish this letter, or else I will never send it off to you. If we don't see each other soon, I'll write you another one about my play.

Vikenty Vikentyevich, I have become anxious and fearful, I keep expecting disasters and I have become superstitious.

I wish you health and a good rest. Greetings to Mariya Germogenovna. I shall look forward to a visit or a call from you. Lyubov Yevgenyevna is in Zubtsov.

12 August 1931. To Moscow
From the writer Vikenty Veresayev

Dear Mikhail Afanasyevich!

I received your letter and sensed, not so much from your words as from the letter itself, how seriously unwell you are, and how troubled your spirits are. As for advice – I don't quite understand what it is you want my advice about. But I still think your hopes of a vacation abroad are completely mad. [. . .]

It is difficult to advise a man in your situation, but all the same I am determined to give you one piece of advice. Supposing a man has been told, 'You can't have children.' Then he says to himself, 'So what's the point of having sexual relations? To hell with it!' And then a monstrous thing happens: his health goes to pieces, he is consumed with exasperation and frustration, he sees naked girls in his sleep and can't think of anything else. Is an artist's desire to write any weaker than sexual desire? And can he, without crippling his whole being, tell himself, 'They won't print me, so I'll give up writing'? That would be a profound mistake.

29 August 1931. From Paris to Moscow
From his brother Ivan

My dear Misha!

I have been wanting to describe my life to you for a long time, to share things with you, and to find out about you and your affairs. I have moved to Paris, where I met up with Kolya after a ten-year interval. I am now working as a musician playing the balalaika, both as a member of an orchestra and as a soloist.

I am married (as you know), and I have a daughter – Ira. She's now about seven. All my family know all about you and love you as their own, sharing in all your joys and griefs. [. . .] I very much want to keep in touch with you, but only so long as I don't hinder you in your work. I am doing some writing myself, or rather I have written things: mostly poetry, and a little prose. I should like to show you what I have written. Only at the moment I am too busy with work (from three until midnight). Things are easier now that I am with Kolya. Before that I felt my loneliness and the fact that I was cut off from everybody.

6 October 1931. From Moscow to Leningrad
To Ruvim Shapiro (a director at the Bolshoy Dramatic
Theatre)

I should like to inform you that *Molière* has been given a

licence by the Chief Repertory Committee for performance in the theatres of Moscow and Leningrad. [. . .]

And so, if your theatre would like to put on *Molière*, I would ask you to arrange to negotiate a contract with me.

26 October 1931. From Moscow to Leningrad
To the writer Yevgeny Zamyatin

What sort of way of carrying on is this – not writing to your good friends? When are you going abroad? I was told that you would be coming to Moscow at the end of October or at the beginning of November. Dash off a line to tell me when. [. . .]

It will be pleasant for a provincial like me to admire the pipe and the suitcase of a real tourist.

28 October 1931. From Leningrad to Moscow
From the writer Yevgeny Zamyatin

Dear Afanasyevich,

And so – hurrah for the three Ms: Mikhail, Maksim [Gorky] and Molière! This splendid combination of three Ms should turn out very profitably: I'm very glad for you. So, you're joining the ranks of the playwrights, while I join those of the Wandering Jews . . .

My distant travels will begin, probably, on 14 November. So that means I should be in Moscow on the 4th or the 5th: that depends on our hearing that we've got the visas (which we still don't have, the devil take them!).

30 October 1931. From Tyarlevo (near Leningrad) to Moscow
From his friend Pavel Popov

I will be very glad to see you in Leningrad, especially since we may be able to be useful to you: A. I. [Anna Ilyinichna Tolstaya-Popova] is currently typing out the variants of *War and Peace*, and you may be able to use some of Tolstoy's draft materials for your work. They might help to reinforce certain images in the scenes you're going to select from the novel. You could arrange with A. I. to look through the necessary variants.

25 December 1931. Moscow
To the writer Aleksey [Maksim] Gorky

Esteemed Aleksey Maksimovich!

My *Molière* has been licensed for performance, at first only in Moscow and Leningrad [. . .].

Knowing what significance your positive report on the play had in its obtaining a licence, I would like to thank you from the bottom of my heart.

I have received permission to send the play to Berlin, and have sent it to Fischer Verlag, with whom I usually enter into contracts regarding the copyright and distribution of my plays abroad.

31 December 1931. Moscow
To Konstantin Stanislavsky (joint Director of the Moscow Arts Theatre)

I wanted to write this letter to you the day after the rehearsal of the party scene in *Dead Souls*. But in the first place I was shy, and secondly I wasn't in the Theatre (I had a cold).

The purpose of this informal letter is to express to you the delight that I have been carrying around with me during these past days. In the space of three hours before my very eyes you transformed the key scene, which had frozen and got stuck, into something alive.

Theatrical magic does exist!

It arouses the highest hopes in me and revives my spirits when I am feeling low. I find it difficult to say what delighted me the most. I don't know, truly. Perhaps your remark about Manilov: 'You mustn't say anything or ask him about anything, because he would instantly glue himself to you' – that was the high point. It's an astonishing definition, precisely in a theatrical sense, and as for your demonstration of how it should be done – that showed the most profound mastery!

I do not worry about Gogol when you are at the rehearsal. Through you he will come. He will come amid laughter in the first scenes of the performance, and in the last he will go off, covered in a shroud of profound meditations. He will come.

19 January 1932. From Paris to Moscow
From his brother Nikolay

All the things meant for Lyubochka (the blouse, the stockings and the little comb) are a present to her from Vanya and me. We would have liked to make a present of the rest to you, Misha, but unfortunately neither Vanya nor I can manage that at the moment; so we will have to resort to the method you suggested, Misha, of a transfer from Berlin. You need to send 500 (five hundred) francs! I quite understand that it's a lot of money, but I see no other solution for the moment. If the sum is too great, or if you don't have that much in reserve, Mikhail, then just transfer as much as you can!

25 January–24 February 1932. From Moscow to Tyarlevo
(near Leningrad)
To his friend Pavel Popov

So here at last a reply is getting written to your last letter. Insomnia, which has now become my true mistress, comes to my aid and guides my pen. But mistresses, as we know, can be unfaithful. Oh, how I would like this one to be unfaithful to me!

And so, dear friend, you ask what one should eat to accompany vodka? Ham. But that's not sufficient. You have to eat it at twilight, sitting on an old, worn settee, amongst old and faithful possessions. A dog should be sitting on the floor by your chair, and you shouldn't be able to hear the trams. It's not yet six in the morning, and there they are, already wailing as they leave the park, and making my accursed dwelling shake. However, I mustn't tempt fate, or else this summer, who knows, I might lose even that – the contract is running out. [. . .]

Have you already heard? Has the news reached you in Leningrad and Tyarlevo? No? Then allow me: on 15 January they rang from the Theatre to inform me that *The Days of the Turbins* is being put back on with all haste. It's unpleasant for me to have to admit it: the news overwhelmed me. I felt physically unwell. A flood of joy, but then immediately I felt anguish as well. My heart, my heart! [. . .]

Then the news leaked out into the town. Mother of God, what happened then! [. . .]

The appalling reactions were of three types. The first took the form 'Congratulations. Now you'll be rich!' That's all right the first time. It's all right the second time. But by the hundredth time it becomes irksome. All the same, we are an uncultured people! What a way to congratulate someone! Especially since congratulations like those will ring hollow to someone in my position for a long time to come, like the very stupidest of taunts. I think about the coming summer and the question of the apartment with dread.

The second line: 'I'll be mortally offended if I don't receive a ticket for the première.' That's just the limit.

And the third is worst of all: it appeared that the inhabitants of Moscow absolutely had to know, 'What does it mean?!' and they began to pester me with the question. They were asking a fine source! And then the population of the city, seeing that neither the author of the play nor anyone else was able or willing to explain, decided to explain it for themselves. And they found such explanations, Pavel Sergeyevich, that my head began to spin. [. . .] And all the same, Pavel Sergeyevich, what does it mean? Do I know?

I know that in the middle of January 1932, for reasons unknown to me, and into a consideration of which I cannot enter, the Government of the USSR issued a wonderful instruction to the Moscow Arts Theatre: that *The Days of the Turbins* should be revived.

For the play's author that means that he – the author – has had a part of his life restored to him. That's all. [. . .]

Today I received your postcard of 20 February 1932. I thank you tenderly for your congratulations!

I will send you this letter, however out of date it has become, and follow it with some more. So now you can see how I work in the epistolary mode . . . agonizingly, as though I were pulling a cart. And so, I send you this letter as 'letter number one'.

**20 February 1932. From Tyarlevo (near Leningrad) to Moscow
From his friend Pavel Popov (postcard)**

I've worn holes in the Moscow newspaper where all you could see was '*The Days of the Turbins* (all tickets sold)' – but then the last three words didn't mean much to me, since I used to see that phrase so often a few years ago. But apart from that I wished I could read something more, since some kind of 'footnote', as editors say, is vital here. All sorts of fantastical rumours are circulating here, which I have tried to quell.

15 March 1932. Moscow
To the writer Vikenty Veresayev

I keep hoping to drop in to see you towards evening to talk about literature, but we're having rehearsals all the time . . .

We're rehearsing in Stanislavsky's house and we finish late.

But just the same, I do sometimes have an agonizing desire to talk to someone.

Yesterday I received the news that my *Molière* has been killed off in Leningrad. The Bolshoy Dramatic Theatre sent me a letter informing me that their Artistic-Political Council has turned down the production and that the Theatre is releasing me from all my contractual obligations.

How did I feel?

My first wish was to grab someone by the throat and start some kind of fight. Then came lucidity. I understood that there was no one to grab, and that I didn't know why or what for. Tilting against windmills is what used to happen in Spain, as you know, and that was a long time ago.

And it's an absurd pastime.

I'm too old.

And the thought that someone might watch from the sidelines with cold and powerful eyes, and might laugh and say, 'Go on, flounder away . . . ' No, no, it's unthinkable!

You have to keep the knowledge of your utter, blinding help-lessness to yourself.

19 March 1932. From Moscow to Tyarlevo (near Leningrad)
To his friend Pavel Popov

What on earth happened?

Above all, it is such a blow to me that I cannot describe it. It would be painful and lengthy.

I had staked everything on that première in April (approximately) on the Fontanka Canal. But my card has lost. The summer has gone up in smoke . . . and, in a word, what more is there to say?

As to the fact that it is a real blow, that's something I'm telling only you. Don't tell anyone else, lest they should play on it and cause me even further harm.

What's more, it means that, to my horror, a permit from the Chief Repertory Committee turns out to be valid for all plays except mine.

It is my pleasant duty to declare that on this occasion I can have no grievance against the organs of the State. Here's the licence.

The State didn't take the play off through its organs of control, and it isn't responsible for the fact that the Theatre took it off. So who did take it off? The Theatre? For pity's sake! What did they pay me 1,200 roubles for, and send a member of the Board of Directors down to Moscow to sign the contract?

Eventually some information arrived from Leningrad. It turns out that the play was taken off not by an organ of the State. *Molière* was destroyed by an utterly unexpected figure!

Molière was killed by a private individual with no authority, a non-political, amateurish and retiring figure whose motives were by no means political. This individual is a dramatist [Vsevolod Vishnevsky]. He appeared in the Theatre and gave them such a fright that they dropped the play. [. . .]

So what is all this?

This is what: I was stabbed from behind in broad daylight on the Fontanka with one of those Finnish knives, while the public stood around in silence. The Theatre, by the way, swears that it shouted 'Help!', but no one came to the rescue. I wouldn't presume to doubt that they did shout, but they shouted very quietly – they might have shouted at least as far as Moscow with a telegram to the People's Commissariat of Education.

And now one or two sympathetic faces have leaned down towards me. They can see the citizen lying in a pool of blood. They say, 'You must shout!' But I feel that to shout when you're lying down is rather undignified. It's not a dramatist's job! [. . .]

When they shot the knight commander of our order of Russian writers [Pushkin] a hundred years ago, they found a deep pistol wound on his body. When a hundred years later they come to undress one of his descendants before dispatching him on his distant journey, they'll find a number of scars from Finnish knives. And they'll all be on his back. Only the weapons change!

A sequel will follow, if you have no objection. My spirits are dejected.

14–20 April 1932. From Moscow to Tyarlevo (near Leningrad) To his friend Pavel Popov

It's five in the morning. I can't sleep. I was lying and talking to myself, so now allow me, dear Pavel Sergeyevich, to talk to you. [. . .]

Every night now I look not ahead, but back, because I can see nothing in the future for myself. In the past I made five fatal mistakes. If it hadn't been for them, [. . .] the very sun would shine on me differently, and I would compose not lying in bed moving my lips soundlessly at dawn, but at my writing-desk, as it should be.

But there's nothing to be done about it now, you can't bring anything back. I just curse myself for those two attacks of timidity which unexpectedly afflicted me like a fainting-fit, and because of which I committed two of the five mistakes. I do have some justification: that the timidity was a chance thing, the product of exhaustion. Over the years of my literary work, I have become weary. I have some justification, but no consolation. [. . .]

I will continue.

And so, exhausted, feeling that it really is necessary and high time to draw some conclusions and make some final decisions, I keep going over my past life and recalling those who were my friends. There are so few of them. I do remember you, I definitely remember you, Pavel Sergeyevich. [. . .]

I know that it's not really the done thing in polite society to talk only about yourself, but I can't write anything or about anything until I have opened my heart to someone. Above all I will write about *The Turbins*, since my entire life now hangs upon that play as on a thread, and every night I offer up prayers to fate that no sword should sever that thread.

But first of all I'm going to a rehearsal, and then I'm going to sleep, and when I've caught up on my sleep I will write you a letter.

24 April 1932. From Moscow to Tyarlevo (near Leningrad) To his friend Pavel Popov

. . . and so my notes. I reckon that the best thing would be if, when you have read them, you threw them into the fire. The stove long ago became my favourite editor. I like it for the fact that, without rejecting anything, it is equally willing to swallow laundry bills, the beginnings of letters and even, shame, oh shame, verses! Ever since I was a child I have hated poetry (I'm not talking about Pushkin, Pushkin isn't poetry!), and if I ever wrote any poems, then they were exclusively satirical, which aroused the indignation of my aunt and the sorrow of my mother, who dreamed only that her sons should become transport engineers.

I don't know whether my late mother knows that her youngest son has become a solo balalaika-player in France, her middle son a scientist, a bacteriologist in that same France, and that her eldest hasn't decided to become anyone at all.

I imagine that she does know. And at times, when in my bitter dreams I see the lampshade, the piano keyboard, the score of *Faust* and her (and I've now seen her three times in my dreams in recent days – why is she disturbing me?), then I want to say to her, 'Come with me to the Arts Theatre. I'll show you a play. And that's all I have to offer.' Peace, Mother?

The play [*The Days of the Turbins*] was revived on 18 February. From Tverskaya Street all the way down to the Theatre men were standing, muttering mechanically, 'Any spare tickets?' It was the same coming down from Dmitrovka Street.

I wasn't in the auditorium. I was in the wings, and the actors were in such a state that they infected me. [. . .]

Then a messenger appeared in the form of an attractive woman. Recently I have perfected to the uttermost a skill that is very difficult to live with. Namely the skill of knowing in advance what someone wants from me as they come towards me. Evidently my nerves have frayed at the ends, and living with my dog has taught me always to be on my guard.

In other words, I know what is going to be said, and the bad thing is that I know that they won't have anything new to say to me. There'll be no surprises, it's all familiar. I only had to glance at her tensely smiling mouth to know that she was going to ask me not to go out and take a bow . . .

The messenger said that K. S. [Stanislavsky] had rung and asked where I was and how I was feeling. I asked her to thank him – I was feeling fine, I was in the wings, and wasn't going to go on stage if I was called.

Oh, how the messenger glowed! And said that K. S. considered that to be a wise decision.

There was no particular wisdom about that decision. It was a very simple decision. I don't want any bows or curtain-calls, in fact there's nothing I want, except for Christ's sake to be left in peace to take hot baths and not to have to think every day about what I am to do with my dog when the contract on my apartment runs out.

One way and another, there's nothing I want.

There were twenty curtain-calls. Afterwards the actors and my acquaintances pestered me with questions: why wouldn't I go out on stage? What sort of a gesture was that? So it turns out that if I had gone out that would have been a gesture, and if I didn't that was also a gesture. I don't know, I don't know what I'm supposed to do.

6 May 1932. From Moscow to Paris
To his brother Nikolay

Dear Kolya,

I would like to ask you to help me with the following matter. The publishers S. Fischer Verlag [. . .], with whom I have a contract concerning the copyright of my play *The Days of the Turbins*, have sent me a letter informing me that a certain

Mr Gréanin, having presented an authorization (?!!!) from the author to the Société des Auteurs et Compositeurs Dramatiques, has *received 3,000 francs on my behalf!* [. . .]

What on earth are they doing to me abroad?

Do you remember that you wrote to me that you didn't like the look of some of the people prowling around the play? Who and what did you mean? Let me know exactly and give me their names. Please help me to bring an end to these attacks on my royalties, and above all to sort out this Mr Gréanin.

7 May 1932. From Moscow to Tyarlevo (near Leningrad) To his friend Pavel Popov

And so, *Dead Souls.* In nine days' time I will be forty-one. It's dreadful, but it's true.

And here, towards the end of my career as a writer, I find myself obliged to write stage adaptations. What a brilliant finale, don't you think? I gaze at the shelves and shudder: whom, oh whom will I have to adapt next? Turgenev, Leskov, the *Brockhaus-Efron Encyclopaedia*? Ostrovsky? But the latter, fortunately, staged himself, obviously foreseeing what would happen to me during 1929–31 . . . Namely . . .

1) *You cannot adapt* Dead Souls. Take that as an axiom from someone who knows the work well. I've been told that there are already 160 stage adaptations of it. That may not be quite accurate, but in any case you can't stage *Dead Souls.*

2) So how is it that I have undertaken to do it?

I didn't undertake to do it, Pavel Sergeyevich. It's a long time since I have undertaken anything, since I do not dispose of a single one of my own steps, and instead it is Fate which grasps me by the throat. As soon as I was appointed to the Moscow Arts Theatre I was given a job as assistant director on *Dead Souls.* [. . .] I had only to take a single glance at the notebook with the version written by the adapter they'd commissioned to do it, for everything to go green before my eyes. [. . .] Well, to cut a long story short, I had to write it myself. [. . .]

You should have seen Nemirovich when he read it! As you can tell, it's not the 161st adaptation, and not an adaptation really at all, but something completely different. [. . .]

Vlad [imir] Ivan [ovich Nemirovich-Danchenko] was in a state of rage and fury. There was a great battle, but all the same they started working on the play in that form. And they've been working on it now for about two years!

8–13 June 1932. From Moscow to Tyarlevo (near Leningrad) To his friend Pavel Popov

I have got muddled in the numbering of my letters, so I'm going to stop doing it. I receive your letters, and they always make me feel good. They arrive alongside admittedly rare but nevertheless tiresome business letters. These can be divided into two categories:

a) Russian letters

b) foreign letters

The first are of a trivially humdrum nature. I have to pay an extra nine roubles for the telephone for a certain month in a certain year. And besides that, why do I not belong to the City Committee of Writers? And if I do belong anywhere, then where, if you please?

I belong to RABIS [the Union of Workers in the Arts], and am glad to belong. Although deep in my heart is the thought that it doesn't matter where I belong. And all these questions and answers simply take up my time.

In other words they're like those mosquitoes that prevent you from enjoying the countryside.

Foreign letters are another matter. When a letter arrives from abroad it lands on my desk like a brick. I know its contents even before I've opened the envelope: some ask what to do, and what next, and how to proceed with such-and-such in such-and-such a place, and the rest inform me from time to time that in this or that place my royalties have been embezzled.

I've been receiving these letters for about five years now and replying to them. But now, this year, I've lost heart. You get fed up with everything in the end. [. . .]

After all, I'm writing into the unknown to people I don't know, to say things that in reality have no force whatsoever. How can I, sitting on Pirogovskaya Street, deal with what's being done on Bülowstrasse or on rue Ballu?

**23 June 1932. From Tyarlevo (near Leningrad) to Moscow
From his friend Pavel Popov**

Dear Mikhail Afanasyevich,

Congratulations on the success of the dress rehearsal of *Dead Souls*. At last we have had news of that, for recently the flow of information about you has dried up. [. . .] We're still hoping to see you in Leningrad.

**30 June 1932. Moscow
To Konstantin Stanislavsky (joint Director of the Moscow
Arts Theatre)**

Dear Konstantin Sergeyevich!

In reply to my request to be given an advance of two and a half thousand roubles Nikolay Vasilyevich [Yegorov] gave me a thousand and won't give me any more – it's enough to make you weep!

I beg you, Konstantin Sergeyevich, to give an instruction to the management to give me a second thousand – without it I really will be facing a catastrophe with my apartment.

And what can I do with Nikolay Vasilyevich? What can I do?!

He says, 'I'll sell my camera and lend you some.'

I don't wish to burden Nikolay Vasilyevich by borrowing money from him or to have to depend on his camera in this difficult business of my apartment!

Believe me, Konstantin Sergeyevich, it gives me no pleasure to ask!

**4 August 1932. From Moscow to Tyarlevo (near Leningrad)
To his friend Pavel Popov**

My dear friend Pavel Sergeyevich,

As soon as Jean-Baptiste Poquelin de Molière releases my soul a little and I get a chance to sort myself out a bit, I will eagerly begin to write to you.

A 200-page biography – and in this heat – and in Moscow too!

And I would like to write to you about important and serious matters, although it's unthinkable for the moment, given the presence of Grimarest, Despois and other foreign tourists on my desk.

6 September 1932. From Moscow
To Yevgeny Shilovsky (Yelena Sergeyevna's husband) (draft)
Dear Yevgeny Aleksandrovich,

I have seen Yelena Sergeyevna at her request, and we have talked things out. We love each other just as much as ever. And we want to get m . . .

4 October 1932. Moscow
To V. Sakhnovsky (at the Moscow Arts Theatre)
Secret. Urgent.

At 3.45 I am getting married at the Register Office. Please let me leave in ten minutes.

Bulgakov's mother, Varvara Mikhaylovna (1869–1922), and father, Afanasy Ivanovich (1859–1907).

The Bulgakov children at the family dacha at Bucha, c. 1904.
Clockwise from top: Mikhail (Misha), Varvara (Varya), Nadezhda
(Nadya), Ivan (Vanya), Yelena (Lyolya), Nikolay (Kolya), Vera.

Bulgakov's first wife, Tatyana Nikolayevna.

Bulgakov's sister
Nadezhda, in Kiev, and
brother Nikolay, in Paris.

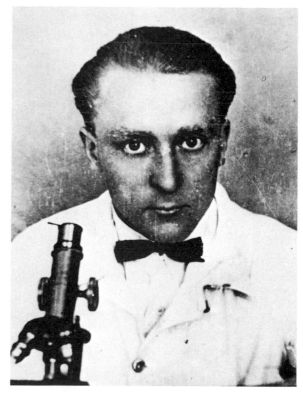

Bulgakov in 1924.

Bulgakov's second wife, Lyubov
Yevgenyevna.

Bulgakov in 1926.

Lyubov Yevgenyevna,
Moscow, 1930.

Bulgakov's third wife, Yelena
Sergeyevna, in her youth.

Bulgakov in 1928.

Bulgakov and Yelena Sergeyevna soon after their marriage in October 1932.

A signed photograph given by
Bulgakov to his boyhood friend
Aleksandr Gdeshinsky, inscribed
'To dear Sasha, M. Bulgakov,
21.IX.39'.

Bulgakov and Yelena Sergeyevna in the late 1930s.

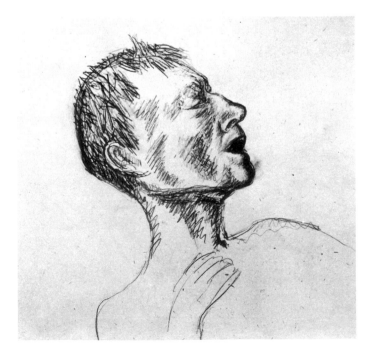

Bulgakov in the last hours of his life, drawn by the stage-designer V. V. Dmitriyev on the night of 9 March 1940.

5

1932–1936

The boost to Bulgakov's spirits provided by the prospect of at last regaining his love had invigorating effects on his work for the rest of 1932. Apart from his work on the prose biography of Molière during that summer, Bulgakov was also nurturing the idea of another work connected with Molière. In July, he had been commissioned by the Zavadsky Theatre Studio to do a translation of *Le Bourgeois Gentilhomme*. Around the time of his marriage to Yelena Sergeyevna, during September, October and the first half of November, Bulgakov tackled this project with vivacity, and what emerged was not so much a translation as a 'Molieriana', as he called it: a pot-pourri of Molierian themes and characters largely based on *Le Bourgeois Gentilhomme*, but also incorporating some of Bulgakov's own reflections on the way in which theatre succeeds in making its audiences suspend their disbelief. The result was an exuberant piece, but it was rejected by the Theatre, presumably because it strayed too far from the original commission.

Undaunted, Bulgakov pressed on with his prose biography of Molière during the winter of 1932–33, and delivered it to the publishers on 5 March 1933. But a month later this work too was rejected, and on similar grounds: the editor Aleksandr Tikhonov found the tone and structure far too playful, and Gorky, to whom the manuscript was sent in Italy for a second opinion, on this occasion agreed with Tikhonov rather than supporting Bulgakov.

The problem may well have been that the general editors of the series, which had only recently been launched, had in mind a collection of thoroughly conventional biographies – such as have indeed characterized the series to this day. Bulgakov, however, had produced a witty and ingenious text. His account opens with a narrator observing the birth of the infant Molière, attended by a midwife who is wholly indifferent to the notion of the child's future renown; and Bulgakov goes on to indulge in a great many digressions on the nature of glory in art as opposed to glory in politics, and on the ups and downs of a playwright's career, which were uncomfortably suggestive of issues of the day in the Soviet Union. 'According to Tikhonov, "fairly transparent hints about our Soviet reality emerge" in my work!' commented Bulgakov sardonically in a letter to Pavel Popov (page 158) in which he describes the fiasco. One might add that it was just as well Tikhonov never saw the – still unpublished – notebook in which Bulgakov wrote the first draft of this biography, where the contemporary references are made even more explicit.

For Bulgakov the rejection of this work was yet another painful blow, seemingly demonstrating that in the 1930s too he was going to be balked in reaching an audience with the works he cared about most passionately. His play about Molière had got bogged down at the Moscow Arts Theatre and was being rehearsed only intermittently and lackadaisically; the adaptation of *Le Bourgeois Gentilhomme* had not found favour; and now the prose biography which had absorbed him so happily was deemed unacceptable. The 'Molière years' between 1929 and 1933 had given him considerable personal satisfaction, but they brought him no material rewards.

One consequence of this complete frustration of all Bulgakov's endeavours since 1929 was that work on the novel that would become *The Master and Margarita* became more intensive, starting from his honeymoon weeks in Leningrad with Yelena Sergeyevna in October 1932. Having, as he declared in his 1930 letter to Stalin, burned the earlier drafts of the novel he had begun in 1928, he now returned to it with renewed excitement, and worked on it in every spare moment that could be snatched from his more mundane commitments. A text that

had apparently started as a satirical novel about the Moscow
cultural scene, and which had involved a Christ and a Devil
figure, now acquired new features. As Marietta Chudakova has
shown, the first full draft, completed between 1932 and 1936,
gained an autobiographical dimension with its new hero, the
unnamed Master. The author of a book containing the story of
Christ and Pilate, as a hero he is flawed by traits of weakness
and cowardice. His talent is saved through the love borne him
by the courageous Margarita, who, by entering into a pact
with the Devil figure – the ultimately benevolent Woland – and
being transformed into a witch, wreaks violent revenge on
the critics who have ruined the Master. Clearly the character
of Margarita is modelled on Yelena Sergeyevna, whose fierce
devotion to Bulgakov has been testified to by all who knew
her. Real experiences, or sometimes just wishful fantasies, from
Bulgakov's life with Yelena Sergeyevna were later frequently
taken up and woven into the complex tapestry of the novel.

An important new source of information distinguishes the
documents presented in this and the last chapter from those in
the earlier part of this book: the diaries that Bulgakov asked
Yelena Sergeyevna to keep from 1 September 1933 onwards,
which provide a detailed chronicle of his daily activities, his
social circle, his meetings with people and his increasing despair.
These diaries have not yet been published as an integral text,
either in their original form or in the version Yelena Sergeyevna
prepared for publication during the 1950s, and although they
have been quoted in a few Soviet publications, no Westerner
gained access to them until 1990. Interleaved with Bulgakov's
correspondence of the period, the diary entries paint an extremely
vivid picture of what it was like to live among the élite of
Moscow's cultural world, in the orbit of the Moscow Arts
Theatre and the Bolshoy. Yet at the same time this was the
era of Stalin's Terror, which became particularly sweeping after
the murder of Kirov in December 1934, a murder we now know
to have been engineered by Stalin himself – who then used it
as an excuse to root out supposed threats to his rule. Yelena
Sergeyevna's diaries portray what it was like to be continually
spied upon and surrounded by informers in a period when arrests,

imprisonments, sentences of internal exile and executions were nightmare everyday occurrences.

After the failure of his Molière projects, Bulgakov's creative work between 1932 and 1936 continued with a succession of lesser works. In the early summer of 1933, for example, a Leningrad music-hall theatre commissioned from him a comedy which became the rather unsatisfactory *Bliss*, a science-fiction play with a somewhat wooden anti-Utopian plot. The play was written between December 1933 and April 1934, by which time the Satire Theatre in Moscow had also signed a contract for it. But neither the Satire Theatre nor the Leningrad theatre was satisfied with the result – the Leningrad director's embarrassed visit to Bulgakov's hotel is described very wittily in a letter to Pavel Popov (page 177) – and in September 1934 Bulgakov was asked to rewrite the text entirely, leaving out the futuristic scenes, but preserving the idea of bringing Ivan the Terrible forward in a time machine to the modern age. By October 1935 the text, now retitled *Ivan Vasilyevich*, was finally submitted to the Repertory Committee, who after much suspicion and hesitation eventually concluded that there was no really subversive content in this amusing but slight comedy, and licensed it for performance. At the end of 1935, rehearsals of *Ivan Vasilyevich* at last got under way at the Satire Theatre. Meanwhile Bulgakov's time in 1933 and 1934 had been taken up with very occasional and half-hearted rehearsals of his *Molière*; with endless rumours that the ban on *Flight* might be lifted; and with work as an actor for the Moscow Arts Theatre. This last was a new departure for him and was something he undertook partly out of financial necessity, but by all accounts he took great pleasure in dressing up and appearing as the judge in a stage adaptation of *The Pickwick Papers*, which he had helped his friend the playwright Natalya Venkstern to write.

During the summer of 1934 another new venture involved Bulgakov's moving into the realm of cinema. He was approached to write a film scenario of Gogol's *Dead Souls* – no doubt as a result of the popularity of his stage adaptation of the novel for the Arts Theatre. But this commission, like the theatre adaptation, turned into a frustrating ordeal: all his most imaginative proposals – such as to exploit the screen's visual potential by means of literal representations of Gogol's hyperbolic metaphors (for example, by giving visual reality to the image of a character advancing on the hero like an army), and once again to use as a framework the image of Gogol leaning against his balcony in Rome – were rejected, and he was forced back, as he had been in the Arts Theatre, on to a more conventional interpretation. What was worse was that the studios rejected three separate drafts of the scenario, and Bulgakov not only ended up having to initiate formal complaints against them for breach of contract, but also had to fight off the film's director, Ivan Pyryev, who kept trying to rewrite the text himself and claim rights over it. His experiences with the other film scenario commissioned from him, an adaptation of Gogol's play *The Government Inspector* for film studios in Kiev, were less painful; amicable relations were maintained throughout, but he was so weary and tied up with other work that he was happy in the end to sign away seventy-five per cent of his rights in the scenario and allow the film's director, M. S. Korostin, to do most of the writing.

In August 1934 Bulgakov began to sketch out plans for a more substantial work. He wanted to write another biographical play about a writer, but this time the subject was to be Russia's national poet, Pushkin. The centenary of Pushkin's death was to fall in 1937 and would certainly be celebrated by a number of theatres: this project, at least, surely could not backfire? Bulgakov resolved to invite his old friend Vikenty Veresayev to be his co-author: this would not only be a mark of his gratitude for Veresayev's financial and moral support in the past, but would also guarantee the project's academic reputation. Veresayev was one of the country's leading experts on Pushkin's life, the author of innumerable biographical studies of the poet and the compiler of a highly-regarded collection of memoirs about him; and after a moment's hesitation he readily agreed. His initial doubts were aroused by Bulgakov's absolute determination that Pushkin himself should not appear on stage during the course of the play; this was partly because Bulgakov feared that such an appearance could lead to a vulgarization of the figure of the poet, but he may also have felt, after all his experiences with his

Molière projects, that it would be safer not to risk attracting the wrath of the critics by presenting an 'incorrect' image of Pushkin. The play that he wrote with Veresayev's help, *Last Days* or *Pushkin*, is a skilful depiction of the forces bearing down on Pushkin during the last days of his life: the hostility of the Court, the fact that both the Tsar and the officer D'Anthès were pursuing his wife Natalya, persecution by the secret police, jealousy in literary circles and financial difficulties – all of which culminated in Pushkin's fighting and perishing in a duel in 1837, a death that has ever since been perceived in Russia as an assassination. But despite all these careful preparations, the writing of this play too ended up being bedevilled with problems, notably when Veresayev decided that his role was being undervalued and he started a ferociously outspoken correspondence on the subject with Bulgakov, accusing him of seeking to play down the social aspects of Pushkin's tragedy. During the summer of 1935, just when Bulgakov thought the play was ready to be delivered to the Vakhtangov Theatre – and to the Arts Theatre, who were hoping to put on a rival production – the letters between him and Veresayev grew more and more bitter. By the end of 1935, however, Veresayev had decided to withdraw his name from the play, while retaining his right to half of the royalties, and the play began to be prepared for production by the Vakhtangov.

The spring of 1935 also brought the apparent culmination of Bulgakov's torments over his play *Molière*. The play had now been in rehearsal for some four years, partly under the direction of Nikolay Gorchakov, and more recently under the direction of Stanislavsky himself. Bulgakov had been appointed an assistant director on the production, and his experience of working closely with Stanislavsky drove him into a frenzy; in his letters he describes graphically how Stanislavsky tried to pressure him into rewriting the text of *Molière* so that the French playwright should clearly be seen on stage 'being a genius'. Stanislavsky also wasted immense amounts of time, as Bulgakov saw it, applying his famous 'method', which took the actors right away from the text into various exercises and improvisations. A few years later Bulgakov would compose a wicked satire on these episodes in his hilarious but unforgiving *Theatrical Novel* (published in

English as *Black Snow*). In 1935, however, he simply lost patience
with Stanislavsky altogether, and after one particularly irksome
rehearsal wrote him an ultimatum demanding that the play be
put on in its original form or not at all. Stanislavsky withdrew
in a huff, and the co-Director of the Theatre, now his arch-rival,
Nemirovich-Danchenko, took over instead.

By the beginning of 1936, the prospect of a public performance
of *Molière*, a work of huge personal significance for Bulgakov,
at last began to seem real. A series of unofficial premières took
place during February and early March; each performance was
more successful than the last, and each ended with at least twenty
curtain-calls. Artistically, the play was a triumph. But the first
few months of 1936 were a particularly savage time for the Soviet
arts: a series of vitriolic articles in *Pravda* attacked a whole range
of leading cultural figures, such as Shostakovich, and the reviews
of *Molière* were unanimously hostile. On the morning of 9 March
1936 an article pouring scorn on Bulgakov's *Molière* appeared
in *Pravda*. By the time he arrived at the Theatre that day, the
management had already cancelled all further performances of
the play, in a prompt action that Bulgakov would never forgive
them. And although plans for the staging of *Pushkin* at the
Vakhtangov and *Ivan Vasilyevich* at the Satire Theatre were
pursued for a little longer, these productions too were soon
axed without ever reaching the stage. This was Bulgakov's most
comprehensive defeat, and it was a blow from which he would
never fully recover.

The years between 1932 and 1936, as portrayed particularly
in Yelena Sergeyevna's diaries, were years full of animation as
well as gloomier or more ominous moments. It is characteristic
of Bulgakov's letters that he very rarely talks about other people
or about matters not directly concerned with his own affairs. As
well as being a symptom of his own self-absorption and a result
of his tendency to use his letters sometimes as a substitute for a
diary – and sometimes, as with his letters to his brother abroad,
as a kind of public statement partly aimed at those who might
well be intercepting them – this silence about others should be
understood as stemming from a general habit of discretion
developed by a great many Soviet citizens. Yelena Sergeyevna's

diaries, by contrast, while clearly suppressing or coding some facts, are much franker than her husband's letters, and they give a marvellous sense of their day-to-day lives. They are helpful, for example, in giving an idea of just which people were regarded by her, and to some extent therefore by him, as true friends. Yakov Leontyev, who worked first at the Moscow Arts Theatre and later in the management of the Bolshoy, figures throughout as a man much loved in their household. Bulgakov's old friends Pavel Popov and Nikolay Lyamin do not elicit especially favourable comments from Yelena Sergeyevna (although Bulgakov clearly chose to see a lot of them); and she reserves some particularly sharp remarks for both Lyamin's and Popov's wives. Notable absentees from among the most regular visitors to the household are Bulgakov's sisters, particularly Nadya and Yelena (Lyolya), who were both living in Moscow; family history has it that Yelena Sergeyevna did not particularly encourage their erstwhile intimacy with Mikhail, an attitude his sisters rather resented.

Regular visitors in the mid-1930s included Dmitriyev, a stage-designer; the doctor Arendt (related by marriage to Leontyev); and writers such as Ilf and Petrov. The poet Akhmatova was an occasional guest when she was visiting the Mandelstams in the apartment-block on Nashchokinsky Street, which Bulgakov and Yelena Sergeyevna finally moved into – to Bulgakov's great relief – in February 1934. Akhmatova was not an intimate friend, but she admired Bulgakov's work and trusted his acumen and integrity when it came to dealing with the Party leadership; more than once she came to him for advice about how to help her friends or family when they fell foul of the secret police. Indeed, Bulgakov established quite a reputation as someone who knew how to compose letters to Stalin, and several people turned to him for assistance, as Zamyatin had done in 1930 when he was drafting the letter that eventually led to his being permitted to leave the USSR.

The Bulgakovs had a particularly complicated relationship with Yelena Sergeyevna's sister Olya (Olga Sergeyevna Bokshanskaya) and her husband Yevgeny Kaluzhsky. Bokshanskaya worked in the Moscow Arts Theatre as a secretary, at first to the management in general, and then to Nemirovich-Danchenko in particular, while Kaluzhsky was an Arts Theatre actor. Olga's blind devotion to Nemirovich-Danchenko and insensitivity to Bulgakov's talent and feelings used to enrage Yelena Sergeyevna; Olga was very sympathetic, for example, to the Communist playwright Afinogenov, a figure whom Bulgakov frequently came across at the Arts Theatre, and whose career always seemed to be taking priority with the Theatre management, causing Bulgakov to feel slighted. Nevertheless, Olga and Yelena Sergeyevna managed to remain in regular and usually civil contact with each other.

Amongst the other regular visitors to the household were a whole series of snoopers and informers – during this period, Kantorovich, Emmanuil Zhukhovitsky and Grisha Konsky – who had perforce to be tolerated, despite the way they insisted on steering the conversation into questions of political conviction. It is almost impossible to imagine the continual tension this situation must have created, and perhaps the only consolation was the pleasure Bulgakov would take from time to time in deliberately shocking them. The attentions of these informers became particularly assiduous following the new American Ambassador William Bullitt's attendance of a performance of *The Days of the Turbins* at the Arts Theatre, which led to a whole series of invitations to social occasions: guests from the American Embassy came to visit the Bulgakovs in their apartment, and they were in turn invited back to a series of glamorous functions. The most remarkable of these was the grand ball thrown by the Ambassador in April 1935; its exoticism clearly provided direct inspiration for Bulgakov's depiction of Satan's ball in *The Master and Margarita*. On this occasion they also made the acquaintance of one of the best-known informers who used to attach himself to foreigners in Moscow, Baron Shteyger, who would figure in *The Master and Margarita* as Baron Maygel. The luxurious lifestyle of the Americans, with their casual talk of travelling all over the globe, gave the Bulgakovs a tantalizing glimpse of a totally different way of life, which Yelena Sergeyevna especially revelled in.

Another relatively glamorous world that Bulgakov and his wife were beginning to move into by the end of 1935 was that of the country's top musicians. They became friends with Melik-Pashayev, Principal Conductor at the Bolshoy Theatre, and also got to know the composers Prokofiev and Shostakovich. At the time of the *Pravda* articles that virtually destroyed both Shostakovich's and Bulgakov's careers early in 1936, Bulgakov's *Pushkin* play was being considered by both Prokofiev and Shostakovich as the potential basis for an opera. For Bulgakov, to whom music was of supreme importance, evenings at home spent making music on their recently-acquired piano with the leading composers of the age were a valuable source of relief amid the gathering gloom.

All in all, this had been an enormously difficult period for him; the cruel, teasing way in which his dream of travelling abroad was snatched away from him – when he had already seen his and Yelena Sergeyevna's passports lying on a desk in the early summer of 1934 – nearly broke his health altogether. When he wrote yet another letter to Stalin, recounting this outrage, it too remained unanswered; whatever sympathetic interest Stalin may once have felt, which had prompted him to help Bulgakov in 1930, had now apparently vanished. Combined with the increasing number of arrests, which since the late 1920s had picked off a large number of his friends and acquaintances – Mandelstam was arrested in May 1934 in the building they both lived in – Bulgakov's sense of being trapped in the USSR, at the mercy of the taunts of his gaolers, brought him to a state of nervous breakdown. He became terrified of going out on his own, and although, after months of suffering, treatment with hypnosis eventually brought the problem under control, it was a condition that later returned at particularly difficult moments. He also began to suffer from an agonizing preoccupation with thoughts of death.

This, then, was his state of mind when the calamity of 9 March 1936 and the suppression of *Molière* hit him. It is perhaps not all that surprising that, even before *Molière* was taken off, Bulgakov had told one of the new Directors of the Arts Theatre, Arkadyev, that the only subject for a play that now really interested him was the theme of Stalin himself.

5 October 1932 – 10 April 1933. From Moscow to Paris
To Lyudmila and Yevgeny Zamyatin (the writer)

Dear Lyudmila Nikolayevna and Zhenya!

I've been writing you this letter since October last year. I began it in your wonderful Astoria Hotel in Leningrad. [. . .]

Well, I have got divorced from Lyubov Yevgenyevna and am married to Yelena Sergeyevna Shilovskaya. I hope that you will love her and look on her kindly, as I do. We are living on Pirogovskaya Street as a threesome – the two of us and her six-year-old son Sergey. We spent the winter by the stove telling fascinating tales of the North Pole and of elephant-hunting; we shot at one another with a toy pistol and were continually ill with flu. During that time I wrote a biography of your fellow Parisian Jean-Baptiste Molière for the series 'Lives of the Great'. At the moment Tikhonov is sitting admiring it.

And so you have succumbed to *Anna Karenina*? My God! The very word 'Tolstoy' horrifies me! I have written an adaptation of *War and Peace*. I now cannot walk past the shelf where Tolstoy stands without shuddering. And you ask when I am planning to visit the West? Just fancy, over the last three months many people have been asking me that question.

14 January 1933. From Moscow to Paris
To his brother Nikolay

Dear Kolya!

I hope that you are alive and well. You've already got used to the fact that news from me comes rarely, and I also have heard nothing of you recently. I trust Ivan and his family are alive and well too.

At the moment I'm finishing a big piece of work – a biography of Molière.

You would oblige me very much if you could find a spare moment to go and have at least a quick look at the Molière monument (the Molière fountain) on rue Richelieu.

I need a brief but exact description of the monument as it looks at present, approximately along the following lines:

The material and colour of Molière's statue.

The material and colour of the figures of the women at the base.

Does water still run in the fountain (the lions' heads at the bottom)?

8 March 1933. From Moscow to Paris
To his brother Nikolay

My dear Kolya!

Our household has been a sick-bay for the whole of the last month. The family's been overwhelmed by flu. Which was why I didn't let you know straight away that I had received your letter which I needed so much, with the description of the fountain.

You touched me infinitely by replying in such detail to all my questions. The photograph is very precious. I send you my thanks and a kiss!

To my great happiness I have at last completed my work on Molière, and I delivered my manuscript on the 5th. It wore me out exceedingly and sapped all my vigour. I can no longer recall for how many years, if you go back and count the beginning of the work on the play [*Molière*], I have been living in the unreal, fairy-tale Paris of the seventeenth century. Now it looks as though I am parting from it for ever.

If fate should carry you to the corner of rue Richelieu and rue Molière, remember me! And give my greetings to Jean-Baptiste de Molière!

13 April 1933, Moscow
To his friend Pavel Popov

Well sir, my Molière period has begun. It started with Tikhonov's review. Dear Patya, this review contains a number of pleasant things. My narrator, who is in charge of the biography, is described as a casual young man, who believes in sorcery and the demonic, possesses occult powers, is fond of risqué stories, uses dubious sources and, what's worse, is inclined to royalism. But that's not all. According to T., 'fairly transparent hints about our Soviet reality emerge' in my work! [. . .]

Having thought the matter over carefully, I decided it would be better not to join battle over it. I just growled about the form of the review, but I didn't bite. And in fact this is what I have done: T. writes that instead of my narrator, I ought to put in 'a serious Soviet historian'. I informed him that I am not a historian, and refused to redo the book. [. . .]

And so, it is my pleasure to bury Jean-Baptiste Molière. It will be better and more peaceful for everyone. I am entirely indifferent to the idea of my book-jacket adorning the window of some shop. In actual fact I am an actor, not a writer. And apart from that I love peace and quiet.

So there's your report on the biography you were interested in.

Please telephone me. We will arrange an evening when we can get together and weave into our conversation at table the names of those glorious comedians Sieurs Lagrange, Brécourt, Du Croisy and the knight commander himself, Jean Molière.

19 May 1933. Moscow
To his friend Pavel Popov

A rumour is circulating that you are going off on holiday. [. . .] I hope you will snatch a moment to drop by to say goodbye. Bring the ill-fated *Molière* with you.

And me? The wind is rustling the foliage by the skin clinic, and my heart misses a beat at the thought of rivers, bridges, seas. There is a gypsy moan in my soul. But it will pass. I can already tell that I shall sit through the whole summer on Pirogovskaya Street writing a comedy (for Leningrad). There will be heat, and banging, and dust and mineral water.

2 August 1933. From Moscow
To the writer Vikenty Veresayev

First of all, I should like to tell you about our trip to Leningrad. The Moscow Arts Theatre were performing *The Days of the Turbins* there in two theatres. They had a great success and full houses, and in consequence I kept getting information that I had become rich. And indeed, the royalties from them should be quite respectable.

And so we went off to Leningrad, knowing how difficult it is to get one's hands on such riches.

At this point not I, but Yelena Sergeyevna, armed with an authorization [she had taken over the running of Bulgakov's business affairs], swept into the second theatre – the Narva House of Culture. The theatre manager twice swore that he would transfer five thousand from my royalties the moment we'd left. As you can guess, he hasn't yet transferred so much as five kopeks. [. . .]

I just dream about the happy day when she will get her way and I, having paid off my remaining debt to you, will be able to say once again what you have done for me, dear Vikenty Vikentyevich.

Oh, I won't ever forget the years 1929–31!

I would get back on my feet sooner, by the way, if it weren't for the necessity of leaving this monstrous pit on Pirogovskaya Street! Because the apartment on Nashchokinsky still isn't ready. They're a year late. A year! They've really mangled me over this.

A demon has taken hold of me. In Leningrad and now here, as I suffocate in these little rooms, I have begun to scribble down all over again page after page of that novel I destroyed three years ago. Why? I don't know. I'm just amusing myself. Let it fall into the river Lethe! Anyway, I will probably put it down again soon.

13 August 1933. From Moscow to Paris
To his brother Nikolay

Could you please help me in one particular matter by taking on power of attorney for me? Mme Maria Reinhardt, an actress [. . .], has translated my play *Zoyka's Apartment* into French and is offering to get it put on in French in the theatre. [. . .] I have agreed to this.

From Yelena Sergeyevna's diary
1 September 1933

Today is the first anniversary of the day when M. A. and I came together again after our separation.

Misha insists that I keep this diary. He himself, after that time in 1926 when they took his diaries away after a search, swore that he would never keep a diary again. For him it is dreadful, incomprehensible, to think that a writer's diary might be confiscated.

14 September 1933. From Moscow to Paris
To his brother Nikolay

The information in the newspapers to the effect that the Moscow Arts Theatre is putting on *Molière* and *Flight* is more or less correct. But the whole business of *Molière* has become so long drawn out (for reasons purely connected with the Theatre) that I have begun to lose hope about the production, and as for *Flight*, then if Fate is kind it will be put on by the spring of 1934. Neither play has any hope, as far as I can see, of being put on in any other theatres in the USSR. There are ominous signs of this.

From Yelena Sergeyevna's diary
22 September 1933

Misha is at the Popovs', and I am heaving books through into the dining-room – the study is damp and they're being ruined.
24 September 1933

This evening we had Olya and Kaluzhsky [Yelena Sergeyevna's sister and brother-in-law] and Lyubasha [Lyubov Yevgenyevna], who today moved into a separate room of her own, next door to us.
27 September 1933

Misha read to Kolya L[yamin] some new chapters from the novel about the Devil, written over the last few days, or rather nights.
28 September 1933

Each evening M. A. tells Sergey stories from a series called 'Bubkin and His Dog Freckle'. Bubkin is an imaginary ideal little boy, a daredevil, prince and knight, and these are his adventures. While Sergey is getting ready for bed each evening Misha asks him, 'Which number story would you like?' 'Um, number seventeen.' 'All right. You mean the one about how Bubkin went to the Bolshoy Theatre with Marshal Voroshilov? Good.' And he begins an improvisation. Kantorovich says that there is a marvellous little boy who could play the part of Bubkin, so he should write it all down! But M. A. is busy with the novel, and in any case he doesn't believe it would be a realistic venture.

10 October 1933

This evening we had Akhmatova, Veresayev, Olya and Kaluzhsky and Patya Popov with Anna Ilyinichna. A reading from the novel. Akhmatova was silent for the whole evening.

12 October 1933

In the morning a call from Olya: Nikolay Erdman and Mass have been arrested. Apparently because of some satirical fables. Misha began to frown. [. . .]

We played tiddly-winks, which is the latest craze.

During the night M. A. burned a portion of his novel.

17 October 1933. Moscow
To the writer Vikenty Veresayev (draft)

Dear Vikenty Vikentyevich,

I recall that once before I treated you to a letter that utterly perplexed you. But that's how it always is: when my literary burden begins to weigh too heavily upon me, I share part of it with Yelena Sergeyevna. But you can weigh down a woman's shoulders only to a certain extent. And then I turn to you.

I have not been as anxious as I am now for a long time. Sleepless nights. At dawn I begin to gaze at the ceiling and stare until life becomes established outside the window – cap, scarf, cap, scarf. God, how dreary!

So what's the problem? The apartment. That's the source of it. And so, in my declining years I've found myself occupying someone else's living space. This one's been handed over and the other one's not ready. A sour physiognomy slides into the apartment from time to time and says, 'It's mine.' Advises us to go to a hotel, and other such platitudes. He's unbearably annoying. And soon this nonsense is going to acquire grandiose proportions, and it'll be impossible to think about any work.

I'm sketching out for myself a scene of evictions, court cases, moving house and other such delights.

From Yelena Sergeyevna's diary
18 October 1933

I went with M. A. and Seryozhka to the new building on Nashchokinsky Street. It's possible we may be able to move in in January.

While we were there someone told us that Erdman is being sent into internal exile in Yeniseysk [in Siberia] for three years.

20 October 1933

M. A. went to see Dr Blyumental and the X-ray department about his kidneys, which have been painful recently. But they said there was nothing wrong.

1 November 1933

A phone call from Ekke [who worked for the publishers of the 'Lives of the Great' series].

'Kamenev likes the Molière biography very much, and he doesn't agree with Tikhonov's opinion of it at all. He's waiting for him to come back from his holiday to talk it over with him. I very much hope that the biography will be published by us after all.'

3 November 1933. From Paris to Moscow
From the writer Yevgeny Zamyatin

Dear Molière Afanasyevich,

I delayed my reply to your kind letter in order to be able to congratulate you simultaneously on the anniversary of October [1917] and on your new household. Ah, youth, youth! Frivolous people!

I was once like you, but now I am being punished for my sins: I've spent two months lying in bed with severe sciatica in my left leg. And it was such a shame: it happened almost on the eve of our departure for a trip to Italy, for which we already had the visas in our pockets. Instead of which it was into bed . . .

[Postscript from his wife Lyudmila] Let Yelena Sergeyevna keep her promise and take you around Europe.

From Yelena Sergeyevna's diary
8 November 1933

M. A. slept through almost the entire day – he's had a lot of sleepless nights. Then he worked on the novel (Margarita's flight). He's been complaining of a headache.

10 November 1933

A letter from Zamyatin in Paris, after a long gap.

13 November 1933

According to Lyubasha, Afinogenov has sent the Moscow Arts Theatre a request not to put on his *Falsehood*. Olya has confirmed the story. Apparently Afinogenov has admitted that the play is incorrectly constructed in political terms.

14 November 1933

M. A. has spoken to Kaluzhsky about his wish to sign up as an actor. He's asked to be given the role of the judge in *Pickwick Papers* and of the Hetman in *The Turbins*. Kaluzhsky responded positively. I am in despair. Bulgakov as an actor.

17 November 1933

It's well below zero. With difficulty we persuaded a man to drive us home for a lot of money and some cigarettes.

6 December 1933

Olya was here. 'Well, what about Molière?' 'Nothing is clear . . . it's very unlikely to go on . . . '

7 December 1933

This evening Dr Damir called. He found M. A. was suffering from extreme exhaustion.

8 December 1933

Knorre [from TRAM] dropped in at the Arts Theatre, called M. A. to one side, and with great subtlety and courtesy offered him a 'splendid subject – about the re-education of thugs in OGPU labour camps'; wouldn't M. A. like to work on it with him? M. A. declined, with no less courtesy.

31 December 1933

Any minute now the Kaluzhskys, Leontyevs and Arendts are coming round.

They came. It was glorious. Zhenya Kaluzhsky and Leontyev were splitting their sides over the indecent comic verses M. A. wrote for the New Year – that is, the verses were perfectly decent, but the rhymes invited other words. The Kaluzhskys stayed the night.

3 January 1934

Zhukhovitsky: 'You ought to go out with some brigade to observe a factory, or to the White Sea Canal.' [. . .] M. A.: 'Not only will I not go to the White Sea Canal, I'm so tired that I won't even go to Malakhovka [outside Moscow].'

8 January 1934

'Soon you'll be going abroad,' Zhukhovitsky began to say animatedly, 'only not with Yelena Sergeyevna!'

'By this cross' (at this point Misha began to cross himself devoutly, although making a Catholic sign of the cross for some reason) 'I won't travel without Yelena Sergeyevna! Even if they thrust a passport into my hands.'

'But why?'

'Because I've got used to visiting those foreign parts with Yelena Sergeyevna. And what's more I will not, as a matter of principle, be placed in the position of a man who is obliged to leave behind a hostage for himself.'

'You're not a modern man, Mikhail Afanasyevich.'

9 January 1934

M. A. is sketching out scene after scene of a play. For which theatre?

'With my name they won't take it anywhere. Even if it turns out well.'

15 January 1934

Misha came home immensely tired from rehearsing *Molière* and *Pickwick*.

6 March 1934. Moscow
To the writer Vikenty Veresayev

I am hoping to show you my new abode before long, as soon as I have settled in a bit more comfortably. An astonishing apartment-block, I swear! There are writers living above and below and behind and in front and alongside. I pray to God that the building will prove indestructible. I am happy to have got out of that damp hole on Pirogovskaya Street. And what bliss, Vikenty Vikentyevich, not to have to travel on the trams!

It's true that it's fairly chilly, there's something not quite right with the toilet and water leaks on to the floor from the cistern, and there'll probably be some other problems as well, but all the same I am happy. So long as the building keeps standing!

Lord, if only spring would hurry up. What a long and exhausting winter it has been. I dream about opening the door on to the balcony.

I am weary, so weary.

6 March 1934. To Moscow
From his friend Pavel Popov

And your apartment is so splendid. It's all the harder for me to admit it, since I was a great fan of Pirogovskaya Street, but all the same I will have to admit it. I hope that by the time we come back to Moscow you will have got some more furniture and the façade of the building is straightened out. Then everything will be all right. [. . .]

The problem of how to combine a bedroom and a study is a very interesting one. To solve it it's not sufficient to push the desk you brought from Pirogovskaya Street under the window. It's much more complicated and fraught than that. And a great deal depends on getting it right, above all your writing.

14 March 1934. From Moscow
To his friend Pavel Popov

This winter has been truly endless. You look out of the window and you want to spit. The grey snow just lies and lies on the roofs. I'm sick of the winter!

The apartment is gradually getting fixed up. But I'm as fed up with the joiners as with the winter. They come and go and bang about.

I've hung a lamp up in the bedroom. As for the study, to hell with it! There's no point in all these studies.

I've already forgotten Pirogovskaya Street. A sure sign that

life there wasn't right. Although there was a lot that was interesting. [. . .]

Molière: well, what is there to say, we're rehearsing. But
rarely, and slowly. And, between you and me, I regard it all
with some gloom. Lyusya [Yelena Sergeyevna] can't talk about
what the Theatre's done to that play without getting angry. But
that period of agitation has long since passed as far as I am
concerned. And were it not for the fact that I have to get a
new play staged in order to stay alive, I should long ago have
ceased thinking about it. If it goes on – well and good, if it
doesn't – too bad. But I work on those rare rehearsals with great
energy and excitement. There's nothing to be done if you have
the theatre in your blood!

From Yelena Sergeyevna's diary
27 March 1934

[Yegorov] said that Stalin was in the [Arts] Theatre a few days
ago, and that he had talked among other things about Bulgakov
and whether he was working for the Theatre.

'I can vouch to you, Yelena Sergeyevna, that amongst the
members of the Government *The Days of the Turbins* is considered to be an outstanding play.'

And altogether Yegorov was behaving in such a way that one
really could believe (despite his horridness) that something very
nice had been said about Bulgakov.

I told him about the new comedy, and that the Satire Theatre
was taking it.

'So what's this, a slap in the face for the Arts Theatre?'

13 April 1934

Yesterday M. A. finished the comedy *Bliss*, for which he had
signed a contract with the Satire Theatre. [. . .]

The other day the film director Pyryev came with a proposal
for a film scenario of *Dead Souls*. M. A. agreed, and will do it
over the summer. [. . .]

We've decided to put in an application for passports for foreign
travel for August and September.

26 April 1934. From Moscow to Zvenigorod (outside Moscow)
To the writer Vikenty Veresayev

This is typewritten because I am not entirely well, so I am lying down and dictating. [. . .] The telephone has been installed, but I won't resort to it; I prefer the post, since the conversation I want to have is longer than a telephone one. I haven't been able to get out anywhere because I have been completely overwhelmed with work. [. . .]

This is what I wanted to ask you, Vikenty Vikentyevich. Is there any possibility of renting a dacha out where you are living, at Zvenigorod? If it's not difficult, could you telephone or write to me about it: from whom, and where, and is there any bathing? We're really thinking about Seryozhka, although of course Yelena Sergeyevna is wanting to get me there too. It's not important to me, since I don't like the charms of the Moscow region and consequently won't get any better there. But to keep them company and to give my wife and Sergey a chance to get some fresh air, I'm prepared to find myself at a dacha. If Zvenigorod's no good, then we'll find something else closer to Moscow.

But next comes the brilliant part. I decided to put in a request for a two-month trip abroad, for August and September. I lay and thought about it for several days, racking my brains, and I asked various people for advice. 'Don't refer to ill-health.' All right, I won't. I can and must refer to one thing only: I must see the world, if only briefly, I have the right to do that. I check with myself, I ask my wife, 'Do I have that right?' And she answers, 'You do.' So what then, should I refer to that?

The whole question is made insanely more complex by the fact that I absolutely must travel with Yelena Sergeyevna. I don't feel well. My neurasthenia and my fear of being alone would turn the trip into a miserable torment. So there's an interesting question: what can I refer to here? Some of my advisers, when they heard the words 'with my wife', simply waved their hands dismissively. But actually there is no reason here for waving hands. It's the truth, and that truth needs to be defended. I don't need any doctors or holiday resorts or sanatoriums, nor anything else of that kind. I know what I need. For two months a different town, a different sun, a different sea, a different hotel, and I believe that in the autumn I would be in a condition to rehearse in Arts Theatre Passage, and maybe even to write.

One person said, 'Ask Nemirovich.' No, I won't ask him! Neither Nemirovich, nor Stanislavsky! They won't lift a finger. Anton Chekhov [who had died in 1904] can ask them if he likes! And so I have to decide. I'll ask Yelena Sergeyevna. She brings me good luck. It's time, it's high time I travelled, Vikenty Vikentyevich! Or otherwise, it will feel so strange – to have reached the sunset of my life!

Don't wish me luck: according to our theatrical superstition, that brings bad luck. [. . .]

Despite a few defects and some damned slipshod work, I am happy in my apartment. There's a lot of sunshine. We're waiting for the gas, since we can't take any baths without it; and it's a disaster for me if I can't take baths – they help a great deal.

28 April 1934. From Moscow
To his friend Pavel Popov

I have put in a request for a trip abroad in August and September. I have been dreaming for a long time about the waves of the Mediterranean, and the museums in Paris, and a quiet hotel, and no acquaintances, and Molière's fountain, and the cafés, and, to put it briefly, simply the possibility of seeing all this. I've been talking to Lyusya for ages now about what a travel book I could write! [. . .]

Though I did once see a writer who had been abroad. He was wearing a beret with a little tail on it. He hadn't brought anything back except that beret! He gave me the impression that he had spent two months sleeping, then he had bought that beret and come home. Not a line or a phrase written, not a thought! Oh, unforgettable Goncharov, where are you now? [. . .]

I beg you not to tell anyone about this for the moment, no one at all. There's no great secrecy, but I simply want to protect myself from the fantastic chattering of all my gossiping acquaintances in Moscow! [. . .] I simply don't want them to be prattling about such an important matter, which for me is a question about my entire future, however brief that may be, as I approach the evening of my life! [. . .]

Ah, Pavel, what letters I will write you! And when I get back in the autumn I will hug you, but I won't buy myself a little tail. Any more than I will buy any knee-breeches. Nor any check socks . . .

From Yelena Sergeyevna's diary
1 May 1934

On 25 April M. A. gave a reading of *Bliss* at the Satire Theatre, which went sluggishly, and they are asking for alterations to be made. [. . .]

We have handed in our request for a two-month trip abroad to Yakov L[eontyev] to be forwarded to Yenukidze.

Olya: 'And why on earth should they give Maka a passport? They issue them to those writers who they can be confident will write a book that is needed in the Soviet Union. But has Maka made any attempt to show that he has changed his views since his telephone call from Stalin?'

1 May 1934. Moscow
To the writer Aleksey [Maksim] Gorky

Much esteemed Aleksey Maksimovich!

The enclosed copy of my application to A. S. Yenukidze will make it clear to you that I am requesting permission to travel abroad for two months.

As I well remember your very valuable favourable comments on my plays *Flight* and *Molière*, I am presuming to trouble you once again with a request to you to give me your support in a matter that for me has a vital and purely literary significance.

In actual fact I really need a slightly longer period for my trip, but I am not asking for that, since it is crucial that I be back at the Moscow Arts Theatre in the autumn in order not to interrupt my work as a director on those plays to which I have been assigned (and in particular on *Molière*).

My nerves are overstrained to such an extent that I am fearful to travel alone, for which reason I request permission for my wife to accompany me.

I am absolutely convinced that this trip would render me capable of working again, and would afford me the possibility, as well as my work in the theatre, of writing a book of travel sketches, the thought of which attracts me.

I have never been abroad.

You would oblige me greatly with a reply.

From Yelena Sergeyevna's diary
11 May 1934
Pyryev: 'M. A., you ought to go and visit a factory and have a look . . .'

(They're all obsessed with this factory!)

18 May 1934
On the desk lay two red passports. I wanted to pay for them, but Borispolets said there was no charge: 'They're being issued on special instructions,' he said respectfully, 'please fill out the form downstairs.' [. . .] Borispolets said that the passports wouldn't be handed over to us today: 'Please come back tomorrow.' [. . .] M. A. kept repeating exultantly, 'So that means that I'm not a captive! It means I will see the world!' [. . .] M. A. held my arm tightly to his side and was laughing and thinking up the first chapter of the book he would bring back from his travels: 'Am I really not a prisoner?'

This is his constant night-time theme: 'I'm a prisoner, I've been artificially blinded.'

At home he dictated to me the first chapter of the book he's planning.

19 May 1934
The reply has been put off until tomorrow.

23 May 1934
The reply has been put off until the 25th.

25 May 1934
Once again there were no passports. We decided to stop going. M. A. is feeling dreadful.

1 June 1934
Pilnyak and his wife have received their passports and left.

We're not able to get on with anything because of this uncertainty.

Akhmatova came to see us. She has come to petition on behalf of Osip Mandelstam, who is in internal exile. [. . .]

There is considerable agitation amongst the writers in Moscow; they're processing applications for a new Writers' Union. Many are not being accepted. [. . .] On 29 May M. A. sent in an application form.

M. A. feels terrible, he's suffering from a fear of death and of solitude. Whenever he can he keeps to his bed.

10 June 1934. Moscow
To Yosif Stalin (draft)

Much esteemed Yosif Vissarionovich!

Allow me to inform you of what has occurred:

I.

At the end of April this year I sent to the Chairman of the Government Commission that runs the Arts Theatre an application, in which I requested permission for a two-month trip abroad together with my wife Yelena Sergeyevna Bulgakova.

In the application I described as the purpose of my trip the fact that I wished to write a book about my travels around Western Europe, with the idea that on my return I would submit it for publication in the USSR.

And since it is the case that I suffer from exhaustion of the nervous system, which is connected with a terror of being on my own, I also requested that my wife be granted permission to accompany me, on the understanding that she would leave behind here for those two months my seven-year-old stepson, whose maintenance and upbringing I am responsible for.

Having sent off the application I began to wait for one of two replies, that is to say, either permission to travel or a refusal of my request, since I imagined that there could be no third reply.

However, what occurred was that which I had not foreseen, that is to say a third alternative.

On 17 May I received a telephone call, during which the following exchange took place:

'Have you put in an application regarding a trip abroad?'

'Yes.'

'Please go to the Foreign Section of the Moscow Regional

Executive Committee, and fill out a form for yourself and for your wife.'

'When should I do that?'

'As soon as possible, since the question of your application is going to be considered on the 21st or the 22nd.'

Overcome with joy as I was, I didn't even enquire as to who was talking, and immediately went and presented myself with my wife at the For. Sec. of the Executive Committee. The official, when he heard that I had been summoned to the F. S. by telephone, asked me to wait, went into the next room, and when he came back asked me to fill in the forms.

When we had done that he accepted them, attaching two photographs to them, and wouldn't take any money, saying, 'These passports will be free.'

He wouldn't take our Soviet passports, saying, 'That comes later, when you exchange them for the passports for foreign travel.'

And then he added the following, word for word: '*You will receive your passports very soon, since there is an instruction about you. You could have had them today*, but it's already late. Give me a ring on the morning of the 18th.'

I said, 'But the 18th isn't a working day.'

To which he replied, 'Well, on the 19th then.'

On the morning of 19 May when we rang, they said, 'The passports aren't here yet. Ring towards the end of the day. If they're here, the passport official will issue them to you.'

When we rang towards the end of the day it emerged that the passports weren't there, and we were asked to ring again on the 23rd.

On the 23rd I went with my wife in person to the F. S., and there learned that the passports weren't there. At that point the official began to make enquiries about them over the telephone, and then asked us to telephone on the 25th or the 27th.

At that point I became wary and asked the official whether it was correct that there was an instruction about me and whether I hadn't misheard on 17 May?

To which I received the reply, 'You will understand that I can't tell you whose instruction it was, *but there is an instruction regarding you and your wife*, just as there is one for the writer Pilnyak.'

At which all my doubts left me, and my joy knew no bounds.

Soon after that I had still further confirmation that permission to travel had been granted. I was informed by the Theatre that someone in the Secretariat of the Central Executive Committee had said, 'The Bulgakovs' case is working out well.'

During this time I received congratulations on the fact that the dream I had had as a writer for so many years, my dream of travelling, something that is vital to every writer, was becoming a reality.

Meanwhile, at the F. S. of the Executive Committee, the reply about our passports was continuing to be deferred from one day to the next, but I reacted with equanimity, assuming that however much they delayed, the passports would eventually appear.

On 7 June the messenger from the Arts Theatre went to the F. S. with a list of actors who were due to receive passports for foreign travel. The Theatre was kind enough to include me and my wife on that list, even though I had submitted my application separately from the Theatre.

During the day the messenger returned, and even from his bewildered and embarrassed face I could see that something had happened.

The messenger informed me that the passports for the actors had been issued, but as far as my wife and I were concerned, he said that we had been REFUSED passports.

On the following day, with no more delay, I received a certificate at the F. S. to the effect that citizen Bulgakov M. A. had been refused permission to leave the country.

After which, rather than wait to hear everyone's expressions of sympathy, surprise and so on, I set off home, able to understand only that I had been landed in a distressing and grotesque situation inappropriate to my years.

2.

The affront that has been offered to me by the F. S. of the Moscow Regional Executive Committee is all the more grievous for the fact that my four years of service in the Moscow Arts

Theatre give no justification for it, which is why I am asking for your protection.

11 June 1934. Moscow
To Yosif Stalin (draft)

I can imagine only one single reason: is it possible that there exists in the organs that control travel abroad a theory that I might remain there for ever? I need scarcely say that in order to settle abroad after making a deceitful application, I would need to part my wife from her child and place her in a horrifying situation, to break up the life of my family, ruin with my own hands my repertory in the Arts Theatre, bring ignominy upon myself – and, above all, for no obvious reason.

But what matters here is something different: I cannot comprehend how, having conceived of one thing, one could request something else. And I have proof of the fact that that is something I cannot understand. It was I who, four years ago, addressed to the Government an application in which I requested either to be given permission to leave the Soviet Union for an indefinite period, or to be allowed to work at the Moscow Arts Theatre. When at that time I was thinking about an open-ended trip, under the pressure of my personal circumstances as a writer, I didn't start writing about a two-month trip . . . I have no guarantees, nor guarantors . . .

20 June 1934. Leningrad
From V. Sakhnovsky (Deputy Director of the Moscow Arts Theatre)

Dear Mikhail Afanasyevich,

Today is the FIVE HUNDREDTH performance of your play. You know how much the Theatre and all our audiences in Moscow and Leningrad love *The Days of the Turbins*. *The Turbins* has become a new *Seagull* for the new generation at the Arts Theatre. You yourself were a witness not long ago, at the première in Leningrad, to the way in which the audience responds to your play, and the Theatre, and particularly the younger Arts Theatre generation, feels more attached to this play than to any other.

You have known for a long time from Konstantin Sergeyevich [Stanislavsky] and Vladimir Ivanovich [Nemirovich-Danchenko] that they both consider you 'one of us' in the Arts Theatre, 'one of us' in your artistic affinities, and for that reason on this day of the FIVE HUNDREDTH performance allow me on behalf of the Theatre to congratulate you as 'one of us', and not only as our beloved dramatist; and in my own name, without inverted commas, allow me to give you a big hug, remembering our three years of amicable work on your other play [*Dead Souls*].

24 June 1934. From Paris to Moscow
From his brother Nikolay

I've made the acquaintance of Yevgeny Ivanovich Zamyatin and seen him a couple of times.

26 June 1934. From Leningrad to Moscow
To Yakov Leontyev (at the Bolshoy Theatre)

Up until now we have not been able to tackle any letters, but there was a reason for this. Both Yelena Sergeyevna and I have been extremely unwell. She began to get dreadful headaches, and I have been suffering from insomnia and all the other delights I brought away with me from Moscow. We began to have treatment with electricity, and the results, touch wood, have been miraculous. We've both begun to come round.

First of all I would like to send you a hug for your precious telegram and wonderful letters (me too).

And so, 500 performances. I had many, many thoughts on that day . . .

In the interval before the scene in the High School Sakhnovsky made a short speech with the curtain down. People applauded quietly so that the audience should not hear. [. . .]

Nemirovich sent a letter of congratulations to the Theatre, in which there was not a whisper about the author. Original, most original, I swear by the 500th performance! [. . .]

The ridiculous 'me too' that has crept on to the first page indicates a tender and unexpected postscript from Yelena Sergeyevna.

26 June 1934. From Leningrad to Moscow
To his friend Pavel Popov

After all that's happened not just I, but my missus, to my great horror, fell ill. She had diabolical migraines, then the pain spread, and she was suffering from insomnia, and so on. We were both obliged to get systematic and serious treatment. We are having electric shock treatment every day, and now we're beginning to get back on our feet.

Well now, we've just had the 500th performance here; it was on the 20th. [. . .] Nemirovich sent his congratulations to the Theatre too. I turned them over and over in my hands until I had satisfied myself that he had not said one word about the author. I imagine that good taste requires that the author should not be mentioned. I didn't know that before, but evidently I am an insufficiently refined person.

The irritating thing is that, without asking me, the Theatre sent him thanks, and from the author as well. I would have given a lot to tear the word 'author' out of there. [. . .]

I am writing a *Dead Souls* for the cinema and will bring the finished thing back with me. After that, all the commotion with *Bliss* will begin. Oh, I have such a lot of work to do! But meanwhile my Margarita is roaming through my mind, and the cat, and flying . . .

10 July 1934. From Leningrad to Moscow
To his friend Pavel Popov

We should reappear in Moscow on about 15 or 17 July. [. . .]

Lyusya insists that the film scenario [*Dead Souls*] came out really well. I showed it to them still in draft form, and it was a good thing that I hadn't bothered about a fair copy. Everything that I liked best about it, that is, the scene with Suvorov's soldiers in the middle of the Nozdryov scene, the separate long ballad about Captain Kopeykin, the funeral service on Sobakevich's estate and, most importantly, Rome with the silhouette [of Gogol] on the balcony – all of that was thrown out! I will succeed only in preserving Kopeykin, and then only by cutting him. But, my God, how I regret Rome!

I let Vaysfeld [from the film studio] and his director have their say, and immediately said that I would redo it the way they wanted, so that they were even rather taken aback.

Something happened here with regard to *Bliss* that simply goes beyond the bounds of reason.

A room at the Astoria. I read it. The Director of the Theatre, who is also the producer, expresses his complete and evidently genuine admiration, intends to put it on, promises money, and says that he'll come back in forty minutes to have supper with me. He arrives forty minutes later, has supper, doesn't say a word about the play, and then disappears into the ground and that's an end of him!

Some people think he's vanished into the fourth dimension.

So that's the kind of miracle that takes place in the world nowadays!

11 July 1934. From Leningrad
To the writer Vikenty Veresayev

I would like to tell you about my unusual adventures this spring.

By the beginning of the spring I had become seriously ill: I began to suffer from insomnia, weakness and finally, which was the filthiest thing I have ever experienced in my life, a fear of solitude, or to be more precise, a fear of being left on my own. It's so repellent that I would prefer to have a leg cut off!

And so of course doctors, sodium bromide and all the rest of it. I was afraid of the streets, couldn't write, found people either exhausting or frightening, couldn't bear to see the newspapers, and had to walk with either Yelena Sergeyevna or Seryozhka holding my arm – it would have been ghastly on my own!

Well, then at the end of April I wrote an application asking to spend two months in France and Rome with Yelena Sergeyevna (I wrote to you about that). Seryozhka would be here, so that would be fine. I sent it off. And then I sent another letter to G[orky]. Although I had little hope of receiving a reply to that one. Something's happened there, as a result of which all our contacts have been broken off. Although it's not hard to guess: someone came and said something, as a result of which a barrier has been erected. And sure enough, I received no reply! [. . .]

On 17 May I was lying on the sofa. The telephone rang and an unknown person, an official I presume, said, 'Did you put in an application? Go to the Foreign Section of the Executive Committee and fill in a form for yourself and your wife.' [. . .]

A state of sheer bliss reigned in our household. Can you imagine: Paris! – the monument to Molière . . . greetings, Monsieur Molière, I have written a book and a play about you; Rome! – greetings, Nikolay Vasilyevich [Gogol], don't be angry, I transformed your *Dead Souls* into a play. True, it doesn't much resemble the one that's being performed in the Theatre, and in fact it's not like it at all, but all the same I did my best . . . The Mediterranean sea! Oh my fathers!

Can you believe it, I sat down and began to sketch out the chapters of a book!

How many of our writers have travelled to Europe, and have come away with less than nothing! Nothing! [. . .]

Then people began to congratulate us, with just a hint of envy: 'Oh, you lucky things!'

'Just a moment,' said I, 'where are the passports, then?'

'Keep calm!' (in chorus)

We stayed calm. My dreams: Rome, a balcony such as Gogol describes, pine-trees, roses . . . a manuscript . . . I'm dictating to Yelena Sergeyevna . . . in the evening we walk, all is quiet and scented . . . in other words, it's just like in a novel!

And then in September there would be a tug at my heart: Kamergersky Street, it's probably drizzling there, the stage is half-lit, who knows, they're probably working on *Molière* in the workshops . . .

And that's when I'd arrive, in that drizzle. With a manuscript in my suitcase, and you can't cap that! [. . .]

They gave a list of names to the messenger and told him to nip off and collect the passports.

So he nipped off, and then he nipped back. His face so horrified me that I was clutching at my heart before he'd even had time to open his mouth.

In other words he brought passports for everybody, and for me a little piece of white paper – M. A. Bulgakov is refused permission. [. . .] I crawled out of the wreckage in such a state that I was not a pleasant sight. But here I have begun to recover.

Before I left I wrote a letter to the General Secretary, in which I recounted all that had happened, and informed him that I wouldn't stay abroad but would come back on time, and asked him to review the matter. There was no reply. But then I cannot even guarantee that my letter reached its destination.

On 13 June I abandoned everything and left for Leningrad. In a couple of days' time we'll be returning to Moscow.

From Yelena Sergeyevna's diary
20 July 1934

On the 17th we returned from Leningrad, where we had spent more than a month living in the Astoria.

24 July 1934. Moscow
From the writer Vikenty Veresayev

I feel so painfully for you! What an endless strain on your nerves! And so much energy gets wasted unnecessarily on it all, which would have been so useful for literary work! Aach! . . . I give you a strong hug and wish you spiritual strength. And what's Italy to you! As if you couldn't arrange peace and quiet and a rest for yourself here. But not in Leningrad, though!

31 July 1934. From Moscow to Paris
To Maria Reinhardt

I have received from my brother the French text of *Zoyka's Apartment* and am rushing to send you some corrections which are vitally important, mistakes I noticed after just a hasty read through the translation. [. . .]

Neither the word 'Lenin' nor the word 'Ilyich' appears in my text. [. . .]

I don't have the word 'Stalin' anywhere, and I request you to strike it out. And in general, if the names of members of the Government of the USSR have been inserted anywhere, I request you to remove them, since their inclusion is utterly inappropriate and is a complete violation of the author's text.

1 August 1934. From Moscow to Paris
To his brother Nikolay

I would ask you emphatically to use all your authority to
ensure the correction of some extremely unpleasant distortions
of my text, namely that the translator has included in the first act
(and possibly elsewhere as well) the names of Lenin and Stalin.
Please ensure that they are struck out immediately. I hope that
I do not need to explain at any length how inappropriate it is to
include the names of members of the Government of the USSR
in a comedy. [. . .]

This summer, and in fact precisely at the moment when this
letter will reach you, I should have been in Paris. I was so close
to it that I had sketched out the entire plan for a two-month
trip. Then I would have sorted out all these matters. But at
the very last moment, completely unexpectedly, and when I
had every hope that the trip would be allowed – I was refused
permission.

If I had been in Paris, I should have been able to show them
the staging myself, I should have been able to provide a complete
interpretation, not just as the author, but also as a director, and
you can be sure that the play would have benefited by it. But
alas, mine is a complex destiny! [. . .]

Send me Zamyatin's address if you can.

Lyusya sends you her greetings. She often questions me,
asking what my brothers are like, and I talk to her about you
and Ivan, and wish that your lives should be happy.

From Yelena Sergeyevna's diary
15 August 1934

We spent the beginning of August with Sergey, living in a
dacha in Zvenigorod. Since the 9th we've been in Moscow, and
now we're wondering whether to go down to Kiev.

They've sent us a copy of the translation of *Zoyka's Apartment*
from Paris. M. A.'s hair stood on end. The translation itself is
generally not bad, but in Ametistov's monologues the translators
have inserted without any authority the names of Lenin and
Stalin, in an unsuitable context. M. A. immediately sent a letter
demanding that the names be removed.

Incidentally, we still don't know whether M. A. has been accepted by the Writers' Union or not. They've been sending occasional notices, and indirectly we heard at first that they wouldn't take him, along with some others, but then that they had accepted him. [. . .]

M. A. had an agonizing time completing *Dead Souls*; he's now delivered a third version to them.

23 August 1934

For M. A. the word 'apartment' has magic powers. There's nothing in the world he's envious of, except a good apartment! It's one of his foibles.

25 August 1934

M. A. is still frightened to out out on his own. [. . .]

A conversation with Afinogenov: 'Mikhail Afanasyevich, why have you not been attending the Congress [of the new Writers' Union]?' 'I am frightened by crowds.' [. . .]

M. A. has got a plan for a play about Pushkin. Only he thinks it absolutely necessary to ask Veresayev to prepare the material for it. M. A feels grateful to him because at a difficult time he came to M. A. and offered him some money as a loan.

So M. A. would like to express his gratitude in this way, although I sense that nothing good will come of it. There's nothing worse than two people working together.

29 August 1934

Zagorsky: why had M. A. not been able to accept Bolshevism . . .

31 August 1934

Zhukhovitsky – who is always present, of course – was pestering M. A. to make a declarative statement that he had accepted Bolshevism.

6 September 1934

M. A. had stomach-ache, he had eaten something that disagreed with him at the dacha. At first he went over Sergey's lessons with him, and then he was teaching him to play chess. [. . .]

In the evening one of our neighbours, the writer L., came round to ask me to type out and send off a letter to the leadership; he's not being published, he's been excluded from everywhere, and his life is difficult. Then came a note from A., who also lives here, asking for money – we found a little at least.

7 September 1934

I accompanied M. A. to the Theatre to a rehearsal of *Pickwick.* [. . .]

After lunch and a sleep he dictated *The Government Inspector* to me.

8 September 1934

On the way to the Theatre we met Sudakov: 'You know, M. A., the situation as regards *Flight* is not bad at all. They're saying we should put it on. Both Yosif Vissarionovich [Stalin] and Avel Sofronovich [Yenukidze] very much approve. So long as Bubnov doesn't interfere.' (?!)

10 September 1934

On the evening of the 9th we had the Moscow cast of *The Turbins*, the American cast of *The Turbins*, Zhukhovitsky – of course – and the Kaluzhskys to visit. We had a candle-lit supper with pies, caviare, sturgeon, veal, sweets, wine, vodka and flowers. We sat very cosily until about four in the morning. [. . .]

M. A. said the evening was like the building of the Tower of Babel – people were talking simultaneously in Russian, English, French and German. Khmelyov was trying to prove to the American Aleksey in atrocious French that art did not exist in the West, that it could be found only here. As evidence he pointed to the example of Stanislavsky . . . [. . .]

All day we've been drifting about like sleepy flies.

11 September 1934

We went to the Popovs'. Annushka sang gypsy waltzes and played the guitar; M. A. is looking for some gypsy music for *Flight*. But will it ever be put on?

15 September 1934

Pyryev has sent a copy of the film scenario of *Dead Souls* back, having made his own alterations to it, but they are very illiterately done; and yet on the cover it says 'M. Bulgakov'.

16 September 1934

In the evening – Lyamin; Misha read him several chapters of the novel. And after he left we had a conversation until seven in the morning, all on the same subject – M. A.'s situation.

17 September 1934

In the evening – Gorchakov. The Satire Theatre is asking M. A. to make a comedy out of *Bliss*, in which Ivan the Terrible should appear in modern Moscow. [. . .]

Ilya [Sudakov] is a real bandit; all his talk about *Flight* was a pack of empty lies. It now turns out that he's got Afinogenov's most recent play, *The Portrait*, in his hands.

13 October 1934

M. A.'s having a bad time with his nerves. He's afraid of open spaces and of being on his own. He's wondering whether to try hypnosis. [. . .]

15 October 1934

M. A.'s nerves are very jumpy, but when we're walking together he saves himself by telling some funny story. [. . .]

This evening M. A. finished dictating to me the film scenario of *The Government Inspector* in draft. [. . .]

At last they've put in gas in our apartment! Sergey was the first to take a bath.

16 October 1934

During the rehearsal [of *Pickwick*] he learned that today for the first time after a long gap they were rehearsing *Molière* – the scene in the cathedral.

He says that he heard the news with indifference. He doesn't believe that the play will ever be put on.

A few days ago Stanislavsky called a meeting about *Molière*, and M. A. came away with the gloomiest of impressions.

18 October 1934

Today we went to see V. V. Veresayev. M. A. had a proposal that he and Veresayev should write a play about Pushkin together, that is that Veresayev should select the material and M. A. would write it.

Mariya Germogenovna immediately greeted the idea with enthusiasm. The old man was very touched, trotted several times up and down his comfortable study, and then gave M. A. a hug.

V. V. really lit up and began to talk about Pushkin, about

his ambiguousness, and about the fact that Natalya Nikolayevna [Pushkin's wife] was by no means a shallow creature, but an unfortunate woman.

At first V. V. was staggered that M. A. had decided to write the play with no Pushkin in it (it would be vulgar otherwise), but agreed once he had thought about it.

20 October 1934

Today we bought a piano.

3 November 1934

There's chaos in the apartment – we've got the decorators in.

Today I went to the dress rehearsal of *Pickwick*. [. . .] The audience laughed at M. A.'s lines (he is playing the judge). Kachalov, Ktorov, Popova and others told me that his acting was that of a professional.

His costume consists of a red gown and a long white curly wig. During the interval afterwards he told me that he had been dreadfully nervous, and that his stool had fallen over – he had knocked it over with his gown as he sat down. He had to begin the scene hanging on to the lectern by his elbows. But then they came to his assistance and picked the stool up.

8 November 1934

In the evening we sat surrounded by all the mess. M. A. was dictating the novel to me – the scene in the cabaret. Sergey was right there, sleeping on the ottoman.

A telephone call: Olya. A long conversation. Right at the end: 'Oh yes, by the way. I've been meaning to say to you for several days. Do you know, it looks as though permission for *Flight* is going to come through. The other day they rang Vladimir Ivanovich [Nemirovich-Danchenko] from the Central Committee and asked his opinion of the play. Well, of course, he praised it to the skies, and said that it was an excellent piece. They replied, "We will bear your opinion in mind."'

14 November 1934

A rehearsal of *Pickwick* in front of Stanislavsky. [. . .]

K. S. has aged a great deal and become thin.

16 November 1934

Today Stanitsyn told M. A. how the old man [Stanislavsky] had reacted to his appearance in the court scene. Stanitsyn was naming all the actors to him. When the judge appeared, Stanislavsky asked, 'And who's that?' 'Bulgakov.' 'Ah.' (Suddenly, turning sharply towards Stanitsyn), 'Which Bulgakov?' 'Mikhail Afanasyevich. The playwright.' 'The writer?!' 'Yes, the writer. He was very keen to have a go.' The old man immediately narrowed his eyes, tittered, and began to watch M. A. Stanitsyn gave a hilarious demonstration of all this to us.

17 November 1934

This evening Akhmatova arrived. Pilnyak had brought her from Leningrad in his car. She told us about Mandelstam's bitter fate. We talked about Pasternak.

19 November 1934

After the hypnosis M. A.'s attacks of terror have begun to disappear, his mood is serene and calm, and he is finding it easy to work. Now – if he could just manage to walk in the streets on his own.

21 November 1934

Today was M. A.'s nameday. Sergey and I gave him – 'half-and-half', as Sergey puts it – some musical scores: *Tannhäuser*, *Ruslan and Lyudmila*, and some others. This was on the evening before.

And today I gave him an Alexander I desk.

In the evening Dr Berg came and tried to instil in him the idea that tomorrow he would go to visit the Leontyevs on his own.

Before that there was a call from Olya, with congratulations and the information that *Flight* hadn't been permitted after all. M. A. took this completely calmly. We weren't able to discover from Olya who had refused it permission.

22 November 1934

At ten in the evening M. A. got up, put on his coat, and went to the Leontyevs on his own.

He hasn't been out on his own for six months.

26 November 1934

In the evening Ilf and Petrov came round for advice about a play they have thought up. Afterwards M. A. went to see Veresayev; V. V. accompanied him back to Smolenskaya Square, and he walked the rest of the way home on his own. He says the fear was less acute.

28 November 1934

In the evening – Dmitriyev. He came from the Arts Theatre and said there was a lot of bustle and excitement there; probably someone had come from the Government, I guess it must have been the General Secretary [Stalin] (to see *The Turbins*).

29 November 1934

Indeed it was the General Secretary, together with Kirov and Zhdanov, who was at *The Turbins* yesterday. I was told so in the Theatre. Yanshin said the company acted well, and that the General Secretary had applauded a lot at the end of the performance.

In the papers there was a very important piece of news: they're abolishing ration cards for bread, and bread will be sold freely.

30 November 1934

During the day M. A. dictated sketches towards a version of *Ivan Vasilyevich* (the reworked *Bliss*).

It turns out that they're planning to put *Molière* on in March. Although there are complications about the sets. [. . .] Gorchakov wants to commission Vilyams to design them. He says it's going to be put on sumptuously – Stanislavsky is insisting on it.

1 December 1934

In the evening there was the première of *Pickwick*. I accompanied M. A. there in a taxi. He stayed until the end of the performance. He came back and told me that during the performance it became known that Kirov had been assassinated in Leningrad.

Many people immediately left the Theatre, amongst them Rykov.

3 December 1934

At half-past three I accompanied M. A. to the Theatre. They're holding a memorial meeting there [for Kirov]. [. . .]

I don't know whether Kirov had been to the theatre in Leningrad, but it's possible that the last play he saw in his life was *The Days of the Turbins*.

9 December 1934

During the day we visited Vikenty Vikentyevich. We took him the last thousand of Misha's debt to him, and both felt relieved when it was done. [. . .]

Now about *Molière*. We told Gorchakov that, according to Olga, they're going to put on *The Portrait*. [. . .] This is one of Vladimir Ivanovich [Nemirovich-Danchenko]'s tricks; he wants to put on a Communist play.

10 December 1934

Gorchakov rang. They're not putting on *The Portrait*, and are pressing on with rehearsals of *Molière*.

14 December 1934

Here's a juicy bit of gossip: apparently Anatoly Kamensky – who went abroad four years ago and didn't come back and started being abusive about the USSR – is now in Moscow!

Misha couldn't restrain himself and said, 'Well comrades, this is quite mystical!'

Zhukhovitsky was very put out and said something stupid, his eyes were darting about and he was dreadfully embarrassed.

I understand him through and through now: more than once Misha and I have caught him out in a lie.

16 December 1934

During the day Misha and Veresayev went to the Vakhtangov Theatre to sign a contract.

17 December 1934

Misha went to a rehearsal of *Molière* while I had a conversation with Yegorov. [. . .] He had the cheek to express surprise that Misha was writing a play for another theatre and not for the Arts Theatre. So to the best of my ability I explained to him all the insults they had subjected Misha to over the last few years, what they had done with *Flight*, and what they were doing with *Molière*, which they have been rehearsing for several years!

22 December 1934

All in all, Misha has been agonizing over these past few days that he won't be able to cope with the work: *The Government Inspector, Ivan Vasilyevich*, and now *Pushkin* coming up.

24 December 1934

We've put up a tree. First of all Misha and I decorated it, laid all the presents out beneath it, switched off the electric light and lit candles on the tree; Misha played a march, and the boys [Seryozhka and Zhenya] flew into the room.

Seryozhka was so excited outside the door he was in tears; he couldn't wait.

There were wild squeals, clattering and shouts! Then, according to the programme, there were performances. Misha had written a text based on *Dead Souls*. [. . .] Misha did my make-up using a cork, lipstick and powder. The curtain was a blanket on the door from the study into the dining-room, and the stage was the study. In order to play the part of my Seryozhka, Misha put on underpants, Seryozhka's coat, which barely reached his waist, and a sailor's jacket. He looked like a huge red cat.

31 December 1934

And so the year is coming to an end. And now, as I walk through our rooms, I frequently catch myself crossing myself and whispering to myself, 'Oh, Lord! Please let things continue like this!'

2 January 1935

An unpleasant experience in the tram this evening, after the theatre. Some type in a hat with a blue star, blind drunk, clearly wanted to make a scene because of my fur coat. There were two women sniggering and egging him on out of curiosity. It's not the first time I've noticed this hatred of fur coats!

4 January 1935

An incredible frost! It's minus 32 degrees Celsius. I went to the Theatre with Misha [. . .]. I was wearing ski trousers, which attracted a great deal of attention amongst the actors. [. . .]

All day I've been recalling a notable conversation with Olga yesterday. [. . .] She said that out of common humanity one ought to feel sorry for Afinogenov. [. . .] I listened to her, said nothing, and just stared at her with such a look! . . . Is she telling me to feel sorry for Afinogenov? Me, the wife of Misha, who has been persecuted and stifled throughout his literary career! [. . .]

I don't know who will ever read these notes of mine. But they mustn't be surprised if I am always writing about practical matters. They won't know of the terrible conditions in which my husband Mikhail Bulgakov had to work.

5 February 1935

According to Misha the session [of hypnosis] was extraordinarily successful.

10 February 1935

Victory! Today Misha went to the performance at the Theatre on his own.

15 February 1935

Zhukhovitsky was here in the evening. The same old, painful conversation on the same subject: Misha's fate. Zhukhovitsky said that Misha should speak out on some contemporary theme and demonstrate his attitude to the modern world. Misha said, 'I'll not do it, so why don't they just leave me in peace!'

2–6 March 1935. From Moscow to Kiev
To his childhood friend Aleksandr Gdeshinsky

Dear Sasha,

Thank you for remembering me, and for your kind invitation.

If you imagine that you reside in Kiev, you are cruelly mistaken! At all events the address office in Kiev has no knowledge of you there.

I was there last August [. . .]. I was in Kiev with only one purpose: to go round my homeland and show my wife the places that I once described. She wanted to see them.

Unfortunately we were able to spend only five days in Kiev. [. . .] And so I went to the hill in the gardens of the Merchants' Assembly, looked at the lights on the river, and recalled my life.

When I walked in the parks during the day I was struck by a strange emotion. My homeland! My melancholy, sweet pleasure and agitation! I would very much like to spend time in that land again. [. . .]

P.S. My wife is called Yelena Sergeyevna. The three of us live together: she and I and eight-year-old Sergey, my stepson – an exceedingly interesting personality. A bandit with a tin revolver, and he's learning the piano.

From Yelena Sergeyevna's diary
5 March 1935
Misha had a difficult rehearsal of *Molière* at Stanislavsky's house. He came back depressed and furious.

14 March 1935. From Moscow
To his friend Pavel Popov
Now Stanislavsky has taken command. They ran through *Molière* for him (except for the last scene, which wasn't ready), and he, instead of giving his opinion of the production and the acting, started to give his opinion of the play.

In the presence of the actors (five years on!) he began to tell me all about the fact that Molière was a genius, and how this genius ought to be depicted in the play.

The actors licked their lips in glee and began to ask that their parts be made larger.

I was overcome with fury. For a heady moment I wanted to fling the notebook down and say to them all, 'You write about geniuses and ungeniuses if you like, but don't teach me how to do it, I won't be able to do it anyway. I'd be better off acting instead of you.'

But you can't, you can't do it. So I stifled it all and began to defend myself.

Three days later the same. He patted my hand and said that I needed to be rubbed up the right way, and then it was the whole business all over again.

In other words I've got to write in something about Molière's significance for the theatre, and somehow I've got to demonstrate that Molière was a genius, and so on.

This is all primitive, feeble and unnecessary. And now I'm sitting in front of my copy of the text, and I can't lift my hand to work on it. I can't not write it in: declaring war would mean wrecking all that work, stirring up a proper commotion, and harming the play itself; but writing green patches into the trousers of a black tail-coat! . . . The devil knows what I should do?!

What on earth is going on, dear citizens?

And by the way, could you tell me when *Molière* is finally going to go on? [. . .]

We didn't eat pancakes. Lyusya has been ill. (She's getting better now.)

And outside the window, alas, it is spring. Sometimes snow-flakes float slantingly down, or there's no snow and there's sun on the dining-table. What will the spring bring? I can hear a voice in myself, I can hear it – nothing!

15 March 1935. From Moscow
To Konstantin Derzhavin (a director at the Krasny Theatre in Leningrad)

And so there are ten scenes in the play about Pushkin. [. . .] The play covers Pushkin's last days and death, but Pushkin never once appears on stage before the spectator.

At the moment nine scenes have been written in rough.

The authors have to deliver the play to the Vakhtangov Theatre not later than 1 December 1935, and the Theatre is obliged to stage it not later than 8 February 1937.

From Yelena Sergeyevna's diary
20 March 1935

B. I. Yarkho did a translation of *Le Bourgeois Gentilhomme* and sent Misha the book with a dedication.

The day before yesterday, I think it was, we learned that he and Shpet have been arrested. We don't know, of course, what for.

26 March 1935

Yesterday Misha and I went to a Wagner concert in the Great Hall of the Conservatoire. [. . .] We sat in the sixth row. I was in a black dress with a low-cut back, which attracted a great deal of attention. One lady said spitefully, 'I detest such things! . . . '
[. . .]

Grisha K[onsky] appeared today without warning at about three. I'm observing him very carefully to see what sort of a fish he is. I can't work it out. He asks questions endlessly. He leads conversations into exactly the same areas, and in just the same manner, as Kantorovich and Zhukhovitsky do. [. . .]

Misha dictated the ninth scene to me today; the scene on the Moyka Canal. [. . .] I'm so glad that he's gone back to Pushkin again. Recently he hasn't been able to dictate at all because of all the agonies he's been enduring with Stanislavsky over *Molière*.

29 March 1935

I went with Misha to the Theatre to collect his salary, then on to a café, then he went to Stanislavsky's while I went into town and then home. During his absence they brought an envelope from the American Embassy with an invitation for Misha and me for 23 April. There was a note at the bottom saying 'Tails or Dinner Jackets'. I'm going to have a black suit made for Misha, because he doesn't have one. It will be interesting to go!

30 March 1935

Today Misha and I went [. . .] to the Torgsin [imported-goods] shop for material for the suit and some other things. We bought very good material, and the shop assistant assured us that it was English and specially made for tail-coats and smoking-jackets, although it was dreadfully expensive – 25 gold roubles a length. Then we bought Misha black shoes to go with the suit. There were no starched shirts.

30 March 1935. Moscow
To his doctor, Semyon Berg

In other words, I feel very well. You have managed it so that I am no longer tortured by my accursed fearfulness. That is now distant and remote. I will come and visit you. I remember our conversations warmly!

From Yelena Sergeyevna's diary
7 April 1935

Akhmatova came to lunch. She has come to petition on behalf of some woman friend of hers who has been sent away from Leningrad into internal exile. [. . .]

Rehearsals of *Molière* are continuing at Stanislavsky's house in Leontyevsky Street, driving Misha to exasperation. Instead of rehearsing the scenes of the play, he occupies the actors in pedagogic exercises and tells them all sorts of irrelevant things which do nothing to make the play progress. Misha has been persuading me that no 'method' and no efforts are going to induce a bad actor to act well. [. . .]

Today I rang *Red Virgin Soil* and was put straight through to Marmush, who, hastily pulling himself together, very courteously informed me that the question of publishing the biography of Molière in their journal was due to be decided on the 10th or the 12th. Misha said, 'You will never see or hear from that man again in your life.'

8 April 1935

I rather liked Pasternak – he is very unusual, not like anyone else I know. Breathing in a special way, he read his translations of Georgian verses. He evidently has a great affection for Misha. When the first toast had been drunk to the host, Pasternak said, 'I would like to drink to Bulgakov.' Our hostess suddenly burst in, 'No, no! We'll drink to Vikenty Vikentyevich [Veresayev] first, and then to Bulgakov,' to which Pasternak obstinately retorted, 'No, I want to drink to Bulgakov. Veresayev is a great man, of course, but he is a lawful phenomenon, whereas Bulgakov is unlawful.'

8 April 1935. From Paris to Moscow
From his brother Nikolay

Dear Mikhail,

With a feeling of great sorrow I note that once again there's not been any word from you for a very long time. [. . .] Are you well, and is everything all right? [. . .] Greetings to you and your family from the Zamyatins, and from my wife and me.

From Yelena Sergeyevna's diary
9 April 1935

Grisha [Konsky] is very intrigued by our invitation to the Embassy. He said he would come to see us off, he just couldn't not, he must see how we looked.

10 April 1935
Sergey has cut his left thumb so badly that Misha decided that he would be permanently scarred and that was the end of his music. Misha was livid, and bawled at him and at us for not taking enough care. Seryozhka stood there pale and panting. Misha put him to bed and bandaged his thumb. We called out Dr Blyumental. We thought it would have to be stitched, but it was all right.

11 April 1935
In the morning Zhukhovitsky rang – 'When could we arrange a day? Bohlen (a Secretary at the American Embassy) would very much like to invite us to lunch.' Instead of replying, Misha immediately invited Bohlen, Thayer (Bullitt [the American Ambassador]'s private secretary) and Zhukhovitsky to come here this evening.

For supper we had caviare, salmon, home-made pâté, radishes, fresh cucumbers, fried mushrooms, vodka and white wine. The Americans speak Russian, Bohlen very well indeed.

The supper began with Misha's showing them the photographs for the passport forms, and saying that tomorrow he was putting in an application for a passport for foreign travel, as he was hoping to go abroad for three months or so.

Zhukhovitsky almost choked. The Americans said we should certainly go. We're dreaming of America . . . Bohlen wants to translate *Zoyka's Apartment* together with Zhukhovitsky.

13 April 1935
Misha went today during the day to see Akhmatova, who is staying at the Mandelstams'. They want to publish a book of Akhmatova's poems, but very selectively. Mandelstam's wife recalled seeing Misha in Baku about fourteen years ago walking along with a sack on his shoulder. That was during a period when he was living in poverty and sold an oil-stove in the bazaar. [. . .]

Today I learned from Olya that apparently, according to Nikolay Vladimirovich Sollogub, my first husband Yury Mamontovich Neyelov has died. How awful: I had almost forgotten all about him, but over the last few days I have recalled him very often.

14 April 1935. From Moscow to Paris
To his brother Nikolay

Dear Nikol!

I am glad to have had news from you. It's a long time since I had any letters from you. And in particular, I didn't receive your February letter.

We're living happily, but I have landed myself with so much work that I'm not coping with it. I fell ill from overwork, but am now feeling better. [. . .]

Thank you very much for writing in such detail about *Zoyka's Apartment*. At one point I did send Reinhardt my commentaries as she requested. But of course that is quite inadequate. My presence is vital.

In the next few days I shall be putting in a request for permission to travel abroad, and shall try to fit it in by the early autumn (in August-September, probably, or October). I would ask you to make contact right away with those theatrical circles that are involved in the production of *Zoyka's Apartment*, to get them to send an invitation through the Soviet Plenipotentiary to the People's Commissariat for Foreign Affairs for me to come to Paris in connection with the production.

I am convinced that if someone in Paris were to tackle this business seriously, then it might help me in my efforts. Is it really impossible to find adequate connections within influential French circles, people who could lend their weight to this invitation?

From Yelena Sergeyevna's diary
17 April 1935

Valera said that if she had met him in the street she wouldn't have recognized Misha, he had changed so much and become healthy, happy and relaxed.

18 April 1935

Yevgeny Aleksandrovich [Shilovsky] told me that Irina Svechina had been arrested. I immediately went to see Aleksandr Andreyevich. He was in a dreadful state: he says that he is quite unable to work, that the house has become 'like a coffin', and so on.

19 April 1935

We had lunch with Bohlen, one of the Secretaries at the American Embassy. His apartment was in an Embassy house, and was bright and beautiful, with an electric gramophone which was also a radio. Of course Zhukhovitsky was there. Then some other Americans from the Embassy came, agreeable people who behaved very simply. Before the meal we were served cocktails. The meal was without soup.

21 April 1935. From Paris to Moscow
From his brother Nikolay

I would be glad to hear about your life, but I am not losing hope of seeing you in person; I have somehow sustained my confidence in this ever since I moved to Paris. For that reason I was extremely glad at what you told me about your efforts to arrange an official trip.

22 April 1935. Moscow
To Konstantin Stanislavsky (joint Director of the Moscow
   Arts Theatre)

Much esteemed Konstantin Sergeyevich!

Today I received an excerpt from the stenographic record of the rehearsal of *Molière* on 17 April 1935, which was sent to me from the Theatre.

Having familiarized myself with it, I find myself obliged to refuse categorically to make any more changes in my play *Molière*, since the alterations sketched out in the record relating to the cabal scene, as well as the alterations to the text sketched out previously in relation to other scenes, utterly destroy, as I have become convinced, my artistic conception, and point to the composition of some entirely new play, which I am incapable of writing, since I am essentially in disagreement with it.

If *Molière* does not suit the Arts Theatre in the form in which it exists at present, although the Theatre accepted it precisely in this form and has been rehearsing it for several years, I would request you to take *Molière* off and to return it to me.

23 April 1935. From Yelena Sergeyevna's diary

The ball at the American Embassy. During the day I went to the hairdresser's, and on the Arbat I went up to the cars to arrange a taxi and a driver came up: 'Yes, madam?' I told him I would give him 40 roubles to take us there in the evening and then come and fetch us at three in the morning. He readily agreed.

I was dressed by the seamstress and Tamara Tomasovna. My evening dress was a rippling dark blue with pale pink flowers, it came out very well. Misha was in a very smart dark suit.

At 11.30 we set off. Once again the driver wouldn't take any money in advance, but said he would come and fetch us. We told him three o'clock, and he asked if that wasn't too early?

Never in my life have I seen such a ball. The Ambassador stood at the top of the stairs to greet his guests. Everyone was wearing tails, and there were only a few jackets and smoking-jackets. Litvinov was in tails, Bubnov in a khaki uniform, and there were a few of our military people.

Bohlen and another American, who turned out to be the military attaché, the former in tails and the latter in a dress uniform with golden aiguillettes, came down the stairs to meet us and received us very cordially.

There were people dancing in a hall with columns, floodlights shining down from the gallery, and behind a net which separated off the orchestra there were live pheasants and other birds. We had supper at separate tables in an enormous dining-room with live bear-cubs in one corner, kid goats, and cockerels in cages. There were accordion-players during supper.

The supper was in a hall where the table laden with food had been covered with a transparent green fabric and lit up from inside. There were masses of tulips and roses. Of course there was an exceptional abundance of food and of champagne. On the top floor (it's an enormous and luxurious house) they had fixed up a *shashlyk* [kebab] stand, and there were people performing dances from the Caucasus.

We wanted to leave at 3.30, but we weren't allowed to leave, so Misha went out and found our driver, who materialized from nowhere, and let him go. And we left at 5.30 in one of the

Embassy cars, having first of all invited some of the Americans from the Embassy to call on us. We were joined in the car by a man we hadn't met, but who is known throughout Moscow and who is always to be found where foreigners are – I think he's called Shteyger. He sat with the driver and we sat in the back. By the time we got back it was already broad daylight.

26 April 1935. Moscow
To Nikolay Gorchakov (director of *Molière* at the Arts Theatre)

I have developed neuralgia as a result of exhaustion, and would therefore earnestly request you to release me from my work as an assistant director for two weeks.

If you consider it necessary for me to put in an application to the Board of Directors about this, then I will do so.

From Yelena Sergeyevna's diary
26 April 1935

Red Virgin Soil has returned the manuscript of the biography of Molière without even a covering letter. On the 20th. I had sent them a telegram asking for it to be returned.

29 April 1935

In the evening we had the wife of Counsellor Wiley, Bohlen, Thayer, Durbrow and one other American, a friend of Bohlen's from Riga whom he asked if he could bring to visit. And, of course, Zhukhovitsky. Mrs Wiley brought me roses, and Bohlen brought Misha whisky and Polish Zubrovka vodka. Misha read the first act of *Zoyka's Apartment* in its final version. [. . .] Misha read in Russian. We had a merry supper. Mrs Wiley invited us to go with her to Turkey; she's leaving in a few days' time to spend a month in Turkey with her husband.

30 April 1935

At 4.30 we arrived on foot at the Embassy, Misha in his dark suit and I in a well-worn black dress. Bohlen had invited us yesterday to come and see a film. [. . .] We were introduced to many people, including the French Ambassador and his wife and the Turkish Ambassador, a fat and very merry

man! [. . .] Mrs Wiley invited us to visit her tomorrow at
10.30 in the evening. Bohlen said he would send a car for us.

3 May 1935

There were about thirty people at the Wileys', including the
Turkish Ambassador, some French writer who had just arrived
in the Soviet Union and, of course, Shteyger. [. . .] We had
champagne, whisky and cognac as we sat, and then there was a
buffet supper: sausages with beans, spaghetti and stewed fruit.
[. . .] The Frenchman [. . .] showed us extraordinary card-
tricks. At first I thought that he'd come to some agreement with
our hostess. But then, when he had performed the trick directly
on me, I came to believe it. And began to feel frightened; it was
quite impossible to explain.

Yesterday Zhukhovitsky dropped in during the day. [. . .] He
had some very hostile things to say about Shteyger, and said that
he would be horrified to meet him in our house. He even pulled
a face as he said it.

8 May 1935. From Moscow to Paris
To his brother Nikolay

As long ago as 31 July and 1 August 1934 I wrote to you
and Reinhardt that I was asking you urgently to correct those
distortions that I had discovered in the French translation of
Zoyka's Apartment. [. . .]

Once again with all seriousness I would ask you to ensure
that the names and surnames I indicated be struck out, both
in the first act and in the others, if they should appear there.
I couldn't believe my eyes when I saw that travestying of
my text.

It is absolutely intolerable that the names of members of the
Soviet Government should figure in a comic text and be spoken
on stage.

From Yelena Sergeyevna's diary
9 May 1935

Over supper Angarsky asked, 'I can't understand it, why is
it that writers nowadays are writing about all sorts of historical
subjects and avoiding modern ones?'

13 May 1935. From Moscow to Paris
To his brother Nikolay

You were asking about *Molière*?

Unfortunately it's all in a muddle. The Arts Theatre, through its own fault, has dragged the rehearsals out for four years (something quite unprecedented!) and even so did not put it on this spring.

Instead of getting on with the play, the rehearsals of which have dragged on for so indecently long, Stanislavsky was seized with a whim and decided to start making corrections to the text. The capacious cup of my patience overflowed, and I refused to make any alterations. What will happen next I don't know.

The apartment? A middling apartment, as Sergey puts it, and it's too small for us, of course, but after Pirogovskaya Street it's sheer bliss! It's light and dry, and we have gas. God, how delightful! I call down a blessing on the person who thought of putting gas into apartments.

From Yelena Sergeyevna's diary
13 May 1935

A few days ago [a theatre] asked M. A. to agree to write a play about the Civil War for the 1937 celebrations [of the anniversary of October 1917]. [. . .] I am very pleased that he has refused, since from bitter experience of the work for the cinema and then with the Molière biography, which was written on commission, I know that at first they always treat you gently, but then they pester you – nothing is right, everything's wrong, and they'll insist on alterations – it's a familiar story! Yes, a literary career is a cross to bear!

15 May 1935

In the evening Volf and Veresayev; Volf arrived with tales of the new Metro, which he had liked enormously – he said, 'I've been feeling proud of it all day.'

17 May 1935

Yekaterina Ivanovna [Sergey's governess], Seryozha and Zhenya [Yelena Sergeyevna's elder son] and I went on the Metro. It's been wonderfully done! It's comfortable and clean and there's plenty of air. I very much liked the escalator, it's such fun to stand on a step and slowly be carried upwards.

And then late in the evening Misha and I went on the Metro to the centre, and bumped into Tata and Kolya [Lyamin]. We travelled together to the Kirov station. There's a huge escalator there, they say it's seventy-two metres deep. When we reached the top, Tata was laughing and insisting that Misha had looked rather nervous and had been holding on to me; and she thought that was funny. She's a terrible fool, and she always has this manner of being ironical about something or another!

18 May 1935

At midday Misha gave a reading of the play about Pushkin. [. . .] The Vakhtangov people listened very well, [. . .] they were very sensitive to the humour and were very moved by the ending. [. . .] But the old folk [the Veresayevs] were dissatisfied, he because he couldn't hear very well.

18 May 1935. Moscow
From the writer Vikenty Veresayev

I left you yesterday feeling greatly dispirited. Of course, you were reading a draft which still has to be polished. But I was struck by the fact that you hadn't considered it necessary to change even those things that we had quite definitely talked about. [. . .] I fear that the true torments of 'co-authorship' are only just beginning. Up to now I have intervened in your work only in a minimal way, realizing that any criticism during the process of writing can only undermine the flow of creativity. However, that doesn't at all mean that I am prepared to content myself with the role of a humble purveyor of material, who does not presume to have any opinion about the quality of the use of that material. [. . .] I would like to hope that the play will nevertheless be called a play by Bulgakov and Veresayev, and that we will manage to reach a successful conclusion, if we only take each other's views into account.

From Yelena Sergeyevna's diary
20 May 1935

Something staggering has happened: Veresayev has sent Misha

an absolutely absurd letter. [. . .] Misha and I both have the same thought, that the old woman has put him up to this. The whole day has been spoiled and work has been disrupted. Misha has been composing a letter to him all day. [. . .] The old man has given me a headache and made me irritable.

20–21 May 1935. Moscow
To the writer Vikenty Veresayev

My dear Vikenty Vikentyevich!

I can only assure you that my astonishment is equal to your dispiritedness. [. . .] You write that you don't wish to content yourself with the role of a humble purveyor of material. But more than once you have said to me that you would take upon yourself the collating of the material for the play, and would leave to me all the dramatist's part. And that's the way we've done it.

However, not only did I always make sure that your material was being used in the most accurate way, but each time I conceded modifications in the drafts at the very first objection on your part, regardless of whether it concerned purely historical aspects or dramatic ones. I objected only in those instances where you were unconvincing in dramatic terms. [. . .]

Altogether we have a serious difference over D'Anthès. You write, 'I find the image of D'Anthès fundamentally incorrect, and as a Pushkin scholar, I cannot take responsibility for it in any way.'

Let me reply to you: I in turn find your image of D'Anthès theatrically impossible. He is so slight, trivial and emasculated that he cannot be set in a serious play. You cannot offer as the murderer of Pushkin, who perished so tragically, a little officer from the ball scene of an operetta. In particular the proposed phrase 'I will kill him in order to free you of him' is something D'Anthès cannot utter. [. . .]

As for reaching a successful conclusion, you're mistaken about that. We already have reached a successful conclusion, at least in the [Vakhtangov] Theatre. The day after the reading I talked with Ruslanov. He spoke of the joy that he and the other listeners had experienced. He spoke, having heard a work that had yet to be finished and polished, of an exceptional success for the author. He lifted my spirits when I felt exhausted. And until I received your letter I was in a very happy frame of mind. But now, I must admit, I am filled with alarm. As I reread your letter and my reply I cannot understand what has provoked all this.

In any case, if we do spoil this success, we will have done it with our own hands, and that will be very sad. Too much back-breaking work has been put into it to wreck a work so casually. [. . .] And all the same I nourish the hope that we will come to some agreement. I wish with all my heart that these letters may sink into oblivion, and that only the play which we have created with such passion should survive.

From Yelena Sergeyevna's diary
21 May 1935
In the evening I visited the Svechins; Irina was released on the 16th at five in the afternoon. She has become limp and apathetic, and has been running a temperature for ten days now. She doesn't laugh any more.
22 May 1935
Yesterday I lay dozing with a hot-water bottle by my head. Patya [Popov] was sitting with Misha. Suddenly the telephone rang. The old man was proposing that they forget the letters.
28 May 1935
Olga rang: the Theatre does want to perform *Molière*. 'There can be no question of handing the play back!' Vladimir Ivanovich [Nemirovich-Danchenko] has asked me to agree to a deadline of 15 January 1936. It would be impossible to get the play ready any sooner. They're taking it away from K. S. [Stanislavsky], and leaving it to the team of directors to put it on. Victory!
29 May 1935
Today Misha completed the first draft of *Pushkin*. The old man came and took a copy, and they agreed that he would come round tomorrow to discuss it.
30 May 1935
At first the conversation was conducted in decidedly sharp tones, and Vikenty Vikentyevich even said that maybe they would have to split up and he would remove his name from

the play (retaining, of course, his half of any profits). But then once again he proposed that they make peace.

1 June 1935

Yesterday, on the 31st, there was a reading [of *Pushkin*]. [. . .] Zhukhovitsky spoke a great deal about Misha's supreme mastery, but he looked quite crushed. [. . .] I am happy with this play. I know it almost by heart and each time I feel very moved by it.

4 June 1935

We went to the Foreign Section to hand in our forms. They accepted the forms, but said they wouldn't consider them until we had brought all the documents.

4 June 1935. From Paris to Moscow
From his brother Nikolay

It's *forbidden* to send money abroad out of Germany (and any violation is even considered to be treason against the State!) in any significant sums. Apparently it's possible to send 10–20 marks a week (or a fortnight). Altogether I fear that you should not place any hopes on the money in Germany as long as these prescribed limits exist, for transfers are unbelievably complex and time-consuming and not without risk for the local inhabitants! Adolf seems to be a bit strapped for cash! [. . .] I am deeply grateful to you for the photograph you sent, thanks to which, at last, we were able to feast our eyes on the two of you.

6 June 1935. Moscow
From the writer Vikenty Veresayev

Don't be afraid – this is a most peaceable letter. I am becoming more and more convinced that there cannot be two bosses with equal rights as far as a single work is concerned. There must be just one boss, and in our case that boss can only be you. [. . .]

It would be so easy to extract ourselves from this dilemma! You called my suggestion that I remove my name from the posters 'a threat'. It isn't a threat, but rather a wish to give you your legitimate freedom to express yourself fully. I repeat that I do not consider myself the author of the play, and it was very unpleasant when you obliged me to take a bow with you and share the applause of the people from the Vakhtangov Theatre; and I now feel that my suggestion that we should each have the right to publish the play in our collected works was entirely wrong – of course it must belong only amongst your works. [. . .] At the same time I consider that the play suffers from a whole series of basic defects, which cannot be remedied by individual modifications any more than you can get a tenor to sing bass, however low he might thrust his chin into his collar.

None of this means, of course, that I am refusing you any such assistance as is within my powers, provided that you will accept it as simple advice which places no obligations on you.

From Yelena Sergeyevna's diary
9 June 1935

Nikolay Vasilyevich Yegorov refused to sign a letter saying that the Theatre had no objections to M. A.'s travelling abroad. What a swine! He can't let a single opportunity go by to play a dirty trick. [. . .] Olya said that Vladimir Ivanovich would probably sign the certificate. And that I should wait.

All right then, we'll wait.

15 June 1935

Today we went to the Foreign Section and delivered all the papers to them. They accepted them along with 440 roubles. They said the reply would take a month. That's a long time to wait!

20 June 1935. From Leningrad to Moscow
From Ilya Sudakov (a director at the Moscow Arts Theatre)

Dear Mikhail Afanasyevich!

I beg you to send me your play about Pushkin. I urge you to arrange things so that I should have the opportunity to work on your play in the Moscow Arts Theatre in parallel with the Vakhtangov Theatre. I will organize things inside the Arts Theatre. I need your help as far as your contract with the Vakhtangov is concerned, I don't know how tied you are to them.

I beg you earnestly to send the play to me in Leningrad. The Astoria. Or, if the worst comes to the worst, to let me have the play at the Kursk station in Moscow when I am on my way to

Kislovodsk. I will let you know the day and the time and the number of the train.

I beg you not to give the play to anyone else in Moscow.

23 June 1935. From Moscow to Leningrad
To Ilya Sudakov (a director at the Moscow Arts Theatre)
Dear Ilya Yakovlevich,

I would let you see my play about Pushkin with great pleasure, but unfortunately I cannot do that at present because the play is still being worked on and will be completed only by the end of the summer. [. . .]

As for your desire to work on it in the Moscow Arts Theatre, then this is the situation: point 5 of my contract with the Vakhtangov says that 'the author undertakes not to give the play to any other Moscow theatre or to publish it before it has been staged at the Vakhtangov Theatre'. As you see, that means that the Vakhtangov has the rights, and if I were to give the play to another theatre then I would have to impose the condition that that theatre didn't stage it before the Vakhtangov.

9 July 1935. From Moscow to Paris
To his brother Nikolay
I wanted to let you know that I have put in an application to the Foreign Section of the Moscow Regional Executive Committee to be given permission to travel abroad with my wife. I dream of spending even a short time at some resort by the sea, because I am so immensely weary. But I won't go on about my weariness, since I am tired even of complaining. Apart from that, of course, I can tell that my presence in Paris, however brief, is quite obviously vital for the production of *Zoyka's Apartment*. I should get a reply in six or seven days.

26 July 1935. From Moscow to Paris
To his brother Nikolay
Dear Nikol!

I am enclosing a photograph of myself with this letter.

In my previous one I told you I had applied for permission to travel abroad.

Unfortunately I have been refused this.

I will tell you about it in more detail next time.

I kiss you and Ivan.

Your Mikhail.

26 July 1935. Moscow
To the writer Vikenty Veresayev

I have been refused permission for my trip abroad (you will clap your hands in astonishment, of course!), and instead of the Seine I find myself on the Klyazma. Well, I suppose it's a river too . . .

And so, I await your news and as a friend wish you the best and most precious thing in the world – good health.

1 August 1935. Moscow
From the writer Vikenty Veresayev

On this occasion I was extremely glad to learn that you were strolling along the banks of the Klyazma rather than the Seine, the Tiber or the Arno. I could not imagine how you could snatch three whole months out of the short time that we have left. The play may be a *chef-d'oeuvre*, but there is still an enormous amount of work to be done on it. After the first two incomparable scenes it goes down and down. The scene of the duel and Pushkin's death was found deeply disappointing by all the people I've read it to, anyway. They say, 'We couldn't restrain our tears over the material you had simply assembled in your book, but with this we remain completely unmoved.' The scene on the Moyka Canal, which should be central, is dreadfully grey, and I'm afraid we're going to come a cropper over it. I tried to write the scene, but I couldn't make it work either. Like a sword of Damocles I have hanging over my head 'that wouldn't work on stage', 'they won't get the point', 'you can't have conversations with a crowd in the background'. I read the play through several times and it became more and more clear to me that many passages are completely unacceptable. So I decided, to hell with it – and began unceremoniously to rework the whole thing, the way I think it ought to be done. And then we'll see what comes out: maybe we'll have two plays that will be quite impossible to reconcile, or maybe we will come to some agreement. [. . .]

Don't be distressed or angry with me; I have got carried away with the work and am working flat out. I reckon to finish by September. And then we will get together. How? As enemies? Or united by the single wish that the play should come out as well as possible?

2 August 1935. Moscow
To the writer Vikenty Veresayev

Your letter of 1 August has just arrived. I am absolutely shattered. It completely contradicts what you wrote to me on 6 June, when you proposed that I alone should put my name to the play. [. . .]

Now it turns out that you are working away writing a parallel play, one that is quite obviously incompatible with the one that is already written, for which two contracts have been agreed, and which the theatres are waiting for in order to start work on it. [. . .]

Let's proceed as you suggested: my name alone will go on the play.

I shall await your reply about this with impatience. I feel I must tell you that time will not wait. Other proposals have arrived apart from the Vakhtangov Theatre's, and precisely in relation to the text that is already written.

I cannot work on a play that is *finished*, and in any case there's no need for it. Anyway, it's quite inconceivable! [. . .]

Vikenty Vikentyevich, why should we part as enemies? It's unnecessary, and there should be no grounds for it.

16 August 1935. Moscow
To the writer Vikenty Veresayev

I have finished studying the material that was handed over to me at your flat. [. . .]

You have gone over the knots of the play, which I had tied with such trouble, over precisely those places where I have avoided head-on attacks, and with the greatest precision you have undone all those knots, after which the costumes simply dropped off the protagonists; and wherever the play had been made most subtle, you have put great fat dots on my 'i's. [. . .]

For what you have written is not a play. [. . .]

I beg you to go back to your June letter and proceed as you yourself suggested, that is, give me the opportunity to put the finishing touches to the play (let me repeat again that it is *finished*), and to deliver it at last to the Vakhtangov Theatre.

You will then look at the final draft, and if as a matter of principle you cannot accept my interpretations, then I alone will put my name to the play. This, as we agreed, will bring no changes in our financial arrangements.

And of course there is absolutely no reason why we should become enemies over this.

The sooner you are able to reply, the easier you will make my work. I am very tired, Vikenty Vikentyevich.

22 August 1935. Moscow
From the writer Vikenty Veresayev

I didn't expect any other reply from you. The basic source of our disagreements is clear to me: it is your chronic blindness to the social aspects of Pushkin's tragedy. You were powerfully afflicted with this blindness before, but now, flushed with the praise of your supporters, you find it even more difficult to feel the defects of your play in this respect. [. . .]

But what's the point in going on! We are speaking different languages. There's just one thing I don't understand. You are deeply convinced that all the things I have suggested are untheatrical. So why do you protest so insistently against my offering my variants to the Theatre for comparison? The Theatre will reject them with a smile, you will have proved that you are right, and all will be fine.

Over the summer I have tired you out and you have tired me out. We are both ready to hate each other. We have nowhere further to go. Do what you like with the play, deliver it to the Theatre in whatever form you feel appropriate. I for my part will retain the right, inasmuch as it will prove possible for me, to campaign for the removal from your beautiful play of its often astonishingly unnecessary violations of historical truth, and for the strengthening of its social background.

27 August 1935. Moscow
To the writer Vikenty Veresayev

. . . As for the variants you are proposing: I have no objections to your offering them to the theatres. If you do decide to do it, you should send the variants to the Vakhtangov Theatre in Moscow and the Krasny Theatre in Leningrad with a letter of explanation and notify me that you have sent them. For my part I will inform the theatres that I categorically refuse to have those variants in the play, since I have concluded that they would be fatally damaging to it.

As for a contract between the co-authors: of course we must draw one up. In view of the fact that by your declaration of hostilities you have created a situation that is difficult and tangled, I will leave it to you to formulate the terms of the contract. We will discuss it, and if there are no differences of opinion we can sign it.

4 September 1935. Moscow
From the writer Vikenty Veresayev

I showed you my variants in draft form, as you could judge from my notes in the margins. They still need to be worked on, but at the moment I find it unpleasant to think about the play. So I will not offer my variants to the theatres. What else do you need for your peace of mind? For me to renounce my 'campaign'? [. . .] Let me know what is needed to end your distress.

From Yelena Sergeyevna's diary
6 September 1935

Today was the 600th performance of *The Turbins*. The Theatre sent Misha no congratulations, nor even any notification.

10 September 1935. Moscow
To the writer Vikenty Veresayev

You ask what I need for my peace of mind? Not just for my peace of mind, but for both co-authors and for the good of the play, I believe that the following is essential: that now, when the crucial moment has arrived when the play reaches the Theatre, it is vital that we refrain everywhere, even in letters, from any harsh criticism of each other's work or any pointed explanations. Otherwise an unhealthy atmosphere may be created around the play, which could threaten the production itself.

Please note that I have very serious grounds for writing this. [. . .]

Along with this letter I am sending to you, and at the same time – in order not to delay – to the theatres, the final text with two names on it. Have a look through it. If you find it appropriate to leave your name on, I will be very glad. If not, then let me know. I will inform the theatres that you have removed your name at your own request.

From Yelena Sergeyevna's diary
11 September 1935

Really, Stanislavsky is a dreadful man. And they have begun to realize that now in the Theatre.

13 September 1935. Moscow
To Nadezhda Radlova (a friend from Leningrad)

Dear Dina!

[. . .] Yes, I finished the play – the one with Veresayev. What a lot of work went into it! It was a tricky thing: Pushkin doesn't appear once on the stage, but all the action centres upon him, and takes place as much as possible because of him.

Lyusya is now tapping energetically at the typewriter, copying it. I put my hand on Lyusya's shoulder to restrain her. She has worn herself out and shared all the excitement with me, burrowing into bookshelves with me and turning pale when I was reading it to the actors.

Now we'll see how fate disposes of this work.

We didn't go away anywhere. Sergey was living in a dacha outside Moscow and we used to drop in on him, but the rain simply poured down like anything.

We cherished a dream of spending some time abroad and put in an application, but were refused.

And so that's the summer over, that's it! And now begins

a complicated and important theatrical season. Straight after Pushkin I've got to put the finishing touches to a comedy [*Ivan Vasilyevich*].

I have an impossible amount of work to do.

Sergey has started school, and apart from that I am toying with the idea of making a pianist of him. He's studying with a good teacher, and plays pieces for four hands with me. We'll have to see what comes of it.

If you come to Moscow, let's see something of you! And instruct Kolya [her husband Nikolay] to show himself too!

From Yelena Sergeyevna's diary
16 September 1935
Olga has returned from Riga. [. . .] She has brought Misha shirts for a tail-coat. In the evening she and Kaluzhsky visited me. Suddenly: Dina Radlova. A conversation about Pushkin, of course. She asked about the contents. Apart from that she talked about Zamyatin, criticizing him for not coming back to the USSR.
20 September 1935
When I came back from the hairdresser's, Misha said that Zakhava had let him know of the Repertory Committee's decision to allow *Pushkin* to be put on. This merits a prayer of thanks to God: at last a joyful day!
24 September 1935
Grisha [Konsky]. In the evening, at his request, Misha read him the first three chapters of the novel [*The Master and Margarita*]. They produced a quite extraordinary effect on Grisha, and I think he wasn't shamming. I wept.
2 October 1935
A joyous evening! Misha gave a reading here of *Ivan Vasilyevich*, with great success. [. . .] Gorchakov was wiping away his tears, and everybody was guffawing.
3 October 1935
This evening Dmitriyev brought Sergey Prokofiev. He made an agreeable impression. There is some question of an opera based on Misha's play (*Pushkin*), and he took the text away with him. [. . .] He invited us to his concert tomorrow at the

Bolshoy Theatre. He'll be playing his music for the ballet *Romeo and Juliet*.

4 October 1935

Prokofiev plays like a real virtuoso. There are marvellous sections in the music. [. . .] Today marks three years since Misha and I registered our marriage.

16 October 1935

This evening – Prokofiev with his wife and Dmitriyev. [. . .] A most interesting conversation about the play. [. . .] Prokofiev is going on tour to Africa, and will return in two months' time. His wife is staying here.

17 October 1935

Misha was at a rehearsal of *Molière*. Amazing news about *Ivan Vasilyevich*. Five people in the Repertory Committee have read the play, and all of them have been hunting to see whether there is anything suspect in it. But they haven't been able to find anything. Misha said, 'What on earth are they looking for?' One marvellous phrase of theirs: 'Wouldn't it be possible for Ivan the Terrible to say somewhere that things are better now than they were then?'

18 October 1935

Misha was sleeping during the day when there was a telephone call from the American Embassy, inviting us to watch a film and to a reception given by Bullitt.

29 October 1935

In the evening came a phone call from Verov: *Ivan Vasilyevich* has been licensed with some slight changes. What joy!

30 October 1935

During the day there was a ring at our door. I went out and there was Akhmatova with such a dreadful face, and so much thinner, that I scarcely recognized her; nor did Misha. It turned out that in one and the same night both her husband (Punin) and her son (Gumilyov) had been arrested. She had come to deliver a letter to Yosif Vissarionovich [Stalin]. She was quite clearly in a confused state and was muttering things to herself.

31 October 1935

Anna Andreyevna [Akhmatova] copied out a letter to Stalin by hand. Then a car came to take her to Pilnyak's.

1 November 1935
Misha read *Ivan Vasilyevich* to the cast at the Satire Theatre.
It was a huge success.

4 November 1935
Akhmatova with a telegram. Punin and Gumilyov had tele-
graphed to say that they were well. That means they've been
released. I am delighted for Akhmatova.

7 November 1935
I accompanied Misha in the morning to the Parade [for the
anniversary of the Revolution]. Later he told me how the
columns crossed the square in a solid wave of several rows. He
saw Stalin on the stands in a grey greatcoat and a military cap.

8 November 1935. Moscow
To his friends Marika and Sergey Yermolinsky
Dear Marika and Seryozha,
Wouldn't you like to go with us to the club today to eat *pelmeni*
[a kind of ravioli]? Come for us at 10 p.m.
If you can't manage it, drop us a reply.
We'll be waiting.

From Yelena Sergeyevna's diary
18 November 1935
The first rehearsal of *Ivan Vasilyevich*.

12 December 1935. Moscow
To the publishers Akademiya
I would like to request the publishers to extend the deadline
for my translation of Molière's *L'Avare* to 10 January 1936.
[. . .]

12 December 1935. From the Atlantic Ocean to Moscow
From his brother Nikolay
Dear Mikhail,
Quite unexpectedly I have been sent on a job to Mexico, and
set off for there on 11 December 1935.
I will be in the USA (New York) and will then go by rail

to Mexico City, where I have to carry out a task for my boss, Professor F. D'Hérelle.

I will be coming back at the beginning of February. [. . .]

I am writing from mid-ocean. The weather is wintry and greyish, there is fog and a wind and we are rolling a bit.

The French ship of the Champlain line is superb: I am travelling first class in all possible luxury and comfort. I am travelling alone, since it was impossible to find the money for the journey for two.

19 December 1935. Moscow
From the writer Vikenty Veresayev

1) In accordance with your express agreement I have decided to remove my name from our play *Aleksandr Pushkin*, which I request should henceforth be called simply: M. Bulgakov, *Aleksandr Pushkin*. I empower you to inform the theatres with whom we have signed contracts of this fact. I will let the Vakhtangov Theatre know myself.

2) In addition to the enclosed formal letter I would like to inform you that my letter to the Vakhtangov Theatre is identical to the letter to you. I am only adding that if my assistance should be needed during the production, then I am at their service.

From Yelena Sergeyevna's diary
21 December 1935

Our life is exceptionally busy. Misha is dictating the translation of *L'Avare* to me for Akademiya. There are rehearsals of *Molière*. Our heads are spinning.

22 December 1935. Moscow
To the writer Vikenty Veresayev

Congratulations with all my heart on your splendid anniversary.

From Yelena Sergeyevna's diary
22 December 1935

Before lunch I sent Veresayev a telegram of congratulations; today is his fiftieth [wedding] anniversary. But I don't want to think about him, he has brought Misha and me so much torment.

3 January 1936

Yesterday Melik[-Pashayev] and Yakov Leontyevich [Leontyev] invited us to the second performance of [Shostakovich's] *Lady Macbeth of Mtsensk*. Yakov Leontyevich sent a car for us. Melik conducts brilliantly. [. . .] Without noticing it, we drank three bottles of champagne [. . .]. Later Melik and Shostakovich joined us. And eventually Dorokhin played a foxtrot on the piano, and I danced with Melik, who told me he was in love with me.

4 January 1936

He [Melik-Pashayev] telephoned Misha and said that the management of the Bolshoy Theatre would like to hear *Pushkin*, and wanted to bring Shostakovich with them. Prokofiev hasn't telephoned again since his return from abroad. If they are going to make an opera out of *Pushkin*, I would rather that Shostakovich did it.

6 January 1936

At two o'clock Yakov Leontyevich [Leontyev], Mutnykh, Shostakovich and Melik-Pashayev came round. At their request Misha read them *Pushkin* (there's an idea of making an opera of it). Shostakovich thanked Misha very much, said that he had liked the play very much indeed, and asked for a copy.

Then we had lunch, and our pies were a wild success. We liked Mutnykh very much, he was simple, merry and agreeable. Altogether it was very nice. Shostakovich played his waltz and polka from *The Bright Stream*, and then Melik also played one of Shostakovich's waltzes. All three pieces are marvellous!

17 January 1936

We only finished typing out *L'Avare* yesterday. Misha has been dictating all this time and is terribly tired, me too.

26 January 1936

Yesterday, quite by chance – an American was moving out of our block – I bought Misha a very elegant and original-looking fur coat for a thousand roubles. The fur is grey – American grizzly bear.

28 January 1936

Today I opened *Pravda* while I was still in bed. In it was an unsigned article entitled 'Cacophony Instead of Music', containing the most harsh criticisms of *Lady Macbeth*. The article speaks about 'a disharmonious, cacophonous torrent' of sounds, and says that the opera is an expression of leftist deformations. I suppose Shostakovich was mistaken to tackle such a gloomy and painful subject. I can imagine what his feelings must be at the moment! [. . .] Arkadyev has been appointed Party Director at the Arts Theatre.

1 February 1936. From Yasnaya Polyana (Tolstoy's estate) to Moscow
From his friends Pavel Popov and Anna Tolstaya

Dear Mikhail Afanasyevich,

The weather keeps changing from snowstorm to thaw and from thaw to frost, from frost to fierce wind, but we remain in the same peaceful mood and in complete ignorance of what is going on in the wider world, and we sit in our rooms, surrounded by white snow and by the white museum, modestly getting on with our work . . . Neither of us is tempted to go to Moscow. It's obvious that we just need to sit quietly here . . . Will you really not come?

From Yelena Sergeyevna's diary
6 February 1936

Yesterday, after innumerable torments, the first, unofficial dress rehearsal of *Molière* took place. Without the bosses. I saw only Arkadyev, Akulov, Secretary of the All-Russian Central Executive Committee, and that scoundrel Litovsky.

It wasn't the show that I had been dreaming of ever since 1930. But Bolduman as Louis XIV and Yanshin as Bouton were excellent. [. . .] People applauded after each scene, and there was loud acclaim at the end. [. . .] After the dress rehearsal we went to a *shashlyk* restaurant with Melik [-Pashayev], and then on to the Bolshoy to *Sadko*; M. A. was very keen to listen to some music. [. . .] M. A. has made a definite decision to write a play about Stalin.

Today in *Pravda* there was an article entitled 'False Notes at the Ballet' about *The Bright Stream*. I feel sorry for Shostakovich, he's been drawn into hack-work; the authors of the ballet libretto were just trying to please.

8 February 1936

Kolya Lyamin. After he had gone, M. A. said he would like to write a play or a novel called 'The Prechistenka District', in order to portray that world of old Moscow which so irritates him.

9 February 1936

Once again a success, and a great one. There were about twenty curtain-calls. The Americans were entranced, and spent a long time thanking us. *21 curtain calls*

11 February 1936

I think there were twenty-one curtain-calls after the end. [. . .] Today in *Soviet Art* there was an article about *Molière* by Litovsky, oozing with malice.

Today Stalin's secretary Poskryobyshev came to see *Molière*. Olya said that according to the Director he very much enjoyed the performance and said that Yosif Vissarionovich [Stalin] absolutely must see it.

**11 February 1936. From Moscow to Yasnaya Polyana
(Tolstoy's estate)**
To his friends Pavel Popov and Anna Tolstaya

I thought and thought – why not come, after all? But it isn't to be. I have a lot of troubles and bother at the moment.

After the thaw here we have had another vile, diabolical frost with wind. I detest and curse it.

Of course, if it were possible to be transported without any effort at all to the snowdrifts of Yasnaya Polyana, then I would sit by the fire and attempt to forget both Molière and Pushkin, and the comedy [*Ivan Vasilyevich*].

No, it's not possible. I envy you, wish you a good rest and thank you for the invitation. [. . .]

Molière has had his première. The dress rehearsals were on the 5th and the 9th. People are talking of a success. I had to go out and take a bow on both occasions, which I find a torture.

Today in *Soviet Art* the first arrow was fired in a review by

Litovsky. He talks about the play disparagingly, with great malice even if it is relatively restrained, and writes inaccurately about the actors, with one exception.

Ivan Vasilyevich is in rehearsal, but I haven't been to the Satire Theatre for ages.

I am trying not to think about Aleksandr Sergeyevich [Pushkin], since my commitments are great enough as it is. I gather the Vakhtangov Theatre has started work on it. It clearly won't be put on at the Moscow Arts Theatre.

I have been feeling unwell, and am so tired that I cannot do a thing: I sit and smoke and dream about felt boots. But I can't sit around for long; I'm off to the performance this evening (the first closed première).

I send you a friendly hug.

Your Mikhail.

From Yelena Sergeyevna's diary
16 February 1936

And so, the official première of *Molière* has taken place. How many years we have waited for it! The auditorium was, as Molière puts it, larded with distinguished persons. [. . .] And apart from that, the audience as a whole was rather select, there were lots of academics, doctors, actors and writers. [. . .] It was a huge success. The people in the wings reckoned that there were twenty-two curtain-calls. They were determined to get the author to take a bow. [. . .] After the performance we had to wait a long time for M. A., who was delayed backstage. Akulov had gone there, and said that the show was superb, but – he asked M. A., 'Will Soviet spectators understand it, is it suitable for them?'

Today, by invitation from the Embassy, we called at 4.30 on the American Ambassador. He has just got back from America. The guests were from the diplomatic corps, and there were just a few Russians. [. . .] Bullitt, as ever, was very courteous, asked all about *Molière*, and asked to be invited to the show.

18 February 1936

M. A. went to the Arts Theatre at Arkadyev's invitation to have a talk. [. . .] He said that the conversation was about what M. A. was going to work on next. M. A. replied that the only subject that interested him at present was Stalin. Arkadyev promised to obtain for him the necessary material. M. A. doesn't believe him.

21 February 1936

During tea in the interval [. . .] Bullitt spoke exceptionally favourably about the play and about M. A. in general, and called him a master.

It was a success. There were just as many curtain-calls; about twenty.

24 February 1936

There was a matinée of *Molière*, and M. A. and I arrived in time for the end of the performance. In the Arts Theatre newspaper *Gorkovets* there were negative reviews of *Molière* by Afinogenov, Vsevolod Ivanov, Olyesha and Gribkov, who writes that the play is 'superfluous on the Soviet stage'. [. . .] Misha's destiny is clear to me: he will be alone and persecuted until the end of his days. [. . .] The performance was a resounding triumph; today there were countless curtain-calls. Bolduman said he was being taken out of the part [of Louis XIV] because of [Gorky's] *Enemies*, which is running in parallel. The best actor in the play!

27 February 1936

The actor Voloshin telephoned and asked to borrow two thousand. These requests will start coming in now. But we are 17 thousand in debt and don't have a kopek of current income; we've been living on advances.

2 March 1936

In *Pravda* they are printing one article after another, and one person after another is being sent flying.

4 March 1936

In the evening a conversation with Yegorov in his office to clarify our finances. The Moscow Arts Theatre is demanding the return of three thousand for *Flight* on the grounds that it has been banned. 'Just show me the ban,' I said. [. . .]

Today a competition was announced in the newspaper to write a textbook on the history of the USSR. M. A. said he would like to write a textbook, so we shall have to prepare material, textbooks and atlases. I am astonished at him. In my opinion it's a completely unrealizable plan.

5 March 1936

At around five there was a telephone call from some woman who gave a false name, hysterically denouncing me to Misha for supposedly having entered into intimate relations with . . . , and she was shouting that I ought to be punished. Misha passed the receiver to me and I heard her last words: 'It's a disgrace, a disgrace, a disgrace!'

How despicable! And of course it's all completely untrue.

6 March 1936

M. A. was supposed to have a meeting with Arkadyev today, but for some reason it was cancelled.

9 March 1936

'Here I will enter a large black cross . . . ' [a quote from *Molière*]

In *Pravda* there was an unsigned article 'Superficial Glitter and False Content'. When we had finished reading it M. A. said, 'That's the end of *Molière* and the end of *Ivan Vasilyevich*.' During the day we went to the Moscow Arts Theatre: *Molière* has been taken off, and won't be performed tomorrow. All their faces were different. In the evening a call from Fedya (Mikhalsky): 'Misha must try to vindicate himself in a letter.' Vindicate what? Misha won't write such a letter. [. . .] Everybody is saying the same thing in a friendly fashion – a vindication. He has nothing to vindicate.

6

1936–1940

Yelena Sergeyevna began her diary entry for 9 March 1936, when Bulgakov's play *Molière* was taken off, with a quotation from the play: 'Here I will enter a large black cross . . . ' One of the characters in *Molière* is the faithful actor Lagrange, known as Registre because he kept a record of the main events affecting Molière's troupe, which he adorned with mysterious symbols as appropriate. The 'large black cross' is inscribed in the record by Lagrange in the closing lines of the play to mark Molière's death. Certainly, the impact of the loss of *Molière*, soon followed by those of *Pushkin* and *Ivan Vasilyevich*, had the effect on Bulgakov of a grievous bereavement. During the late spring of 1936 there were tentative conversations about resurrecting both *Molière* and *Pushkin*, but only on condition that Bulgakov make various changes to the texts; and he, by now entirely disillusioned by these proposals for cosmetic changes that would suddenly make everything all right, categorically refused. In May an official from the Party Central Committee attended a dress rehearsal of *Ivan Vasilyevich* and banned it on the spot.

Bulgakov and Yelena Sergeyevna decided to get away from Moscow for a time, and spent the first two weeks of June in Kiev – although to finance even this modest expedition Bulgakov was obliged to agree to a new contract with the Moscow Arts Theatre for an adaptation of *The Merry Wives of Windsor*. On their return from Kiev they were greeted with a proposal from the Leningrad composer Boris Asafyev for Bulgakov to write the libretto for an opera – for the Bolshoy Theatre – on the subject of Minin and Pozharsky, the leaders of a seventeenth-century uprising to liberate Moscow from the Poles. This latter project quite appealed to Bulgakov, who now attended the opera and the ballet or concerts rather more frequently than the theatre. He set to and finished the libretto by the middle of July, before going away once more on holiday, this time together with a group from the Arts Theatre, to Sukhumi on the Black Sea. There he began to tackle *The Merry Wives*, beginning with an attempt to translate Shakespeare's linguistically very demanding opening scene; but as Yelena Sergeyevna recorded, the tactless and overbearing manner of Nikolay Gorchakov, who had worked as a director on both *Molière* and *Ivan Vasilyevich*, caused Bulgakov's patience to snap. He and Yelena Sergeyevna flew back to Moscow (the only time Bulgakov travelled by aeroplane, so far as we know), and within days of their return Bulgakov sent in his resignation to the Moscow Arts Theatre and broke off his contract with them for *The Merry Wives of Windsor*. Six years after the telephone conversation with Stalin that had earned him the one job he had said he really wanted if he was going to stay in the USSR, Bulgakov now parted company with the Arts Theatre on the most acrimonious terms, carrying away with him a scornful, bitter dislike for the Theatre's two founders, Stanislavsky and Nemirovich-Danchenko.

By the time the tenth anniversary of the première of *The Days of the Turbins* came round on 5 October 1936, an occasion that only fuelled his resentment of the Theatre, Bulgakov had signed a new contract which committed him to writing one opera libretto a year for the Bolshoy Theatre. This was brought about through Bulgakov's friendship with Yakov Leontyev, who worked in the management of the Bolshoy, and through whom he came to be friends with other figures in the management such as Samuil Samosud and Vladimir Mutnykh. With the *Minin* libretto already under his belt and steps being taken at the Bolshoy to get it staged, Bulgakov embarked on his first commissioned project, a libretto entitled *The Black Sea*, which was to deal with the White Army's defeat by the Reds at Perekop in the Crimea in 1920.

He completed this libretto the following spring and delivered it to the Bolshoy in March 1937. At the very end of 1936, news came from Bulgakov's brother Nikolay that the production in Paris of *Zoyka's Apartment*, which had been planned for some years, now looked as though it was finally going to be staged. In the context of Stalin's Terror, manifestations of which were being noted thick and fast in Yelena Sergeyevna's diary and included the arrest of Bulgakov's old friend Nikolay Lyamin, it is not difficult to understand why Bulgakov wrote back hastily, reiterating yet again his insistence that any references to Lenin or Stalin interpolated into his text must be cut out.

But the work that really engaged his thoughts through the winter of 1936 and the spring of 1937 was the second of the two novels he was writing more or less in secret. The first complete draft of the future *Master and Margarita* had been finished early in the summer of 1936, before Bulgakov went to Sukhumi, and he was not working much on it at present, although he gave occasional readings of portions of the text to selected friends. Instead, he now returned to an idea he had first had in the summer of 1929, after the first bannings of all his plays: that of an autobiographical novel in which he would describe his own career and his impressions of the Moscow Arts Theatre. By 1936, his experiences of the latter had allowed him to accumulate more than enough rich material, and he began composing a text that was an act of gleeful revenge on Stanislavsky and Nemirovich-Danchenko, parodying their every eccentricity. The novel was originally called *A Theatrical Novel*, but soon acquired the new title *The Notes of a Dead Man* – far more appropriate from an author who felt that he had been strangled along with his hero Molière.

Most of the staff of the Moscow Arts Theatre could recognize themselves and their colleagues mirrored in Bulgakov's witty and inventive portrayal of the Theatre as an institution entirely at the mercy of the whims and neurotic temperaments of its two feuding Directors. Bulgakov's friends and acquaintances – his sister-in-law Olga and her husband Kaluzhsky; Pavel Markov, the Literary Director of the Theatre; Fedya Mikhalsky, the administrator with an unerring eye when it came to deciding who should or should not be given tickets; and stage-designers associated with the Arts Theatre, such as Dmitriyev and Vilyams – all clamoured to attend readings at the Bulgakovs' apartment, and the hilarity of such evenings did something to alleviate the wretchedness of those years. As with *The Master and Margarita*, Bulgakov never allowed the text of this novel to leave his apartment, so that the two novels were known to his contemporaries only ever through the author's own (much extolled) readings. Bulgakov never finished the *Theatrical Novel/Notes of a Dead Man*, setting it aside in order to get back to *The Master and Margarita*. Happily, however, enough of the text was completed for even a reader unfamiliar with the Moscow Arts Theatre to enjoy its entertaining satire and witty portraiture.

The year 1937 is one of the blackest in Soviet history, and Yelena Sergeyevna's diaries give an impression of just one household's awareness of the endless succession of arrests and trials that took place. She adds very little by way of comment, but her very laconicism is chilling. As more such memoir materials emerge from Soviet archives during the 1990s, we shall be able to put together a grim picture of the extent to which every household was touched by the arrest and disappearance of loved ones as well as public figures. Yelena Sergeyevna, who through her marriage to Yevgeny Shilovsky had been acquainted with members of Moscow's military élite, records the show trials mounted against Marshal Tukhachevsky and his associates (1937) in much the same apparently dispassionate tones as she had earlier recorded the Zinoviev and Kamenev trials (1936) and would later, in 1938, register the trial of Bukharin and Rykov, and that of Yagoda, the particularly sadistic head of the NKVD (formerly OGPU). Friends were also affected, of course: Nikolay Lyamin, who two years after his arrest wrote somewhat pathetically to Bulgakov to re-establish contact from his internal exile in Kaluga; and Dmitriyev, whose wife Yelizaveta (Veta) was arrested, with the result that he too became liable to an automatic sentence of internal exile. Dmitriyev rather goes down in Yelena Sergeyevna's opinion after this calamity, presumably because she feels he has not behaved entirely honourably over the affair.

As Moscow's cultural establishment was subjected to wave after wave of arrests, an unforeseen concomitant was that a number of Bulgakov's erstwhile opponents fell from their positions, and Yelena Sergeyevna can scarcely contain her delight when 'Nemesis', as she puts it, overtakes people like the critic Litovsky, who had hounded Bulgakov so systematically throughout his career. She is clearly not too unhappy when successive heads of the Moscow Arts Theatre such as Arkadyev and Boyarsky are dismissed and arrested, or when figures such as Kerzhentsev, who had tried so hard to bully Bulgakov into being a writer subservient to the requirements of the State, fall from grace. Nor can she and Bulgakov have felt many regrets when Dobranitsky, a mysterious emissary from the Party's Central Committee, who had attached himself to the Bulgakovs and continually tried to raise Bulgakov's hopes and persuade him to write a work of propaganda, was arrested; this came shortly after the arrest of the man who was evidently Dobranitsky's controller, Angarov. But private relish in particular instances was not, according to Bulgakov's code of honour, to be translated into public triumphalism; and he resisted all pressure to take part at writers' meetings in the dressing-down of the playwright Kirshon, who had also done much to harm him in the past.

As 1937 proceeded, Bulgakov tried to carry on with his work for the Bolshoy Theatre, and wrote his next libretto, *Peter the Great*, in time to deliver it in September of that year. The text was rejected by Kerzhentsev, not just on operatic grounds, which Bulgakov was prepared to consider, but also on a whole range of political grounds, which left him in helpless despair. In October, as in May, he contemplated addressing a further letter to Stalin, but by now the prospect appeared too dangerous. He would write only one more letter to Stalin, a very cautious and respectful missive written in February 1938, no longer about himself, but in an attempt to persuade Stalin to relax the restrictions still in force on the movements of the satirical playwright Nikolay Erdman, who with his brother Boris, a stage-designer, had become a close friend of Bulgakov's in recent years. His previous letters to Stalin had already been characterized by a highly stylized manner of writing, and this one concerning Erdman (page 266) goes even further in its archaic formality.

The year 1937 was also marked by a legal battle with a theatre in Kharkov which was claiming damages over the withdrawal of the Pushkin play; by a commission from the Vakhtangov Theatre for a stage adaptation of *Don Quixote*, a job that Bulgakov undertook with great interest and satisfaction and completed the following summer; and, towards the end of the year, by a revival of his hopes that *Minin and Pozharsky* – which had been pushed aside at the Bolshoy by a proposed production of *Ivan Susanin*, an opera on a similar theme to *Minin* – might be staged. This last led to a hectic correspondence with the Leningrad composer Asafyev, a nervous individual sensitive to every slight, who was reluctant to come down to Moscow to fight on the opera's behalf; although Asafyev did eventually come, Bulgakov's *Minin and Pozharsky* never in the end reached the stage. Meanwhile, Bulgakov continued working with great determination throughout the second half of 1937 and the first half of 1938 on *The Master and Margarita*, revising from beginning to end the draft he had completed in 1936 and polishing it at every opportunity. Clearly the novel's concerns with the integrity of the artist, with the survival of true art despite oppression, with faith in love, and with the vital relevance of the stories of Christ and Pilate to a Soviet Union where all conception of good and evil seemed to have vanished, had acquired an even greater urgency during the period of the Terror.

During the summer of 1938 Bulgakov reached a crucial stage in the composition of the novel. For only the second time in their married life he parted from Yelena Sergeyevna, who went to a dacha in Lebedyan – on the Don south of Moscow – to try to regain her health, while he remained in Moscow to dictate a revised version of *The Master and Margarita* to her sister Olga, an accomplished typist. As a result of this separation – which was interrupted for a month in the middle of the summer when Bulgakov joined Yelena Sergeyevna in Lebedyan – we have at our disposal a unique account of Bulgakov's emotions as the work progressed, in the shape of the letters he wrote, sometimes several a day, to his wife. He gives an amusing depiction of the atmosphere in which the work proceeded, with Olga Sergeyevna remaining thoroughly disapproving throughout; but he also communicates his sense of the scale of his own achievement as the final draft takes shape on the typewriter.

When the summer of 1938 was over, their life returned to its familiar course. First there was the predictable trouble with Bulgakov's *Don Quixote*, which was finally passed by the Repertory Committee in November, but then fell into a kind of limbo at the Vakhtangov Theatre, despite all their declared enthusiasm for the text; and once more Bulgakov's hopes of seeing a play actually staged gradually vanished. It was performed only after his death, in a production in Leningrad starring the actor Nikolay Cherkasov (Eisenstein's Ivan the Terrible), when it won considerable acclaim. In September 1938 the composer Isaak Dunayevsky suggested to Bulgakov that they work together on a libretto based on Maupassant's short story *Mlle Fifi*; and Bulgakov duly completed it, under the title *Rachel*, in March 1939. It was the only one of his libretti ever to be staged – although again only after his death.

The last chapter in Bulgakov's life centres around his play *Batum*, which dealt with an episode in the life of the young Stalin. Bulgakov had first mentioned his idea of writing a play about Stalin in the spring of 1936, to the authorities at the Arts Theatre, who spoke of the possibility of helping him to gain access to the necessary material – although he remained sceptical about this. Once Bulgakov had parted company so bitterly with the Arts Theatre, he did not mention the project again. But in September 1938, Pavel Markov and Vitaly Vilenkin approached him and asked whether he would not, despite everything, write another play for the Theatre. It then emerged that they were desperately seeking a play about Stalin to mark his sixtieth birthday at the end of 1939, and that they had come to Bulgakov, remembering his earlier interest in the idea, in the hope that at least he would write something of tolerable quality.

This request presented Bulgakov with a terrible dilemma. First of all, he felt he had to pour out once again all his grievances against the Arts Theatre; he also had an understandable fear that the writing of such a play would be a very dangerous undertaking in itself. For a long time he adamantly refused. And yet it seems clear that at the same time he was tremendously excited by the prospect of writing about Stalin, the figure who had so dominated his career, intervening to save it in 1930, but subsequently presiding over his gradual strangulation as a writer. In fact, by the time the Theatre persuaded Bulgakov to accept the commission, he had already started to sketch out the play.

That Bulgakov should have written a play about Stalin has been a matter of some embarrassment in the Soviet Union, where on standard censorship grounds the play could be neither mentioned nor published until the late 1980s, but where liberal opinion too has sometimes been reluctant to examine the question, fearing that it might have to conclude that Bulgakov demeaned himself in a dreadful compromise with the tyrant and sacrificed his artistic integrity. What can fairly be stated is that the text is not just a blind eulogy of Stalin. It is a relatively straightforward historical piece which does not underestimate Stalin's talents for leadership at the beginning of his rise to power; set for the most part in Batum between 1898 and 1904, it considers the reasons for his emergence as a leader. For Bulgakov, the figure of Stalin was bound to be an all-absorbing one, fulfilling a similar role in his life as a writer to the parts Louis XIV and Tsar Nicholas I had played in the lives of Molière and Pushkin. A large proportion of all Bulgakov's writing draws on history and biography or autobiography, and seeks to understand the problems of good and evil, and of guilt and responsibility in the interplay between the individual and the State. The real significance of *Batum* for Bulgakov must have been that at last he had some sort of licence to reflect publicly on the tyrant, and perhaps above all to confront the nature of his own relationship with Stalin. If his wife's diaries are read alongside the text, it does not feel as though Bulgakov was here compromising his integrity. It is difficult to imagine how things would have turned out if the play had ever actually been staged; but whatever had happened, it seems that somehow it was inevitable that Bulgakov should perish in this last enterprise.

The documents in this chapter movingly record the catastrophe that struck as Bulgakov and Yelena Sergeyevna set off by train for Batum in August 1939 with colleagues from the Moscow Arts Theatre; they had been sent to do some additional research on the subject after the play had apparently been approved. At the last minute, word was received from Stalin that he did not wish the play to be performed; the trip by the brigade (as it was officially called) was cancelled and the Theatre summoned them straight back to Moscow. The blow was so devastating that Bulgakov's health immediately collapsed. At first he was alarmed by the thought that they were returning to Moscow to their deaths – a reasonable supposition if Stalin was displeased by the portrayal of himself in the play. Fresh in the Bulgakovs' minds would have been the news of the arrest in June of Meyerkhold, followed in July by the appalling mutilation and murder of his wife Zinaida Raykh – a murder that was never investigated, and which was widely perceived as 'a general threat to wives' (Robert Conquest, *The Great Terror*). But when they got back to their apartment, no arrest awaited them, just ominous silence.

Soon however, the calamity took on different dimensions. Bulgakov, even in the car on the way back to Moscow, complained that he found the light hard to bear, and on their return he had to lie in a darkened room for some days and only later managed to get back on his feet. In a vivid letter (page 295) written to Bulgakov's brother Nikolay in Paris over twenty years after his death, and published by Grigory Fayman in 1990, Yelena Sergeyevna describes how in September 1939 they decided to go to Leningrad for a change of scene if nothing else; shortly after they arrived Bulgakov's eyesight began rapidly to deteriorate, and the oculist who examined him diagnosed a grave illness and told them to return to Moscow immediately. Bulgakov had clearly long ago anticipated this, and as a trained doctor knew all too well how his illness – the same disease of the kidneys that had killed his father – would progress. In Moscow the specialists insisted that he ought to be admitted to hospital, but said that in any case he would die in a matter of days.

In actual fact, Bulgakov lived for another six months. He refused to go into hospital, but did agree to spend some time in the sanatorium at Barvikha, outside Moscow, where Yelena Sergeyevna could be with him all the time. From there he dictated several letters to his closest friends and relatives: Aleksandr (Sasha) Gdeshinsky, who delighted him by sending at his request detailed recollections of their childhood in Kiev, including accounts of the music that was performed at concerts they had attended together; Pavel Popov, who in December sent him a very moving tribute (page 291); and his sister Lyolya (Yelena), who helped Yelena Sergeyevna to tend him at the end. In December 1939, Bulgakov returned home. He had not been able to read, nor scarcely to write, for some months. Once or twice more he went out on the street, with a stick and in dark glasses, but soon he was unable to leave his bed, emaciated, weak, and in dreadful pain all over his body. Nevertheless, up until about two weeks before he died, Bulgakov continued to dictate occasional corrections to *The Master and Margarita*, evidently believing to the end that one day his greatest novel, like the rest of his works, would receive the audience and the reception it deserved. Neither he nor his devoted Margarita, as she sat on a pillow on the floor beside his bed, copying the last revisions into a notebook as his death approached, could possibly have imagined that it would take as long as a quarter of a century – until just before Yelena Sergeyevna herself died in 1970 – before *The Master and Margarita* was published.

Bulgakov died on 10 March 1940. He was buried in the plot allocated to the Moscow Arts Theatre in the cemetery of the Novo-Devichy Convent. In April 1940 the poet Anna Akhmatova brought Yelena Sergeyevna a poem she had written in Bulgakov's memory, of which the following literal translation is a part:

> I offer this to you in place of graveside roses,
> Instead of smoking incense;
> You lived so severely, and to the end you carried
> Your magnificent disdain.
> You drank wine, you were an incomparable jester,
> And gasped for breath between stifling walls,
> And you yourself let in your awesome guest,
> And with her you remained alone.

From Yelena Sergeyevna's diary
10 March 1936

It now turns out that rumours were circulating that *Molière* was going to be taken off at the very beginning of March. Clearly *Ivan Vasilyevich* will be taken off as well.

11 March 1936

In *Soviet Art* today *Molière* is described as a squalid and mendacious play. How are we to live? How is M. A. to go on working?

11 March 1936. Moscow
From the writer Vikenty Veresayev

I am deeply shocked by the taking off of your play. Your creative path seems to be unremittingly difficult. I wish you spiritual strength to bear this new blow. I embrace you warmly.

12 March 1936. Moscow
To the writer Vikenty Veresayev

Dear Vikenty Vikentyevich,

I have just received your letter and was deeply touched! It is a very serious blow. According to the information I received yesterday, it seems that apart from *Molière* they are also taking off the comedy *Ivan Vasilyevich* at the Satire Theatre, which was absolutely ready to be premièred.

It's not clear to me what will happen next.

I thank you with all seriousness for your letter and embrace you as a friend. I wish you all the best.

From Yelena Sergeyevna's diary
13 March 1936

In the evening, Zhukhovitsky. He made an utterly loathsome impression on me. He tells lies at every turn, comes round to elicit information, and I sense that he will do us some harm. There can be no doubt about his role.

14 March 1936

We were invited again to Bullitt's at 4.30, but decided not to go; we didn't want to listen to their sympathy and enquiries.

In the evening we went to the Bolshoy to *Natalka-poltavka* [*Natasha from Poltava*], performed by the Kiev Opera on tour. [. . .] Before the start of the second act Stalin, Molotov and Ordzhonikidze appeared in the Government Box opposite us. I kept thinking about Stalin and dreaming that he would think of Misha, and our fate would be transformed. When it was over, all the performers gathered on the stage and gave Stalin an ovation, in which the whole theatre then joined. Stalin waved cordially to the performers and applauded them.

16 March 1936

After waiting for some time, M. A. was asked to go into the office. They spoke for about an hour and a half. Kerzhentsev criticized both *Molière* and *Pushkin*; at this, M. A. realized that the rehearsals of *Pushkin* were also to be suspended. [. . .] He didn't argue about the quality of the play, didn't complain or ask for anything. Then Kerzhentsev asked a question about his future plans. M. A. told him about the play about Stalin and his work on the textbook.

A pointless meeting.

18 March 1936

In *Soviet Art* for 17 March there was an unpleasantly-phrased paragraph about *Pushkin*.

M. A. telephoned Veresayev to suggest that he send a letter to the editor to say that the play had been signed by Bulgakov alone, in order to protect Veresayev from attacks, but Vikenty Vikentyevich said that was not necessary.

3 April 1936

They've arrested Kolya Lyamin.

5 April 1936

M. A. is dictating alterations to *Ivan Vasilyevich*. They want some modifications. Goodness knows what Gorchakov has dreamed up: he wants to include a Young Pioneer girl in the comedy as a positive figure. M. A. flatly refused to take that sort of despicable step!

18 April 1936

M. A. talked with Gorchakov and Rafalovich about *Molière*. They want to start performances up again. They've asked for some slight modifications: a toning down of the incest theme. *Paris vaut bien une messe!* M. A. is thinking of agreeing to the modifications.

13 May 1936

An in-house dress rehearsal of *Ivan Vasilyevich*. [. . .] The production still makes the same cheerless impression. Apart from our family – M. A., Yevgeny and Sergey, Yekaterina Ivanovna and me – the only people watching the performance were Boyarsky and Angarov from the Party Central Committee. Towards the end of the play, without even taking his coat off, holding a military cap and a briefcase in his hands, Furer came into the auditorium; apparently he's also from the Party Central Committee.

As soon as the performance was over the play was banned. Gorchakov told us that Furer had immediately said, 'I don't advise you to put it on.'

19 May 1936

Ruslanov came with a request: wouldn't it be possible to make alterations to *Pushkin?* M. A. refused *categorically*. He's made an agreement with the Moscow Arts Theatre to do a translation of *The Merry Wives of Windsor*, and to create a Shakespeariana rather like the Molieriana in his *Follies of Jourdain* [Bulgakov's adaptation of *Le Bourgeois Gentilhomme*]. It's very sad that M. A. has had to sign this contract. But we need money to take a trip to Kiev: unless he gets some sort of a rest he'll collapse living like this.

12 June 1936

Today we came back from Kiev; the city had a consoling effect. [. . .] On our way back we bought a copy of the magazine *Theatre and Drama* in the train. In the leader *Molière* was described as 'low-grade falsification'. Then a few more vile things including a thoroughly dirty attack from Meyerkhold on M. A. How Meyerkhold used to beg M. A. for a play in the old days, every one he wrote!

16 June 1936

The composer B. Asafyev with a proposal for a libretto (and he would do the music) for an opera, *Minin and Pozharsky*. This is Dmitriyev's matchmaking.

10 July 1936. From Polenovo (a holiday resort) to Moscow
From the composer Boris Asafyev

Melik-Pashayev [the conductor] arrived here yesterday and gave me a welcome piece of news, that you have finished *Minin and Pozharsky*. Allow me to congratulate you on this account and send you my greetings. On the 11th, that is tomorrow, Mutnykh is coming back here and I will arrange with him how we should meet. I can't wait! . . .

23 July 1936. From Leningrad to Moscow
From the composer Boris Asafyev

I am writing to you to say once again that I am sincerely excited and stimulated by your libretto. You mustn't get anxious or alarmed. I will write the opera, just let me rest a little and give me a little more time to think really deeply about your text in relation to the musical action, that is to get a distinct feeling for that action. I will write to you about all my ideas. Don't be angry if I pester you.

I implore you not to torment yourself. If only I knew how to calm you! I can promise you that in my life too there have been such 'states', so I think I have the right to feel for you and to sympathize: after all, I too am a loner. Other composers don't recognize me. And nor do most of the musicologists.

From Yelena Sergeyevna's diary
26 July 1936

Tomorrow we are leaving Moscow for Sinop, near Sukhumi. *Minin* is finished. M. A. wrote it in exactly one month, in dreadful heat.

17 August 1936. From Sukhumi (on the Black Sea) to Moscow
To Yakov Leontyev (at the Bolshoy Theatre)

Dear Yakov Leontyevich!

I can feel that my poor old head has had a good rest. Now I am beginning to talk to my friends again, those I remember with affection. [. . .]

The Sinop is a splendid hotel. It's possible to have a really good rest here. There's a park; billiards; balconies; the sea is close; it's spacious; it's clean; and there's only one draw-back – the food. It's dull. And monotonous. You will agree that mysterious words on a menu bring no consolation – *zwebel klops*, *boeuf Stroganoff*, stuffed . . . , *languette piquante* etc. All these words conceal one and the same thing – complete rubbish. And a great many people, including myself, just carry on taking our medicinal drops from abroad, and feed on rice pudding and bilberry jelly.

All the rest is fine. Few people don't enjoy it here. But amongst them is my sister-in-law Olga. She burst in here with such a clatter that even I, with all my fantastical imagination, was taken aback. And now from morning to night she calls imprecations down upon the entire seaboard – the mountains, the sky, the air, the magnolias, the cypresses, and Zhenya for having brought her here, and the balcony because there's a palm-tree near to it. She says that everyone should be moved out of here and the area should be planted with citrus trees. In other words, there's nothing she likes – apart from Nemirovich, of course. She began by very nearly drowning. And if it hadn't been for Yershov, who threw himself into the water fully-clothed and dragged her out, there would have been a nice little contre-temps. Lyusya is well, which I am very glad of. Ours is a difficult life, and I will be happy if she recovers her strength here.

At first I didn't do any reading and tried not to think about anything, to forget it all, but now I have begun a translation of *The Merry Wives of Windsor* for the Moscow Arts Theatre. Incidentally, about the Arts Theatre. There is amazing news from there. My protectors and benefactors have been displaying such class that I can only gape. But I'll tell you about all that when we next meet. Lyusya has been saying to me that you are a prophet!

Ah, dear Yakov Leontyevich, what is going to happen to me this autumn? Should I go and visit a fortune-teller perhaps?

What about *Minin*? I sent Asafyev a small addition to one of the scenes in a letter. Is he working?

We're planning to leave here on 27 or 28 August via Tiflis and Vladikavkaz (now renamed Ordzhonikidze).

If you had time to write to me here I should be delighted. Lyusya sends the warmest and friendliest greetings to all your family. Don't forget!

From Yelena Sergeyevna's diary
1 September 1936

Today we flew back to Moscow from the Caucasus. [. . .] I am extremely unwell; I am never going to get into an aeroplane again. M. A. coped splendidly with the flight, feasting with a good appetite on pies and fruit.

The end of our stay in Sinop was spoiled by Gorchakov. He wanted to persuade M. A. to write two or even three new scenes for *Molière*. M. A. refused – 'I won't shift a comma in it.' Then came a conversation about *The Merry Wives*, which M. A. had begun to translate while he was there. [. . .] 'You must put a bit of hanky-panky in! . . . You're much too coy, maître . . . Hee-hee-hee . . . ' On the following day M. A. told Gorchakov that he was refusing to continue work on the translation and on *The Merry Wives* altogether. Gorchakov was furious. A conversation with Markov, who said that the Theatre would be able to protect the translation from Gorchakov's encroachments. 'That's all a pack of lies. The Theatre's not capable of protecting me from anything.'

M. A. abandoned work. We left for Tiflis, and from there travelled by car over the Georgian Military Highway. We stayed in Vladikavkaz, where M. A. had once suffered so much. And then came back to Moscow.

9 September 1936

What should M. A. do next? [. . .] M. A. feels like leaving the Moscow Arts Theatre. He finds it painful to be there after the destruction of *Molière*: 'It's the graveyard of my plays.'

14 September 1936

During the conversation M. A. said that perhaps he was going to part company with the Moscow Arts Theatre. Samosud [from the Bolshoy Theatre]: 'We'll take you on in any capacity. How about as a tenor?' At half-past two in the morning Yakov L[eontyev] telephoned to send us greetings; he was playing billiards with Mutnykh somewhere or other.

15 September 1936. Moscow
To Mikhail Arkadyev (one of the Directors of the Moscow Arts Theatre)

Dear Mikhail Pavlovich,

Now that I've thoroughly considered the matter that you and I have talked about, I have come to the firm conclusion that, given the distressed condition I find myself in, which has been brought about by the devastation inflicted on my plays, I no longer feel capable of working in the Moscow Arts Theatre; I simply find it painful to be there.

Yesterday I also thought over the whole question of *The Merry Wives* again, and I can see that it will be impossible for me to steel myself. I am not going to do the translation. I would therefore ask you to take steps to annul my contract, and also to accept the enclosed letter requesting that I be relieved of my duties at the Moscow Arts Theatre.

From Yelena Sergeyevna's diary
15 September 1936

This morning M. A. wrote Arkadyev a letter withdrawing from his post at the Theatre and from his work on *The Merry Wives*. [. . .] We saw Rafalovich. He was staggered at the news that M. A. was leaving. M. A. told me that he wrote that letter to the Moscow Arts Theatre 'with a certain voluptousness, even'.

Now it remains for him to decide what to do about the Bolshoy Theatre. M. A. says he can't remain suspended in a vacuum, and that he must have some sort of environment around him, preferably a theatrical one. And that he is attracted by the music at the Bolshoy.

1 October 1936.

Contracts were signed concerning work at the Bolshoy and a libretto entitled *The Black Sea*.

2 October 1936. Moscow
To the writer Vikenty Veresayev

I hope that you are well and had a holiday this summer.

I succeeded in spending a month on the Black Sea. Unfortunately Yelena Sergeyevna had bad luck travelling with me. She brought back some infection from the south and has been ill for a whole month. Now she is feeling better, and I am gradually beginning to sort out the chaos that was created by my defeat as a playwright.

I have left the Moscow Arts Theatre. It was painful for me to work in the place where they ruined *Molière*. I have refused to fulfil my contract for the translation of *The Merry Wives*. I had begun to feel hemmed in in Arts Theatre Passage, they've played too many tricks with me.

And now I'm going to work as a writer of opera libretti. So, if it must be libretti, that's what it has to be!

I'm sending you with this letter a certificate from the theatre in Kiev about the tax they deducted from us. May Pushkin rest in peace, and may we do the same! I won't disturb him, so let him not disturb me.

I've managed to find Chekhov's correspondence with Knipper [-Chekhova]. I'll bring it round to you with the other books and my debt as soon as Yelena Sergeyevna is recovered. She will bring some order into our finances, for *The Merry Wives* is a real millstone – I have to return the advance on the contract.

I send you a hug and wishes that your work should be productive.

From Yelena Sergeyevna's diary
5 October 1936

Today is the tenth anniversary of the première of *The Turbins*. It was first performed on 5 October 1926. M. A. is in a wretched state. Needless to say, it didn't even occur to the Theatre to mark the day in any way.

5 October 1936. Moscow
To Yakov Leontyev (at the Bolshoy Theatre)

Many thanks, dear Yakov Leontyevich, for your kind and thoughtful letter.

Both contracts were signed on 25 September, and I have already started work. Let's hope that it will be successful!

Moscow, as always, confers everyday cares upon me. Amongst other things I am awaiting with interest the arrival of Asafyev.

I don't know what state his work is in. According to Dmitriyev he's recovering after an illness.

There has been a cryptic silence from Arts Theatre Passage, interrupted, to be sure, by a mild conversation with their legal adviser about the return of five thousand for *The Merry Wives*. With the greatest of pleasure, say I – take it out of my royalties.

My sister-in-law, protectress and benefactress, who was cooing caresses and tendernesses down the telephone, when she heard about the Bolshoy Theatre bellowed 'What?!' so terrifyingly that Lyusya trembled. From which I can only conclude that they don't like the Bolshoy Theatre.

But never mind, let them all be drowned in the Lethe. That's all they deserve.

I just don't know whether, as they go down, they will play any more dirty tricks on me, or whether they will submerge without a squeak. Probably the former, just to keep up standards.

Today's a special occasion for me. It's exactly ten years since the première of the *Turbins*. My tenth anniversary.

I am sitting at my inkwell and waiting for the door to open and for a delegation to appear from Stanislavsky and Nemirovich with a speech and a valuable gift in tribute. The speech will make mention of all my crippled or ruined plays and a list will be adduced of all the joys that they, Stan. and Nem., have brought me during ten years in Arts Theatre Passage. The valuable gift will take the form of a large saucepan made of some precious metal (copper, for example), filled with all the blood they have sucked from me over the ten years.

Come and see me soon, dear friend, and I will show it all to you. Get better quickly!

5 October 1936. Moscow
To his friend Pavel Popov

Greetings, Pavel!

Let me continue the agreeable conversation that was begun over the telephone. All the same, you might have rung me!

I have been through a dreadful commotion and torment and reflections, which ended up with my resigning from the Arts

Theatre and tearing up the contract for the translation of *The Merry Wives*.

Enough! There's a limit to everything.

Give me a ring, Pavel! We'll arrange when you can come round. I have been missing you. Yelena Sergeyevna was unwell for a long time, but is now getting better.

Tell them to bring a bottle of Clicquot up from your cellar and drink to the health of *The Days of the Turbins*; the play is celebrating its tenth anniversary today. I take my greasy writer's skull-cap off to the missus, my wife congratulates me, and that's an end to the anniversary.

From Yelena Sergeyevna's diary
14 October 1936

A conversation. A conversation that was melancholy and alarming – because of its subtext, naturally. M. A. said that he was not being given the opportunity to work in his native land, and that all his works got banned. Stavsky [Secretary of the Writers' Union] said that someone somewhere was going to discuss M. A.'s works. His entire conversation consists of evasions, standard formulations and cunning.

17 October 1936. From Leningrad to Moscow
From the composer Boris Asafyev (telegram)

Yesterday sixteenth finished our opera. Greetings. Asafyev.

3–4 November 1936. Moscow
To Yelena Sergeyevna

Mysya! I've never eaten anything so delightful. Thank you for a marvellous supper. Your loving . . .

On the night of 3–4 November.

From Yelena Sergeyevna's diary
13 November 1936

I accompanied M. A. to Spaso-Peskovsky [Street], to a reception given by Bullitt.

17 November 1936

A reception given by the military attaché Faymonville at the residence of the American Ambassador. Two films. [. . .] Later on [. . .] Kerzhentsev came up to M. A. and said that he was having doubts about *The Black Sea*. Oh, we are so weary of all this!

18 November 1936

I am delighted that retribution has been visited upon that vile reptile Litovsky.

19 November 1936

In the evening M. A. was playing chess with Topi [his friend Sergey Topleninov]. Yakov Leontyevich telephoned and said that Kerzhentsev had mentioned the idea of *Minin* in the Government Box, and that it had met with approval. Evidently the conversation was with Yosif Vissarionovich [Stalin]. Incidentally, I was remembering that soon after the taking off of *Molière* Yakov Leontyevich had told us that, according to his friend Mogilny, Stalin had apparently said, 'What's this about another play of Bulgakov's being taken off? It's a pity; he's a talented author.' It seems quite plausible. Otherwise it would be difficult to explain all these conversations and suggestions about revivals.

22 November 1936

We're having massages every day; it helps the nerves. We talk about our dreadful life, and we read the newspapers.

25 November 1936

The opening of the Congress of Soviets. At about half-past five, a huge din from the radio in the apartment downstairs; Stalin's name is greeted with an ovation. At the beginning of his speech: another ovation.

26 November 1936

In the evening we had Ilf and Petrov, with their wives, and the Yermolinskys round. [. . .] Ilf and Petrov are not just marvellous writers, but also marvellous people; decent, benevolent, honourable as writers as in life, clever and witty.

28 November 1936

Yakov Leontyev telephoned during lunch and said that the Bolshoy management was sending Melik [-Pashayev] and M. A. to Leningrad to listen to *Minin*; M. A. was to go at Asafyev's request. And so they went off today on the *Red Arrow*. This is the first time M. A. and I have been parted since 1932.

29 November 1936

I sent M. A. a telegram. He telephoned me at two in the morning. He said the music was good, that there were some very strong passages in it; that the journey was disagreeable, the weather was appalling, and that he wasn't liking the city this time.

1 December 1936

He's back. [. . .] M. A. brought some funny masks back from Leningrad as a present for Sergey, and now he's started wearing them himself.

9 December 1936. From Paris to Moscow
From his brother Nikolay

Dear Mikhail,

After a long lull and period of waiting, the question of the production of *Zoyka's Apartment* has arisen once again. The thing is that the director at the Vieux Colombier theatre is intending to begin performing it in January of next year (1937). [. . .]

Yevgeny Ivanovich [Zamyatin] is suffering from heart trouble, and I've been treating him and visiting him: he and his wife send you their greetings.

From Yelena Sergeyevna's diary
22 December 1936

They telephoned from *Literaturnaya Gazeta* to ask M. A. to write a few words about the sinking of the *Komsomol*.

23 December 1936. Moscow
To the editor of *Literaturnaya Gazeta*

I was shocked by the news of the sinking of the Soviet merchant ship *Komsomol*. But I am sure that my words of indignation will not help anything. I should like to add my voice to those of all who consider that it is vital to dispatch a squadron into Spanish waters.

Soviet naval vessels will be able to escort our merchant craft and inspire respect for the Soviet flag, as well as, if necessary, reminding people how deep and dangerous are the waters in which warmongers sail.

M. Bulgakov (writer).

From Yelena Sergeyevna's diary
1 January 1937

We saw the New Year in at home. Zhenichka [Yelena Sergeyevna's elder son] came. We lit candles on the tree. There were presents, surprises, big balloons and games with masks.

M. A. and the children made a great din smashing cups with '1936' written on them, which had been specially bought and painted for the occasion. [. . .]

God grant that 1937 should be a happier year than the last one!

3 January 1937. From Moscow to Paris
To his brother Nikolay

Dear Kolya,

I have delayed in replying to your letter of 9 December 1936 because our Sergey has been ill – he's had scarlet fever.

Above all I would ask with the utmost seriousness that you personally check through the French text of *Zoyka's Apartment* and inform me that there are not and will not be permitted any distortions or arbitrary interpolations bearing an anti-Soviet character, which would consequently be unacceptable and disagreeable to me as a citizen of the USSR. That's the most important thing.

And now the second thing: if the play really is going to be put on in Paris, I should prefer assorted individuals not to get any chance to embezzle my royalties. [. . .]

I hope that my letters to you and to Bloch will help to protect my royalties and hinder any attempts to divert them to Germany.

There is a suggestion that the Moscow Arts Theatre might visit Paris, but I don't know whether it will come off or not. Since the autumn I have had no connection with the Arts Theatre. I resigned because it was too painful for me to work there after the ruining of *Molière*. At the moment I am working as a staff librettist at the Bolshoy Opera Theatre.

Sergey's scarlet fever is nearly better. I hope that there won't be any complications, and then things will get easier. I will write to you again in the next few days.

9 January 1937. From Moscow to Leningrad
To the composer Boris Asafyev

Dear Boris Vladimirovich!

Don't be angry with me for not having written to you until now. I didn't write because I really didn't know what to write.

I'm now sitting inserting a new scene into *Minin* as well as the alterations they have demanded.

Things are hard for me, and I feel terrible. Obsessive thoughts about my ruined literary life and about my hopeless future give rise to other black thoughts. What should I write to you in a letter? What?

I value your work and wish for you with all my heart that which is dwindling in me – strength.

29 January 1937. Moscow
To his friend Pavel Popov

Dear Pavel!

Let me know when I can come and visit you. I miss you. Give me a ring and we can arrange to see each other either here or in your flat.

After the death of *Molière* all is quiet and melancholy here, and I can see no way forward.

From Yelena Sergeyevna's diary
7 February 1937

M. A. has begun to write a novel about theatrical life. As long ago as 1929, when I was spending the summer in Yessentuki, M. A. wrote and said there was a present waiting for me . . . When I arrived back he showed me a notebook, the beginning of an epistolary novel, and he said that was the present, and he was going to write this theatrical novel.

And so now he has got the notebook out again, and is writing eagerly.

Quite a lot of it is written already. [. . .] For my part, I am wildly enthusiastic about it, and hang on every word!

12 February 1937

This is M. A.'s sore point: 'I am a prisoner . . . they'll never let me out of here . . . I'll never see the world . . . ' [. . .] M. A. is in a dreadful state. 'They won't perform me at home, while abroad they rob me.'

18 February 1937

Aleksandrov telephoned to tell us that Ordzhonikidze had died of a heart attack [it was actually suicide]. Everyone is staggered.

11 March 1937. Moscow
From Vasily Sakhnovsky (at the Moscow Arts Theatre)

I have learned from Yosif (I mean Yosif Rayevsky) that a certain novel devoted to a theatre I am interested in has flowed out of someone's pen. I was walking along the street with Yosif and laughed heartily. And quite r-r-right too!

From Yelena Sergeyevna's diary
18 March 1937

After working frenziedly M. A. has finished *The Black Sea*.

21 March 1937

A phone call from Mutnykh; he wants to talk about *Minin*. [. . .] M. A. said he'd heard that Zamyatin had died in Paris.

24 March 1937. From Moscow to Leningrad
To the composer Boris Asafyev

The Theatre has received both scenes.

Melik [-Pashayev] played one of them, the Kostroma scene, at my house. I embrace and salute you, it's brilliantly written! How splendid the finale is – long may you flourish, glorious citizens of Kostroma!!

Do you know, despite all the troubles with which I am paying for my life as a writer, despite my exhaustion and gloom – I am keeping a constant eye on *Minin* and am doing all I can to get the opera staged.

24 March 1937. Moscow
To his friend Pavel Popov

I haven't written to you before this because our life is always frantically busy and full of difficult and disagreeable problems. Many people told me that 1936 had been a bad year for me supposedly because it was a leap year – there's some sort of superstition about it. But now I can see that, as far as I am concerned, 1937 is going to be in every way a match for its predecessor.

Amongst other things, I am going to court on 2 April – some sharks from a theatre in Kharkov are making an attempt to extract money from me by playing on my misfortune over *Pushkin*. Nowadays I cannot hear the word 'Pushkin' without a shudder, and hourly I curse myself for having had the ill-fated thought of writing a play about him. Some of my well-wishers have adopted a rather strange way of consoling me. More than once I have heard their suspiciously unctuous voices: 'Never mind, it will all get printed after your death!' I am very grateful to them, of course!

I would like to have a break. Yelena Sergeyevna and I invite you and Anna Ilyinichna to come round on the 28th at 10 p.m. to drink tea. Drop me a line or ring to say whether you can come.

From Yelena Sergeyevna's diary
28 March 1937

My conclusions are that we are entirely alone, and that our situation is terrifying.

30 March 1937

Conversations with M. A. about what we are to do. [. . .]

Oh, yes, I forgot to write about this! We've been told how Meyerkhold confessed all his sins at a meeting of Party activists in the Organization of Cultural Workers. It was so shameful that at first people thought he was mocking them. He's an astonishing reptile!

1 April 1937

An invitation to the American Embassy to a fancy-dress ball organized by the Ambassador's daughter. In the evening Mrs Kennan telephoned M. A. I talked to her about what to wear: 'Tails, of course?' She replied with a strong accent (we were speaking Russian), 'Oh no, I think a smoking-jacket will do.' And where are we to get a smoking-jacket? And patent-leather shoes? And proper collars? It's quite clear that I won't be able to go; and probably Misha would feel uncomfortable in an ordinary jacket.

4 April 1937. Moscow
To the writer Vikenty Veresayev

I wanted to let you know that we have won our case in the City Court, and that the Kharkov Russian Drama Theatre's suit has been rejected. [. . .]

No one appeared in court from the Kharkov side, to my regret: I would have liked to feast my eyes on one of those who began this affair! What people! [. . .]

So that's it – I hope that we shan't have to go back to it any more. I am very exhausted and brooding. My most recent attempts to write for the dramatic theatre were sheer Don Quixotism on my part. And I will not repeat them . . . You won't see me any more on the theatrical front. I've had experience and I've been through too much . . .

From Yelena Sergeyevna's diary
4 April 1937

In the papers was the news that Yagoda has been dismissed from his post and faces prosecution for actions he has committed of a criminal nature. [. . .]

In the elections for President of the Moscow Writers' Group, Kirshon failed to win. It is gratifying to think that Nemesis does exist after all for these people – like Kirshon!

7 April 1937

A telephone call from the Central Committee summoning Misha to see Angarov. He went. According to him they had a long conversation which was irksome because it was so completely unproductive. Misha talked about what they had done to *Pushkin*, while Angarov replied in such a way that it was clear that he wanted to guide Misha into the correct paths. Amongst other things, talking about *Minin*, he said, 'Why do you not love the Russian people?' and kept saying that the Poles were portrayed very attractively in the libretto.

The most important thing wasn't said: [. . .] what Misha must say, and probably put in writing, to the Central Committee, or what sort of steps he's supposed to take. But Misha's view is that his position offers no hope. They have crushed him, and they want to compel him to write in a way that he will not write.

10 April 1937

Misha will never see Europe.

14 April 1937

Painful news: Ilf has died. He was suffering from very bad tuberculosis.

15 April 1937

A telephone call from the Soviet Writers' Club asking M. A. to be part of the guard of honour around the coffin.

19 April 1937

The wife of the poet Mandelstam came to visit M. A. He's in internal exile and has already spent more than two years in Voronezh, apparently. She is in an extremely difficult position and is without work.

20 April 1937

A staggering event at the Bolshoy Theatre: Mutnykh has been arrested.

21 April 1937

A rumour that Kirshon and Afinogenov are in trouble. They say that Averbakh has been arrested. Is it possible that Nemesis has been visited upon Kirshon?

22 April 1937

Markov [. . .] pestered Misha terribly to show him the section of the novel [*A Theatrical Novel*] that is about him; he was late for the reading. Markov told us that in the Box (evidently at *Anna Karenina*) there was a conversation about the [Moscow Arts Theatre's] trip to Paris, and supposedly Stalin was in favour of their taking *The Turbins*, but Molotov objected.

23 April 1937

Yes, Nemesis has come. There are very bad stories in the press about Kirshon and Afinogenov.

25 April 1937

We were in the Bolshoy Theatre, and on our way home [. . .] we met Valentin Katayev. Of course we talked about Kirshon. There is a rumour that Kryuchkov, Gorky's former assistant, has been arrested. I don't know what Kryuchkov has been up to, but today in the *Moscow Evening News* he is called a filthy operator.

27 April 1937

Olyesha caught us up. He was trying to persuade Misha to go to the meeting of Moscow playwrights which is starting today, and at which they are going to deal with Kirshon. He was trying to persuade Misha to speak, and to tell them that Kirshon was the main organizer of M. A.'s persecution. That's more or less true, but of course Misha has no intention of speaking.

28 April 1937

Misha has been in very low spirits indeed for the last few days, which makes me despair. But I'm prepared to admit myself that our future looks bleak.

30 April 1937

Today there was good, sunny weather, so we went on a riverboat along the Moskva. It was very soothing.

2 May 1937

During the day M. A. sorted through old newspapers in his library. [. . .] Today Misha took a firm decision to write a letter about his plight as a writer. I think he's absolutely right. We can't go on living like this. All this time I've been telling M. A. that he's been defending himself at the cost of eating away at himself.

6 May 1937

For the last few days M. A. has been working on a letter to the Government.

7 May 1937

Today in *Pravda* there was an article by P. Markov about the Moscow Arts Theatre. There was not a single word in it about *The Turbins*, and when he listed the Soviet dramatists who have been performed in the Arts Theatre, Bulgakov's name wasn't there!

9 May 1937

In the evening Vilyams and his wife and Shebalin were here. M. A. read them the first chapters (not in full) of his novel about Christ and the Devil (it doesn't yet have a title, but that's how I describe it to myself).

10 May 1937. From Moscow to Leningrad
To the composer Boris Asafyev

Dear Boris Vladimirovich,

I am dictating this because I find it easier to work that way. I have now been suffering from complete nervous exhaustion for a month. That is the only explanation for the delay in replying to your last letter. I keep putting off this letter and others from one day to the next. I didn't have the strength to sit down at my desk. And there was no sense in sending a telegram, since there was nothing urgent to say. You know all too well what feeling tormented is like, and will of course cease to be angry with me.

A new factor has appeared on the horizon, and that's *Ivan Susanin*, which has begun to be spoken of persistently in the Theatre. If it is pushed through then we must face up to the truth, *Minin* won't be put on. Kerzhentsev talked to me on the telephone yesterday, and it emerged that he hadn't read the final version of the libretto. They sent him a copy from the Bolshoy yesterday. [. . .]

You must come to talk with Kerzhentsev and Samosud (of course you already know that Mutnykh is no longer a Director of the Bolshoy Theatre and has been arrested).

From Yelena Sergeyevna's diary
12 May 1937

At home this evening. M. A. is sitting working at his letter to Stalin.

13 May 1937

In the evening M. A. began revising the novel [*The Master and Margarita*], starting from the very beginning.

14 May 1937

A highly fascinating conversation. Dobranitsky constructed the whole thing along the following lines: we've been very guilty in relation to you, but it all happened because the leaders on the cultural front were people such as Kirshon, Litovsky and others. But now we're rooting them out and we must remedy this state of affairs by bringing you back to the drama front; after all, it's turned out that you and we (that is, the dramatist Bulgakov and the Party) have had common enemies, and furthermore a common theme concerns us: 'the motherland' – and so on and so forth.

M. A. says that he is very clever and quick on the uptake, and that in M. A.'s opinion his conversation was a more intelligent attempt than previous ones to get him to write, if not a propaganda play, then at least a pro-Soviet one.

He wouldn't name the figure who was standing behind him, and Misha didn't attempt to ask. But M. A. says it is Angarov and no one else, if indeed there is anyone there at all.

Apart from anything else, D[obranitsky] said that there had been some discussion of the question of getting Erdman back to work.

15 May 1937

During the day Dmitriyev came, and said, 'Write a propaganda play!' Misha said, 'Tell me, who sent you?' Dmitriyev burst out laughing. I like him very much.

16 May 1937

In the papers I read that Kirshon, Lerner, Sapashkov and Gorodetsky are to face criminal charges for their activities in the copyright administration. Now there's a place where they have sucked Misha's blood, and mine, in recent times. [. . .]

In the evening Dmitriyev dropped in before the *Red Arrow*. Over supper he was booming on that M. A. should appeal to the authorities, but that he should send off the beginning of the history textbook beforehand. [. . .] But appeal for what, on what grounds?

M. A. is in a dreadful state. Once again he has become afraid of walking in the street on his own.

23 May 1937

M. A. went out to walk up and down the backstreets, to practise walking on his own, while Dobranitsky got down to reading *Pushkin*. [. . .] 'You'll see, I won't disappear. I consider it my duty, a matter of Party conscience, to do all that I can to remedy the mistake that has been made with regard to Bulgakov.'

26 May 1937

Today in the newspaper a report that Afinogenov has been excluded from the Party.

4 June 1937

In the evening the Dmitriyevs and Anna Akhmatova, who read three or four of her lyrical poems.

5 June 1937

[On the dismissal of the President of the Repertory Committee] Litovsky is one of the vilest monsters I have encountered through Misha's literary career. [. . .] Dobranitsky is taking an enormous interest in Misha.

6 June 1937

In the morning I picked up the newspapers, glanced at *Pravda* and rushed to wake Misha. A shattering piece of news: Arkadyev has been dismissed from the Moscow Arts Theatre.

10 June 1937

Dobranitsky came to bring M. A. some books on the Civil War. He quizzes M. A. about his convictions and is quite evidently a political agitator. It's a riddle for us, who is he exactly?

11 June 1937

[On the Tukhachevsky case] There was a meeting after the rehearsals. In the resolution they demanded the highest sanction against the traitors.

12 June 1937

In *Pravda* there is a report that Tukhachevsky and the others have been sentenced to be shot.

15 June 1937

M. A. is currently working on the material for a libretto, *Peter the Great*.

24 June 1937. Moscow
From Vasily Kuza (at the Vakhtangov Theatre)

. . . *Don Quixote.* We are no less excited by that idea than by *Nana* . . . In conversation with me you said that it was very difficult . . . Think about it in earnest. We could sign a contract with you straight away and give you a deadline of one and a half to two years to adapt *Don Quixote.*

From Yelena Sergeyevna's diary
25 June 1937

[On Zhukhovitsky] It has long been clear to M. A. and to me who he is, but we were curious to see what he would do. He began with a speech from which it emerged that he'd been told to pass on a threat: that *The Turbins* would be taken off if M. A. didn't write a propaganda play. To which M. A. replied, 'Oh, well, I shall have to sell the chandelier.' Then about *Pushkin*; he quizzed him about how and why the play had been taken off, and by whom? *Pushkin* again! What's going on?! And then about *Zoyka's Apartment*, how and what . . . We said it was a long time since we'd heard anything. His conversation is a combination of lies and provocations.

M. A. is busy studying the moon at the moment, he's been observing it with binoculars for the novel. There's a full moon at the moment.

8 July 1937

M. A. took Seryozhka to the river, where they went canoeing; both of them were thrilled.

13 July 1937

I dropped in today to the Moscow Arts Theatre [. . .] and saw Olga. She said that Arkadyev had been arrested. So there's an end to a career for you.

15 July 1937. From Moscow to Paris
To his brother Nikolay

I am extremely puzzled and worried. After your telegram, which I received on 7 April 1937 – '*Documents reçus attendez lettre Nicolas*' – I haven't had any news from Paris, neither from you, nor from the Société [des Auteurs et Compositeurs Dramatiques]. I don't know what's happening about *Zoyka*, nor what's happening about the copyright.

Your silence alarms me. Please send me some news.

I send you a kiss.

Your Mikhail.

17 July 1937. From Zhitomir (in the Ukraine) to Moscow To Yakov Leontyev (at the Bolshoy Theatre) and his family

Dear friends,

It's delightful here! And so, revelling in the sun and the little river, the acacias, the limes and the sweet air, and in the hope of recovering from our exhaustion, Lyusya and I both kiss you tenderly and will write in more detail later.

From Yelena Sergeyevna's diary
14 August 1937

Today we returned from Zhitomir. Praskovya appalled us with the news that Sergey has appendicitis. [. . .] Praskovya told us that the writer Klychkov, who lives in our block, has been arrested. I don't know this Klychkov.

15 August 1937

Misha said there were rumours in town about arrests of writers; some man called Zatudin or Zatubin, Bruno Yasensky, Ivan Katayev and someone else as well. They're not names that mean much to me.

16 August 1937

Ardov said that Bukhov had been arrested. In his time this Bukhov made a repellent impression on me.

17 August 1937

Boyarsky has been appointed the new Director of the Moscow Arts Theatre.

18 August 1937

Misha has heard that Adriyan Pyotrovsky has been imprisoned in Leningrad.

20 August 1937

It poured constantly with cold autumn rain.

Dobranitsky telephoned and came round. It turns out that

Angarov has been arrested. [. . .] Dobranitsky stubbornly
predicts that there will now be changes for the better in M. A.'s
literary destiny, while M. A. just as stubbornly refuses to believe
it. Dobranitsky asked this question: 'And do you regret the fact
that during your conversation of 1930 you didn't say that you
would like to emigrate?' M. A. replied, 'It is I who should ask
you whether I should regret it or not. If you say that writers fall
silent abroad, then isn't it all the same to me whether I remain
silent in my native land or in another country?'

30 August 1937
According to Smirnov, 'Aroseyev has fallen seriously ill and
won't be coming back' – which means that Aroseyev, the former
Chairman of the All-Union Society for Cultural Relations with
Foreign Countries, has been arrested.

2 September 1937
In the newspaper there was a report of the suicide of
Lyubchenko, the President of the Ukrainian Council of People's
Commissars.

5 September 1937
Misha was told that Abram Efros has been arrested. We don't
know [. . .] There are a lot of lies about.

6 September 1937
[Smirnov] told us that Litovsky had been arrested. I don't
know if it's true. If only it were!

17 September 1937. Moscow
To Platon Kerzhentsev (at the Bolshoy Theatre)
I enclose a copy of the opera libretto *Peter the Great*, which I
have written and delivered to the Bolshoy Theatre, in accordance
with the agreement whereby I am obliged to write one libretto
a year for the Bolshoy Theatre, and would request you to read
through it.

From Yelena Sergeyevna's diary
19 September 1937
Dmitriyev arrived and came to lunch. He said he'd seen
Litovsky in Leningrad, which means that Smirnov was quite
wrong to say that he'd been arrested.

19 September 1937. Moscow
From Platon Kerzhentsev (at the Bolshoy Theatre)

1. One gets no sense of the common people (even in the battle of Poltava), so you must provide two to three appropriate figures (a peasant, a workman, a soldier and so on) and crowd scenes.

2. It's not clear who Peter was supported by (in part – the merchants) and who was against him (some of the boyars, the Church).

3. The roles of his associates are weak (in particular the role of Menshikov).

4. It is not shown that the new State was created out of the cruel exploitation of the people (and in general you should base yourself on comrade Stalin's formulation).

5. Many scenes are not really finished, they lack dramatic action. More sharp conflicts and tragedy are needed.

6. The ending is excessively idyllic – here too you must have some sort of song by the oppressed people. Here you ought to bring out more the coming state revolutions and periods of interregnum (the division of power between the ruling classes and other groups).

7. It wouldn't be a bad thing to indicate episodically the role of foreign powers (spying and, for example, their attempts to use Aleksey).

8. It needs to be stressed more distinctly that Aleksey and company support the values of the past (and be precise about what those values represent).

9. You need to show more of the various facets of Peter's work, his work in economics and other civilizing undertakings. (Scene 2 is schematic.)

10. The language is much too modern – you need to add more of the flavour of the age.

It's only a very first approximation to the theme; a great deal of work still needs to be done.

From Yelena Sergeyevna's diary
23 September 1937

Agonizing attempts to find a way out. A letter to the authorities? Abandoning the theatre? Correcting the novel [*The Master and Margarita*] and submitting it? There's nothing we can do, it's a desperate situation.

During the day we went on a river-boat with Sergey. The weather was beautiful. It calms the nerves.

25 September 1937

Rumours that Kirshon has been arrested. M. A. doesn't believe it.

27 September 1937

An astonishing phone call from Smirnov, who said that he had had a word about *Flight*, and that a request had come for a copy of it. Where from? He said he couldn't tell us over the telephone. We decided to make a copy of the text. M. A. and I are racking our brains to try to understand what this means.

28 September 1937

Olyesha telephoned Misha to ask his advice about his distress; his nerves are shattered, and apart from that he has suffered a tragedy. He didn't say so, but I know from the newspapers and from people's stories that his stepson threw himself out of a window and fell to his death.

2 October 1937. From Moscow to Leningrad
To the composer Boris Asafyev

I apologize that this is typed. I have caught a cold and am laid up, so am dictating.

I haven't written to you before this because until very recently I just didn't know what was happening with my *Peter*. And then, in addition, some casual but urgent work landed on me all of a sudden, and it has consumed the last few days.

Let me begin at the end: my *Peter* is no more, that is to say the typed libretto is lying in front of me, but there's no use, as they say, to be had from it.

And now in proper order: when I had finished the work I sent one copy to the Bolshoy and sent another to Kerzhentsev in order to speed things up. Kerzhentsev has sent me a critical analysis of the work, consisting of ten points. Principally, what can be said about them is that they are exceedingly difficult to put into effect, and in any case mean that the whole job has got to be done again from scratch, and I have got to

plunge myself back up to my neck in the historical material.
[. . .]

Now I find myself at a crossroads. Should I redo it or not,
should I tackle something else, or should I abandon it all? In
all probability necessity will oblige me to redo it, but I cannot
vouch that I will have any success.

I agree with a lot of what [Melik-] Pashayev said when he read
the libretto. There are purely operatic defects, but I reckon that
they can be remedied. The real problem lies in Kerzhentsev's
points.

Now the question of the composer. The Theatre told me that
I must hand the libretto in, and that the question of the choice
of composer was a matter for the Committee and the Theatre.
With all the conviction I could muster I told them how desirable
it would be if you were to do the opera. That was all I could
do. But of course the Committee will decide. [. . .]

And now I am sitting and seeking a way out, but there is no
evident way out for me. I need to decide not just the question of
Peter. Over the last seven years I have created sixteen works in
different genres, and they have all perished. This is an impossible
situation, and in our home everything looks utterly hopeless and
sombre.

From Yelena Sergeyevna's diary
3 October 1937

M. A. and I keep talking about *Flight*. What does it mean?
Has something changed politically? Why do they need the play?
Nothing will come of it.

4 October 1937. Moscow
From the writer Vikenty Veresayev

Dear Mikhail Afanasyevich!

Eighteen months ago you borrowed a thousand roubles from
me, counting on the fact that you would be able to return it in
the autumn. This did not prove possible because the Shakespeare
business went wrong.

My own circumstances have now taken a sharp turn for the

worse. My biography of Pushkin has been banned, they don't want to reprint my previous things, and I'm not writing fiction at the moment. I have undertaken a translation of the *Iliad* and the *Odyssey*. It's a job that will take about six or seven years, and until it is completed it won't keep me fed.

If at all possible, I would ask you earnestly to return the loan.

5 October 1937. Moscow
To the writer Vikenty Veresayev

Dear Vikenty Vikentyevich,

I have just received your letter and will bring the money I owe you tomorrow (or I may manage to do it today).

I beg you to forgive me for having delayed so long; nothing ever seems to work out.

I was very distressed at what you wrote about the Pushkin biography and the rest. I know from experience the cost of such blows.

Not long ago I totted it up: over the last seven years I have created sixteen things, and all of them have perished, except one, and that was the adaptation of Gogol! It would be naïve to think that a seventeenth or nineteenth thing would succeed.

I am working hard, but it has no sense or purpose to it. Which is why I am in a state of apathy.

From Yelena Sergeyevna's diary
5 October 1937

He must write a letter to the authorities. But that's frightening.

6 October 1937

A conversation about the dramatist Mikitenko, whose career, judging from the newspapers, has come to an end. A case rather like Kirshon's!

13 October 1937

A report in the newspapers that Bubnov has been dismissed.

16 October 1937

A long conversation with Kerzhentsev about *Peter* and about *Minin*, the gist of which is that it's all got to be redone.

21 October 1937

My birthday. Misha and Sergey gave me flowers.

23 October 1937

Misha is close to deciding to leave the Bolshoy Theatre. Working on librettos is dreadful! Make some corrections to the novel (the Devil, the Master, Margarita) and submit it?

5 November 1937

Pilnyak has been arrested.

11 November 1937

It turns out that Dobranitsky has been arrested, and Nina and the child have moved in with the Troitskys. [. . .] In the evening Misha sorted through his books and I dusted them, and we were altogether 'domestic'.

12 November 1937

In the evening M. A. worked on his novel about the Master and Margarita.

15 November 1937

Grisha [Konsky] telephoned and said he was missing us, and asked if he could come round. He came, but behaved extremely strangely. Misha was working in his room. Grisha latched on to the bookshelves and it was impossible to tear him away from them. Later, when M. A. was talking on the telephone, he went into the study, up to the writing-desk, and took out an album and began to examine it closely, then had a thorough look over the writing-desk and even tried to peep into an envelope full of cards which was lying on the desk. A regular Bitkov [a police spy in Bulgakov's *Pushkin*]! And it's a pity, because on the whole he's talented, as well as being sharp and clever.

24 November 1937

Yakov Leontyevich telephoned and said that the General Secretary had been at the dress rehearsal of *Virgin Soil Upturned* [a stage adaptation of Sholokhov's novel] today, and in conversation with Kerzhentsev had said, ' . . . and there's Bulgakov, who wrote *Minin and Pozharsky* . . . ' Yakov was delighted that Misha's name had been mentioned, so, being a kind person, he telephoned.

14 December 1937

Kerzhentsev summoned M. A. to see him and informed him

that he had reported to a highly-placed figure about *Minin* and was now asking M. A. to make the necessary alterations to the libretto. He said the Poles were all right (although last time he said that they were not all right). [. . .]

As for *Quixote*, he said that it would have to done in such a way that you could feel contemporary Spain (?!).

15 December 1937. From Leningrad to Moscow
From the composer Boris Afasyev

True, I have the sense that you have been advised not to associate with me, but after all, we're not talking about some new libretto of yours. Maybe *Minin* should simply be forgotten and destroyed? Well, I am ready if you like. After all, I asked that the score be returned to me and that your text be released from my music. And then I would be free, and you too.

From Yelena Sergeyevna's diary
16 December 1937

A letter has arrived from Asafyev which is one long wail! [. . .] You can tell that he is so overwrought that he has reached the end of his tether.

17 December 1937

In the newspaper (*Pravda*) there was an article by Kerzhentsev, 'An Alien Theatre', about Meyerkhold. A harsh critique of Meyerkhold's entire theatrical career. His theatre will undoubtedly be closed down.

18 December 1937. From Moscow to Leningrad
To the composer Boris Asafyev

I have received your letter of the 15th, which greatly surprised me. Your supposition that I had been advised not to associate with you is completely without foundation. Absolutely nobody has given me any such advice, and if it had entered anybody's head to advise me in that way, then I am the sort of man who, let me tell you, is capable of not obeying! And I was sure that you knew me well enough to know that I was not like the rest. I send you a reproach!

And now I have an important piece of news for you about *Minin*. On 14 December I was asked to go and see Kerzhentsev, who informed me that he had made a report about the work on *Minin* and asked me on the spot to embark urgently on the alterations to the libretto that he is insisting on. [. . .]

I don't know what awaits *Minin* in the future, but for today I have the distinct impression that wheels have begun to turn.

19 December 1937. From Leningrad to Moscow
From the composer Boris Asafyev

I will categorically ignore the first angry paragraph of your letter. Of course nobody *literally* gave you such advice, and of course you wouldn't have obeyed under direct pressure. But I don't know your new opera libretto [*Peter the Great*], and it might have been that you felt uncomfortable about letting me see it, even though you have kept me informed about your new work. And then one of the composers in Leningrad showed me sketches commissioned by the Bolshoy Theatre from him for an opera on your libretto. Don't take all this as a reproach. But I do consider that I know Bulgakov and that I value his true worth. And, simply, I love him. [. . .]

Heartfelt greetings. Don't be offended; having to struggle at the age of fifty-three for recognition and for the right to be a composer and for the right to compose not just ballets, but operas and symphonies too – it's not an easy matter. Greetings to your wife. I will await news.

25 December 1937. From Moscow to Leningrad
To the composer Boris Asafyev

On 21 December I sent you a letter in which I warned you that you needed to leave for Moscow at once. I waited for the only possible reply – a telegram announcing your departure. It didn't come. Do you mean to say that the exceptional seriousness of the matter of *Minin* is not clear to you? I am astounded. Are such letters written for no reason?

I have just sent you a telegram urging you to leave for Moscow. It means that there is something very important, if I summon you like this.

I repeat: you must leave for Moscow immediately.

I would like you to know that in this instance my concern is for you, and to remember that I warned you of the vital necessity of coming.

From Yelena Sergeyevna's diary
31 December 1937

The year is coming to an end. It has left a bitter taste in my mouth.

1 January 1938

My black evening dress had a terrific effect on Olga, but, alas, I've nothing to wear it for any more and I shall have to sell it.

8 January 1938

Today there was a Committee resolution about the liquidation of the Meyerkhold Theatre.

16 January 1938

Yesterday, at last, Asafyev appeared.

17 January 1938

As we walked home along Bryusov Street we saw Meyerkhold walking along with Raykh [his wife]. Dmitriyev detached himself and ran over to them. You can't stop yourself wondering: what will happen to Meyerkhold after the closing of his theatre, where will they put him?

19 January 1938

Yesterday there was a devastating item of news about Kerzhentsev. In Zhdanov's speech during the Session he was called a commercial traveller. His career is at an end! My God, how much muddle and harm he has caused the arts! And who will be put in his place? [. . .]

M. A. read passages from the theatrical novel. Erdman stayed the night.

20 January 1938

Once again his constant wretchedness at the skilful way in which so many people, Stanislavsky and Nemirovich first among them, have destroyed him as a playwright.

25 January 1938

They say that Shumyatsky has been arrested, with his wife as well. [. . .] [On Shostakovich's article 'A Report on my Creative Work'] I consider Shostakovich a genius. But to write such an article!

28 January 1938

They say that Ravichev (or Rabichev), Kerzhentsev's assistant, has shot himself.

29 January 1938

This evening we're going to listen to [Shostakovich's] fifth symphony [subtitled 'A Soviet Artist's Practical Creative Reply to Just Criticism'] which has created such a sensation.

31 January 1938

M. A. is composing a letter to Y. V. Stalin asking for N. Erdman's fate to be eased.

4 February 1938. Moscow
To Yosif Stalin

To Yosif Vissarionovich Stalin
From the playwright Mikhail Afanasyevich Bulgakov

Deeply esteemed Yosif Vissarionovich!

Permit me to address to you a request concerning the playwright Nikolay Robertovich Erdman, who has fully served his three-year sentence of exile in the towns of Yeniseysk and Tomsk, and who is currently resident in the town of Kalinin.

Confident in the fact that literary gifts are extremely highly prized in our fatherland, and knowing at the same time that the writer Nikolay Erdman is currently deprived of the opportunity to practise his skills as the result of the negative attitude that has developed towards him, and which has been sharply voiced in the press, I take the liberty of asking you to give your attention to his fate.

In the hope that the lot of the writer N. Erdman might be alleviated if you were to think it worthwhile considering this request, I ask wholeheartedly for N. Erdman to be given the possibility of returning to Moscow and of working in literature without hindrance, so that he may put behind him his solitary state and his spiritual depression.

M. Bulgakov.

From Yelena Sergeyevna's diary
5 February 1938

Today I took and delivered to the Central Committee of the Party Misha's letter addressed to Stalin about easing the fate of Nikolay Erdman.

6 February 1938

In the morning a telephone call from Dmitriyev, asking if he could come round immediately. He arrived completely crushed. It turned out that they had arrested his wife, Yelisaveta Isayevna. He wants to try to plead for her.

9 February 1938

Misha [. . .] is correcting the novel about Woland [*The Master and Margarita*].

10 February 1938

Dmitriyev came round during the day. He's trying to think how to intercede for his wife. Poor thing!

12 February 1938

Dmitriyev dropped in briefly before the train. Recently he has begun to irritate me, and I don't like it when conversations turn into chatter about petty squabbles.

21 February 1938

The woman from the Theatre buffet has been arrested.

23 February 1938

There's some nonsense in the ballet at the Bolshoy: Kudryavtsev, [. . .] Smoltsova and someone else have been arrested.

Misha says Dr Blyumental has been arrested.

It's quiet at home. Misha and I are going to have supper and then go to bed.

28 February 1938

[On the announcement of the show trials of Bukharin, Rykov and Yagoda and of the others accused of bringing about the deaths of Gorky, Menzhinsky and Kuybyshev] All day I have been reeling under the impact of this information.

1 March 1938

Misha was at Angarsky's today, and they have arranged to read the beginning of the novel. It looks as though Misha has now settled for the title *The Master and Margarita*. There is of course no hope of getting it published. Misha is now correcting it at night and is forging ahead with it, he wants to complete it during March.

5 March 1938

Dmitriyev was here in the evening. As before he is crushed by the arrest of his wife, and is trying to think what to do to find out about her fate or help her.

6 March 1938

Over the past few days Misha has been working on the novel in every spare moment.

7 March 1938

Grisha [Konsky] was here this evening. Rafalovich from the Arts Theatre has been arrested.

10 March 1938

Each morning I pick up the newspaper and am horrified at what a bestial creature Yagoda is!

12 March 1938

In the evening Dmitriyev came to ask advice about the letter he wants to send to Y. V. Stalin concerning this business with Veta. I typed the letter out for him [. . .] since Misha said that no one in the OGPU would believe that the letter had been written by the artist Dmitriyev – the handwriting was that of a housemaid! Although maybe that would precisely help . . .

13 March 1938

The sentencing [in the Bukharin trial]; they've all been condemned to the firing squad except Rakovsky, Bessonov and Pletnyov.

18 March 1938

Misha is unwell, and is sitting over the novel.

19 March 1938

The novel. Influenza.

22 March 1938

A ceremonial envelope from the American Ambassador; there will be a ball on 26 March. Misha and I laughed about his shiny black suit trousers and about the fact that I have shortened my long lacy dress. Neither of us will go, although, of course, it would have been interesting to see it.

31 March 1938

Seryozha [Yermolinsky] says that the ancient chapters [those in *The Master and Margarita* set in Jerusalem] are an extraordinary achievement.

21 April 1938

Today Dmitriyev, of course. Misha says he's already begun to reconcile himself to his calamity.

3 May 1938

Angarsky asked M. A. to read the novel (*The Master and Margarita*). M. A. read the first three chapters. Angarsky immediately said, 'Well, you can't publish that.' 'Why not?' 'You can't.'

Letters written in the summer of 1938 from Bulgakov in Moscow to Yelena Sergeyevna in Lebedyan (south of Moscow)

27 May 1938

Dearest Lyusenka,

I send you a big kiss! My one anxiety is how you disembarked with your retinue. Are you alive and well after that train? I thought there would be a telegram today, but Nastya says, 'What telegram? They're busy shopping in the market.'[. . .]

In the evening – the scene of Susanin in the wood at the Bolshoy, and then to Yakov Leontyevich's.

At night – Pilate. Ah, what difficult and involved material! That was yesterday. And today, I fear, will prove typical of my summer.

At eleven in the morning – Solovyov with his libretto (the director is Ivanov). Two hours of the most exhausting conversation, with all sorts of intricate problems. Then the telephone started: Mordvinov about Pototsky, the composer Yurovsky about his *Opanas*, Olga about the typing of the novel, Yevgeny [his elder stepson] inviting himself to lunch tomorrow, and Gorodetsky, also about *Opanas*.

In the middle of all this – Seryozha Yermolinsky. We went for a stroll, then he had lunch with me. He borrowed some old magazines, invited me to their dacha, and we talked about you.

This evening – Pilate. It wasn't very fruitful. Solovyov had distracted me. There is a gap in my material. It's a good thing it's not in the second chapter. I hope I'll manage to fill it in between typing sessions. [. . .]

So, and now the night has come. I'm tired. The water in the bathroom is making a noise. It's time to sleep. I kiss you, my friend. I implore you to rest. Don't think about theatres, nor about Nemirovich nor about playwrights, and don't read anything except soiled and well-thumbed novels in translation (or maybe they don't have any in Lebedyan?). May the sun in Lebedyan be like a sunflower over you, and may the sunflowers (if there are any in Lebedyan!) be like the sun.

Your M.

Kiss Sergey, and tell him that I entrust him with the job of looking after you!

30 May 1938

Dearest Lyusenka!

I have received Sergey's postcard with a picture of a knife and two people kissing and yours, where you write about exerting yourself settling in. You're not tiring yourself with all this?

The novel is already being typed. Olga's working well. I'm waiting for her now. I'm getting to the end of the second chapter.

Nastya has been very assiduous in looking after me. I send you a big kiss, my friend. I'm hurrying to give the postcard to Nastya.

Your M.

1–2 June 1938

Today, dear Lyu, your long letter of the 31st arrived. I wanted to get down to a long letter of my own as soon as I had finished dictating, but I don't have the energy. Even Olga, with her unique powers of endurance as a typist, has run out of steam today. The letter will be for tomorrow, but now – into a bath, a bath.

We've done 132 typed pages. Roughly speaking, that's about a third of the novel (if you include the trimming down of over-lengthy passages). [. . .]

In my dreams I shall endeavour to see the sun (of Lebedyan) and sunflowers. I send you a big kiss.

Your M.

2 June 1938

My dear Lyu!

First, you will see glued into a corner the image of a lady, or rather a portion of that lady, which I have saved from being destroyed. I think constantly of that lady, and in order to think about her more conveniently, I keep such fragments in front of me. [. . .]

Let's start with the novel. About a third, as I said in my postcard, has been typed. And you have to give Olga her due, she works very well. We compose for several hours at a time, and my head is filled with a quiet moan of weariness, but it's good weariness, not a torment.

And so everything, you might think, is fine, and suddenly from the wings one of the evil geniuses emerges on to the stage . . .

With your typical shrewdness you will instantly exclaim, 'Nemirovich!'

And you are quite right. It's him, precisely.

The thing is that, as I knew and said, all your sister's tales about how ill he was, and how the doctors were concealing . . . and so on, were complete rubbish, just typical Karlsbad-Marienbad trivial codswallop. He's as healthy as one of Gogol's coach-builders, and is just pining in Barvikha with nothing to do and pestering Olga with all sorts of nonsense.

Feeling thoroughly at a loose end in Barvikha, where there's no Hotel Astoria, no actors and actresses or anything, he has begun threatening to arrive in Moscow on the 7th. And your sister has already declared triumphantly that from now on there will begin to be disruptions to our work. And that's not all: she also added, glowing with happiness, that perhaps he would 'whisk her off to Leningrad on the 15th'!

It would be a good thing if Woland were to fly down over Barvikha! Alas, that sort of thing happens only in my novel!

A break in the typing would be the end!

I will lose the thread of the correcting and all the connections. Whatever happens the typing must be completed.

My mind is already working feverishly on the problem of where to find another typist, but of course it will be impossible to find one anywhere.

He's already dragged your sister off to Barvikha today, and I'm losing the day.

I think I should know today whether he's going off to Leningrad or not.

The novel must be finished! Now! Now! [. . .]

Oh dear, I wrote to you that you shouldn't think about the Theatre or about Nemirovich, and here I am writing about him. But whoever would have thought that he would manage even to do some damage to the novel! But never mind, never mind, don't upset yourself – I will finish the novel.

3 June 1938

Yes, the novel . . . My fingers itch unbearably to describe the atmosphere in which it is being transferred on to typed sheets, but unfortunately I must renounce that! Or I would have provided you with some entertainment! [. . .]

A magnificent phrase: 'You ought to show Vladimir Ivanovich [Nemirovich-Danchenko] the novel' (this at a moment when I was uncertain and pensive).

Of course, of course! I'm simply burning with impatience to show the novel to that philistine.

3 June 1938
To his stepson Sergey Shilovsky

Secret letter
For Sergey's eyes only

Dear Sergey!

Thank you for the letter and drawings. Please write again or I shall get bored.

Write to me in secret, please, to give me your opinion as to whether Masya is getting better and whether she has put on any weight or not.

I send you a kiss!

Your UncMich.

13 June 1938

I'm dictating the twenty-first chapter. I'm buried under this novel. I've thought it all through and it's all clear to me. I've completely withdrawn into myself, and I would be able to unlock myself only to one person, but she isn't here! She's growing sunflowers!

I kiss them both – the person and the sunflowers.

14–15 June 1938

Lyu! You shouldn't bathe three times! Sit in the shade and don't wear yourself out going to the market. They'll manage to buy eggs without you . . .

Sit and admire the landscape all around, and think of me. Don't walk too much. So your health is good? Write and tell me! [. . .]

Sist. (joyfully, triumphantly): 'I wrote to Vladimir Ivanovich to say that you were terribly flattered that Vladimir Ivanovich had sent his respects to you.'

There ensued a huge scene made by me. A demand that she should not dare to write in my name things I had not said. I informed her that I wasn't flattered, and reminded her of how I had been included without warning in the Turbins' letter of congratulations sent to Nemirovich from Leningrad.

S.'s total stupefaction that for the first time in her life someone was creating a scene and it wasn't her. She muttered that I 'hadn't understood!' and that she could 'show me a copy'.

Sist. (in businesslike tones): 'I've already sent Zhenya [her husband] a letter saying that I couldn't see the main direction in your novel yet.'

I (in a strangulated voice): 'Oh, why's that?'

Sist. (not noticing my look): 'Well, yes. That is, I'm not saying that it won't emerge. After all, I haven't got to the end yet. But I can't see it for the moment.'

I (to myself): '. . . . .!' [. . .]

In front of me lie 327 typed pages (about twenty-two chapters). If I remain in good health, the typing will soon be finished. Then the most important thing remains – my revision of it, which will be considerable and lengthy and painstaking, and might involve retyping some pages.

'And what will come of it?' you ask. I don't know. In all probability you will put it away in the writing-desk or in the cupboard where the corpses of my plays lie, and from time to time you will remember. However, we cannot know our future.

I have already formed my judgement on the work, and if I can lift the end a little as well, then I will consider that the piece is worthy to be revised and to be put away into the darkness of a drawer.

For the moment I am interested in your judgement, and no one can tell whether I shall ever know the judgement of the reading public.

My esteemed copyist has particularly helped me to reach the sternest possible judgement on the work. In the course of 327 pages she smiled once, on page 245 ('Glorious sea. . .'). Why that precisely should have amused her I do not know. I am not confident that she will ever succeed in discovering any sort of main direction in the novel, but on the other hand I am certain that utter disapproval of the work on her part has been guaranteed. This found expression in the cryptic remark 'This novel is your own private affair.' (?!) Presumably she meant by this that she was not to blame. [. . .]

Ku! I kiss you tenderly for your invitation and for your concern. My only joyous dream is of seeing you, and I will try to do all I can to achieve it. But I can't promise that I will succeed. The thing is, Ku, that I have begun to feel unwell, and if it's going to be like today and yesterday, for example, then I am unlikely to get away. I didn't want to write to you about it, but I can't not. But I hope I will feel better all the same, and then I'll try. [. . .]

Oh dear, Ku, you can't see from a distance what this last sunset novel has done to your husband at the end of his dreadful life in literature.

I send you a big kiss.

Your M.

22 June 1938

This evening Mark Leopoldovich [their doctor] is going to look at me, and then all will be a bit clearer. [. . .]

Ku! What revision of the novel can I possible do in Lebedyan? And *Don Quixote* isn't very likely either. I can't bear to think about a typewriter!

If I do manage to come, then it will be for a short time. And, what's more, I'm incapable not only of writing anything, but even of reading anything. I need absolute peace (your expression, which I liked). That's right, absolute peace! I can't bear to look at *Don Quixote* at all at the moment . . .

I kiss you, my beautiful and charming Helen!

Your M.

P.S. Look what the novel's done to me! Just now I began to tear up scrap paper and look, I've torn up your letter! I'm gluing it tenderly together again. Kisses.

[Bulgakov then spent a month with Yelena Sergeyevna in Lebedyan]

22 July 1938

Well, we got back to Moscow this morning at 8 a.m. It was stifling. We took a taxi, Yevgeny [his elder stepson] back to Rzhevsky Street, and I – home. I wanted to quench my thirst with tea and then go straight to the Sandunovsky Baths, and from there to Lavrushinsky Street, but after the tea I collapsed and went to sleep. After my sleep I felt brighter and went to the Sandunovsky Baths. The hot water and barber were sheer delight. But those bites are a real misery! The one from Lebedyan hasn't gone down at all, and in the railway carriage some flying beast bit me on the sole of my foot so that my foot has swollen and I am limping. What a devil!

I've just realized that I'm writing nonsense! It must be very interesting to read about the sole of my foot! I'm sorry.

I contemplated Moscow with interest. All was as it should be. You can tell that a lot of people are away. People's clothes show that they are exhausted by the heat. No ties, white trousers everywhere and shiny faces. My telephone calls have shown that many of the people I would like to see are not here. [. . .]

So there you are. I kiss you tenderly and remember the moon by the church as I plunge into my Moscow preoccupations.

23 July 1938

I am gazing greedily at the Spanish copy of *Don Quixote*. Now I'm going to get down to it. It's stifling. But Nastya has got hold of ice and some Beryozovskaya mineral water.

24 July 1938

Dear Ku! Thank you for your affectionate night-time post-cards. Of course I enjoyed it! I think of you and kiss you! Once I had thrown off the irksome business of the papers concerning the apartment, I began to feel marvellous and am working easily on *Quixote*. Everything is very convenient. There's no banging about from upstairs for the moment, the telephone is silent, and I have dictionaries spread out all around me. I drink tea with excellent jam, and am polishing Sancho until he gleams. Then I'll go over Don Quixote himself, and then over the rest of them, so that they will play like those dragonflies over the river-bank – do you remember? But the air here! It's not heat, but stuffiness which is sticky, viscous and heavy. When you're plunging into the water, think of me . . .

26 July 1938

Dear Ku, I've just received your telegram and postcard with the news of Sergey's accident. He's an astonishing lad! I hope it heals quickly. You didn't strain yourself carrying him? For he's as heavy as a chest of drawers! And incidentally, Ku, how's your health? Write and tell me!

I haven't read the play to anybody, and don't intend to until you and I have made a typed copy of it. [. . .]

The evening brings no relief from the stuffiness. It's half-past ten now and all the windows are open, but hardly any air comes into the rooms. And anyway the air is such that it might as well not come in. Nastya's taken to sleeping on the balcony.

Until tomorrow, Ku! I kiss you, and tell Sergey I asked you to stroke his head for me.

M.

30 July 1938

You can feel sorry for me. It's an inferno here. Not only does there seem to be no end to the heat, but it's getting worse with each day. At night moths fly in through the open windows and drown in the jam, and are followed by some sort of little green flies which expire on the books. Nastasya's going around with a wet cloth on her head, snivelling. She says that a man collapsed and someone else as well in one queue. It's become difficult to work. [. . .]

Dmitriyev is very insistent that I should visit him in Leningrad. And in the heat of the moment I was inclined to do it. Judging by our telephone conversation, everything has worked out badly for him. And he can't come to Moscow. But now I can see that the stars are against this trip; the main thing is that I feel terrible, and I am simply physically incapable of performing such an exploit. And what's more a whole range of things may be going to come together over the next few days. So I'm going to beat a retreat and continue to attack *Quixote* instead. [. . .]

I went to visit the Fyodorovs at their dacha. They met me charmingly as ever, but oh, the countryside around Moscow! Dacha villages full of smoke, littered with paper and covered in dust, and all this for dozens of miles. And the bathing! I remembered the Don and the sandy river-bed there.

And the dachas are like hen-coops! I came back after the sun had already set and gazed out of the window and felt so melancholy. And thought of you particularly vividly. If only I could sit and talk to you now! I've no more strength to write, I'm exhausted. I'll write about S., the Theatre, the novel and other things in the next letter.

4 August 1938

What do you mean, Lebedyan? I'm sitting here on tenterhooks in a state of alarm about your health, and cannot wait for your

Lebedyan term to come to an end. There's no possibility of my coming to Lebedyan! I'm extremely unhappy that you're not here with me at the moment, and my only consolation is that you are having a rest. But your health! Now what's the matter? I'm in a bad mood, preoccupied, and weighed down by all sorts of stresses. I'm sad that you're not here.

I send you a big kiss!

M.

6–7 August 1938

My dear friend Lyusi!

One of the reasons that I haven't been able to get down to a long letter before now was Dmitriyev. He landed on me from Leningrad with the news that he was being sent to live in Tadzhikistan. He's now lobbying through Moskvin as a Deputy and through the Moscow Arts Theatre for a review of the decision, and there is a hope that since they haven't got anything against him, and he has been ordered to live there as the husband of a spouse in [internal] exile, and also because of his unquestionable significance as a theatrical designer, his lot may be alleviated.

[. . . Bulgakov goes on to talk once again about his fury at the role Stanislavsky and Nemirovich-Danchenko had played in the taking off of *Molière* . . .]

By chance I have come across an article about the fantastic in Hoffmann. I'm keeping it for you, knowing that it will astound you as it did me. I am right in *The Master and Margarita*! You will understand what that realization means to me – I am right!

I am breaking off this letter and crossing out what I have written about Stanislavsky. It's not the moment to write about him – he has just died.

Your M.

8 August 1938

Dmitriyev's arrival turned my life into a complete nightmare. *Quixote* ground to a halt, so did various important ideas, I couldn't collect my thoughts to write letters, my head was full of the telephone ringing, and then the same questions and answers twenty times over. I feel sorry for him, he's completely crushed, but he drove me to the point where I became physically ill!

This evening he's going back to Leningrad, having obtained through the Moscow Arts Theatre a delay in his case, which should lead, I hope, to a rescinding of the decision to exile him. He was supposed to go yesterday, but he was summoned to the Arts Theatre to decorate the hall in mourning [for Stanislavsky].

I did all I could to help him with advice and sympathy, and now, I must admit to you, I am just dreaming of switching on the lamp, plunging into silence, and awaiting your return. [. . .]

And so you're leaving on the 14th? Excellent. There's no point in sitting there any more. Ku, if it's not too difficult, could you get some headache powders there and bring them with you?

9 August 1938

This is my first morning without Dmitriyev. You won't understand what happiness that is, since you weren't here during this nightmare, which I will tell you about in detail when I see you. It's enough that I have begun to suffer from complete insomnia. He left saying that he would come back again in a few days, and I am seriously concerned about how I am going to protect my work and peace. There's a limit to everything! [. . .]

As you can understand, I am still very much under the impact of Konstantin [Stanislavsky]'s death. And I keep thinking and thinking. [. . .] . . . my thoughts are heavy and obsessive, about my fate in literature, and about what the Moscow Arts Theatre has done to me . . .

From Yelena Sergeyevna's diary
15 August 1938

A basket of flowers from Misha, and the joy of being reunited with him. We recalled the summer, and the month that Misha spent with us there. [. . .] And, finally, Misha's utterly depressing story about how Dmitriyev was nearly the end of him and disrupted the work on *Don Quixote* by landing on him for an entire week with his problems (he'd been designated for internal exile to somewhere in Tadzhikistan as the husband of a wife in exile). Complete disappointment in Dmitriyev as a person; but then how many such disappointments we have suffered!

23 August 1938

Katayev started a conversation about Misha's situation. Its purport was quite clear: that Misha must, in Katayev's view, write some short story and submit it, and altogether he should return to the bosom of [Soviet] writers with a new work – 'the quarrel has gone on too long' – and so on. All this we have heard before, we know it all, and it's all too easy to understand! And it's all so tiresome!

4 September 1938

On the 3rd Nikolay Robertovich [Erdman] came to ask Misha's advice about a letter he wants to write requesting that his conviction be struck off the record.

5 September 1938

Today is the 800th performance of *The Turbins*. [. . .] We received congratulations over the telephone from Olga, Fedya [Mikhalsky] and Grisha [Konsky].

10 September 1938

Yesterday Markov and Vilenkin came. They arrived after ten and sat until five in the morning. At first the evening was excruciatingly painful for them. They had come to ask Misha to write a play for the Moscow Arts Theatre. 'I will never consent to it, it's against my interests to do it and it's dangerous for me. And I already know how things will develop afterwards.' [. . .] Then Misha told them everything he thought about the Arts Theatre's treatment of him; all their sins and boorish behaviour. And he added, 'But that's all in the past now, I've forgotten and forgiven it. But I won't write for you.' [. . . Markov:] 'But didn't you want to write a play about Stalin?' Misha replied that there would be a problem about the material he would need for such a play – how was it to be obtained? [. . .] He said, 'It's very difficult, although I can already see quite a lot of the play.'

12 September 1938

. . . the man's written twelve plays and works at a furious pace, and he's got nothing to show for it except a pair of worn trousers.

14 September 1938

After a very long gap Lida R. telephoned and said that Ivan Al. and Nina R. [Dobranitsky's wife] had been arrested, and that she had been left with Nina's little boy Andryusha on her hands. She asked me to come and visit her.

18 September 1938

Weariness and despair about our own situation!

21 September 1938

Hitler wants to attack Czechoslovakia. Is it really possible there will be a war? [. . .]

Amidst all the busy work, he keeps harping back to one and the same subject: his ruined literary career. Misha blames himself for everything, but I find this painful; I know perfectly well that it is others who have ruined him.

22 September 1938

[On the composer Dunayevsky's telephoning to propose a libretto based on Maupassant's *Mlle Fifi* (*Rachel*)] This is an acceptable proposal. Misha has already obtained some of the material, and tonight he has already been telling me the content of all five scenes.

28 September 1938

Yesterday, of course, we sat up until late. Markov and Vilenkin came and tried to prove that everything was different now. [. . .] Misha must write the play precisely at this moment.

4 October 1938

My mood today is murderous, and Misha woke feeling the same. All this, is, of course, natural, you cannot live without seeing the results of your labours.

20 October 1938

All has become clear. The Moscow Arts Theatre desperately

needs a play about Lenin and Stalin. And since the plays of the other authors are extremely weak, they are hoping that Misha will bail them out.

We had what was for us a melancholy and painful conversation about *Flight*; amongst other things, Misha said that his vision had been blinkered, that he would never see the rest of the world outside his own country, and that this was a dreadful thing.

23 October 1938

In *Pravda* an article by Markov about the Moscow Arts Theatre, in which are listed Soviet plays and their authors, but no *Turbins*.

This is persecution by silence.

26 October 1938

[On the Arts Theatre's fortieth anniversary celebrations] I mean to say, just think of it! They haven't included *The Turbins* amongst the celebration performances, even though it's now been running for over twelve years and has been performed over 800 times! There is not a single article about the anniversary in which the author's name or the title of the play has been mentioned.

1 November 1938

I called on [. . .] the Deputy Director of the Literary Fund to talk about paper. In the Literary Fund shop they wouldn't sell me any, saying that Misha had already received more than the quota, which, it turns out, amounts to four kilograms of paper a year.

What is he supposed to work on?

5 November 1938

A telephone call from Kuza to say that *Don Quixote* has been licensed for performance by the Chief Repertory Committee and by the Committee for Arts Affairs. [. . .] What an unpleasant book Stanislavsky's *An Actor Prepares* is. It's superfluous. Even if you were to learn it off by heart you still wouldn't become an actor. And it's deadly dull.

11 November 1938

The beginning of Sakhnovsky's speech: 'I have been sent to you on behalf of the Moscow Arts Theatre by Nemirovich and by Boyarsky to say to you, "Come back to us, come to work for us." '

24 November 1938

Dmitriyev has had his passport returned to him.

1 December 1938. From Moscow to Leningrad
To the composer Isaak Dunayevsky

I am putting the finishing touches to *Rachel* and hope it will be ready any day now. I would very much like to see you. As soon as you are in Moscow, please, give me a ring. Both *Rachel* and I miss you.

From Yelena Sergeyevna's diary
8 January 1939.

A painful and pessimistic mood over the last few days.

18 January 1939. From Leningrad to Moscow
From the composer Isaak Dunayevsky

I consider the first act of our opera a *chef-d'oeuvre* both textually and dramatically. [. . .] I implore you not to pay any attention to my *apparent* lack of interest. Let the absence of the music not hinder your splendid inspiration; the thing is that I always take a long time to launch myself on the path of creativity. [. . .]

9 February 1939. From Kaluga (200 kilometres south-west
of Moscow) to Moscow
From his friend Nikolay Lyamin

Having returned from my distant travels, I have found a peaceful refuge in the town of Kaluga. [. . .] My mood is quiet, or rather I have no mood at all. I don't know what I am going to do. [. . .] In the future I shall do what fate ordains, which is what I always do anyway. [. . .] For some reason it seems to me that an eternity has passed since I've seen anyone. I kiss you all very, very hard, you, Lyusya and Seryozha.

Your Kolya.

11 March 1939. Moscow
To the writer Vikenty Veresayev

Not infrequently I have a great desire to talk with you, but I am somehow shy of doing that because, as with any writer who has been destroyed and persecuted, my thoughts are all the time directed towards one gloomy subject, my situation, and that becomes wearisome for those around me.

Having become convinced over the last few years of the fact that not a single line of mine will ever be printed or staged, I am trying to develop an attitude of indifference towards this fact. And it seems as though I have achieved some significant success.

One of my recent endeavours has been a *Don Quixote* based on Cervantes, written to a commission from the Vakhtangov Theatre. And it's now lying there and will lie until it rots, despite the fact that they received it with enthusiasm and that it is furnished with a stamp from the Repertory Committee.

They have inserted it into such a distant corner of their plan that it is perfectly clear that it won't be put on. Nor will it be put on anywhere else. This causes me no grief at all, since I have already become used to considering each of my works from just one angle – how great will the unpleasantnesses be that it will bring me? And if I cannot foresee any major ones, then I am heartily grateful even for that.

At the moment I am engaged on a job that is entirely senseless from the point of view of everyday life – I am doing a final revision of my novel.

All the same, however much you might try to throttle yourself, it's difficult to stop seizing your pen. I am tormented by an obscure desire to settle my final accounts in literature.

What are you working on? Have you finished your translation?

I would like to see you. Are you ever free in the evenings? I will give you a ring and drop in.

Keep well, and I wish you fruitful work.

27 March 1939. Moscow
To the Board of Directors of the Bolshoy Theatre

I enclose for the attention of the Board of Directors my next libretto, for the opera *Rachel*, based on Maupassant.

8 April 1939. Moscow
To Vasily Kuza (at the Vakhtangov Theatre)

The situation as regards *Don Quixote* is beginning to cause me anxiety, and I would ask you to write and tell me what you are going to do about the play. When will it be put on? And will it be put on at all?

From Yelena Sergeyevna's diary
19 April 1939

We had a good supper and were merry. We sat for a long time. But Grisha! He's a proper Bitkov!
6 May 1939

Yesterday before the reading Olga told me that [Natalya] Venkstern had been arrested.

19 May 1939. From Paris to Moscow
From his brother Nikolay

My dear Mikhail,

I received your registered letter of 9 May with great joy, as I have had no news from you for over eighteen months.

I can tell from what you say that you haven't been receiving my letters.

From Yelena Sergeyevna's diary
20 May 1939

This morning Dmitriyev came with news of Veta. Evidently she is no longer alive.

In the town there is a rumour that Babel has been arrested.
21 May 1939

Misha is sitting at the moment (ten in the evening) over his play about Stalin.
5 June 1939

Yesterday Olga came, and we had a notable conversation about Misha's situation and about his Stalin play. The Theatre is clearly anxious about the question, and is keenly interested in the play about Stalin which Misha is already sketching out.

13 June 1939

Misha's mood is dreadful.

23 June 1939

Apparently Meyerkhold has been arrested.

7 July 1939

They say that Boyarsky has been arrested. I must say that he's a man I have always found very unpleasant.

14 July 1939. From Moscow to Novy Petergof
To Vitaly Vilenkin (of the Moscow Arts Theatre)

The results of my reading [of the play *Batum*] can evidently be considered, if I am not mistaken, propitious. After the reading Grigory Mikhaylovich [Kalishyan] asked me to speed up my work on the revision and the typing so as to deliver the play to the Moscow Arts Theatre by 1 August without fail. And today (we had a meeting) he asked me to move the deadline forward to 25 July. [. . .]

Sergey underwent an operation yesterday (a huge boil on his stomach). In a couple of days' time he will leave for Anapa with his governess.

Things will get quieter in the apartment and I will transform my notebooks, which are scribbled all over with jottings, into an elegant typed copy.

I am tired. Occasionally I go out to Serebryany Bor, bathe, and come straight back. And as for a proper holiday – we don't know anything about that yet. [. . .]

Growing weary, I push the notebook away and wonder, what will be the fate of this play? Have a guess. A lot of work has been put into it.

From Yelena Sergeyevna's diary
17 July 1939

There is a rumour that Zinaida Raykh [Meyerkhold's wife] has been brutally murdered.

5 August 1939

Nikolay [Erdman] telephoned and then came round. [. . .] Nikolay had a depressing piece of news: he has been refused permission to live in Moscow.

13 August 1939

Can we really be leaving tomorrow [for Batum]? I can't believe this happiness.

14 August 1939

Eight o'clock in the morning. Last packing. The car will come at eleven – and then the train!

14 August 1939. From Moscow to the train
From Grigory Kalishyan (at the Moscow Arts Theatre)
(telegram)

Need for journey cancelled. Return to Moscow.

From Yelena Sergeyevna's diary
15 August 1939

After two hours, at Serpukhov, while the four of us were having a meal in our compartment, a postwoman entered the compartment and asked, 'Is there a "bukhgalter" ['accountant', a mistake for 'Bulgakov'] here?' and held out an express telegram.

Misha read it (and sat reading it for a long time), and said that there was no need for us to travel any further. [. . .]

In the car we were thinking, 'What are we going towards? Something completely unknown?' Misha had one hand over his eyes to block out the sun, and held on to me with the other hand, saying, 'What is it that we are rushing to meet? Death, perhaps?' After three hours of furious driving, that is, by eight in the evening, we were back in the apartment. Misha wouldn't allow the lights to be switched on, so we lit candles.

Misha is in a dreadful state.

Early this morning he told me he was incapable of going out anywhere. He spent the day in the darkened apartment, he can't bear the light.

17 August 1939

Sakhnovsky and Vilenkin. [. . . Sakhnovsky] began to tell us that the play had met with a harshly critical reception at the top. It was unacceptable to turn a figure such as Stalin into a fictional character, and it was unacceptable to place him in made-up situations and put made-up words in his mouth. The play was not to be staged nor published. The second thing was that at the top they considered that Bulgakov had submitted this play out of a wish to rebuild bridges and improve people's opinions of him.

This accusation is as difficult to prove as his innocence. How could it be proved that M. A. had no intention of building any bridges, but simply wanted, as a dramatist, to write a play he found interesting because of the material, and with a hero, and that the play should not lie in his desk drawer, but should be performed on stage?! [. . .]

Misha is considering a letter to the authorities.

22 August 1939

[Kalishyan] was trying to persuade him to write a play about ordinary Soviet people. [. . .] Misha was in a bad mood after this conversation. [. . .] Today there was a report in the newspapers about the negotiations with Germany and Ribbentrop's visit.

23 August 1939

I am cleaning the apartment as vigorously as I can, I find it easier when I occupy myself with physical work. [. . .] Misha is forcing himself stubbornly to study foreign languages – evidently with the same purpose as me with my cleaning.

24 August 1939

Today in the newspapers it said that the non-aggression pact with Germany had been signed.

25 August 1939

Everyone in the Theatre looks at me with sympathy as though I were a widow.

27 August 1939

Misha feels crushed. He says that he has really been knocked off his feet. It's never been like this before.

7 September 1939. Moscow
To the Board of Directors of the Bolshoy Theatre

Owing to poor health I request leave from 10 September to 5 October this year.

26 September 1939. From Moscow to Kiev
To his boyhood friend Aleksandr Gdeshinsky
Any news from you would be agreeable, especially now, when only the illuminated dial of the radio, through which music reaches me, links me with the outside world.

From Yelena Sergeyevna's diary
29 September 1939
I will go straight to Misha's grave illness. [. . .] World events are seething all around us, but they reach us only indistinctly, so struck down are we by our own misfortune.

1 October 1939. From Kaluga (200 kilometres south-west
of Moscow) to Moscow
From Nikolay Lyamin
Such is fate. [. . .] It is so distressing to think of you lying in a dark room and worrying.

3 October 1939. From Kiev to Moscow
From his boyhood friend Aleksandr Gdeshinsky
Dear Misha!
I was very upset and saddened by your letter. Where do such misfortunes come from to afflict a man? I believe and want to think that you will get over it.

4 October 1939. Moscow
To his friend Pavel Popov
Thank you, dear Pavel, for your kind letter. My letter, unfortunately, cannot be a detailed one as I am plagued by headaches. For that reason I simply embrace you and send my greetings to Anna Ilyinichna.

1 December 1939. From the sanatorium at Barvikha to
Moscow
To his friend and neighbour Aleksey Fayko
Dear friends!
Thank you for your friendly concern, for the embroidered skull-cap and for your affectionate care for Sergey.

This is the state of my affairs: I have begun to feel better here, so that hope has even awakened in me. A considerable improvement has been observed in the left eye. The right one, which is more badly affected, is dragging slowly along behind it. I have already been out in the open air in the wood. But then I was struck down by flu. We are hoping that it will pass without trace.

For the moment reading is forbidden me. Writing – as you can see, I'm dictating to Yelena Sergeyevna – also. For the moment I wish you the best, well, of course, health above all else!

1 December 1939. From the sanatorium at Barvikha
To his friend Pavel Popov

Dear Patya,

I am dictating, but sparingly, as I have flu which, to my great happiness, seems to be drawing to a close. An improvement (in my eyes) has been observed in the course of my main illness. Thanks to that, hope has awoken in me that I am returning to life.

When you sit in your study reading a book – think of me. I have been deprived of that happiness for two and half months now. If you were to write, which I would be very glad of, write straight to our flat in Moscow.

Your Mikhail.

3 December 1939. From the sanatorium at Barvikha to
Moscow
To his sister Yelena

Dear Lyolya!

Here is some news of me. A considerable improvement has been observed in my left eye. The right eye is lagging behind, but also seems to be trying to do something useful. According to the doctor it turns out that if there is an improvement in the eyes, that means there is an improvement in the functioning of the kidneys. And if that's the case, then I feel a new hope stirring in me that on this occasion I will get away from the old crone with the scythe and finish one or two things that I would like to finish.

At the moment I have been kept in bed for a bit by flu, but otherwise I had begun to go out and had been for a walk in the wood. And had grown significantly stronger.

So, what is Barvikha? It's a comfortable, magnificently equipped clinical sanatorium. Most of all I am longing to get home, of course! East, West, home's best, as they say.

I am being treated painstakingly, largely with a specially selected and blended diet. Mostly vegetables in all forms, and fruits. The one and the other are fearfully dull, but they say there's no other way, that otherwise they won't be able to set me up again properly. And anyway, it's so important for me to be able to read and write that I am even prepared to chew such rubbish as carrots.

It's not clear how long we will have to spend here. If you would like to write to me, which I would be very glad of, write directly to our Moscow apartment. Greetings to Varya and Nadya.

5 December 1939. From Moscow to the sanatorium at Barvikha
From his friend Pavel Popov

Dear Maka,

I was very touched by your letter. I think of you constantly. Not just now, but before and always; at table, in bed, and in the street. Whether I see you or not, you are what makes life beautiful for me. I fear that you may not suspect what you mean to me. When a Russian was once asked whether he didn't belong to a tribe of barbarians, he replied, 'If the past of my race contains people such as Pushkin and Gogol, I cannot consider myself a barbarian.'

In former times an Aleutian bishop was asked, by someone who met him on Kuznetsky Bridge Street – and he had come from the wilds of the north – how he liked Moscow. He replied, 'It lacks people,' that is, there were no real people.

And in the same way, being your contemporary, one does not feel that there is a lack of people: reading the lines you have written, one knows that a genuine literary culture still exists; transported by fantasy to the places you describe, one understands that the creative imagination has not dried up, that the lamp lit by the Romantics, by Hoffmann and others, still burns and gleams, and that altogether the art of words has not forsaken mankind . . . For me you stand on a pedestal that no other artists have attained, even though they may be masters at feeling themselves not just the centre of an audience, but the centre of the universe.

I even feel awed that I am acquainted with you, that I allow myself to joke with you, and that I use the intimate form of address to you; am I not thereby profaning the reverence I feel for you? But what am I doing writing all this? Your every word, even if casually uttered, is a work of art, whatever it is that you are speaking about. Everything else relating to literature is shallow beside you. So how could I not think of you and feel for you? One historian whose lectures I went to as a student wrote in his memoirs of how he had taken leave for a long period of time from his teacher, academician Golubinsky: 'I kissed the hand of the man who had written the history of the Russian Church.' And in the just same way I have always wanted, as I still want, to kiss the hand of the man who wrote *Molière*.

6 December 1939. From the sanatorium at Barvikha
To his friend Pavel Popov

Yes, dear Pavel, you should never try to plan things in advance. Both of us have been laid low by flu, and everything's fallen to pieces as far as fresh air and making further progress are concerned. I feel poorly and I lie in bed all the time, dreaming only of getting back to Moscow and taking a rest from the very hard regime, and from all the various procedures with which they have finally worn me out after three months. Enough treatments!

Reading and writing are, as before, strictly forbidden me and, as they say here, will be forbidden 'for a long time'.

Now there's a little phrase that is full of uncertainty! Would you like to translate for me what 'for a long time' means?

I am going to try to be back in Moscow, whatever happens, by 20 December.

12 December 1939. From Moscow to the sanatorium at
Barvikha
From his friend Pavel Popov

Today I visited Vikenty Vikentyevich [Veresayev] and learned an interesting piece of news concerning you which I hadn't known before, that is about your *Pushkin* and the fact that it has been included in the plan for 1940. [. . .] V. V. was very kind, and talked about you very sympathetically and touchingly.

Thank you for your letter. I kiss Yelena Sergeyevna's hands, and embrace you at long distance. Did you receive my previous letter, it may have crossed with your last one?

Your loving Pavel.

25 December 1939. Moscow
To his sister Yelena

I've been back in Moscow since the 18th. Come and visit me. Make an arrangement with Lyusya about when would suit you. I won't write much, I'm saving my eyes.

Your M.

28 December 1939. From Moscow to Kiev
To his boyhood friend Aleksandr Gdeshinsky

Until now I have been unable to reply to you, my dear friend, and to thank you for all the information you kindly sent to me. So here I am, back from the sanatorium. And how am I? To tell you frankly and in secret, I am consumed by the thought that I have come back to die.

This does not suit me for one reason: that it is painful, tedious and banal. As you know, there is only one decent way of dying, and that is with the help of a firearm, but unfortunately I do not possess such a thing.

To be more precise about my illness: I can clearly perceive within me a struggle going on between the symptoms of life and of death. In particular on the side of life there has been an improvement in my sight.

But enough about my illness!

I will add just one thing: that towards the end of my life I have come to experience yet another disappointment – in therapeutic medicine.

I won't call the doctors murderers, that would be too harsh, but I will willingly call them casual, untalented hacks.

There are exceptions, of course, but they are rare!

But what use are those exceptions if these allopaths not only have no means of combating ailments like mine, but sometimes cannot even diagnose what the ailment is?

Time will pass and people will laugh at our therapeutic medicine as they do at Molière's doctors. What I have said does not apply to surgeons, oculists or dentists. Nor to the best of doctors, Yelena Sergeyevna. But she can't manage on her own, so I have adopted a new faith and moved over to homeopathy. But most of all may God help us poor invalids!

Please write to me, I beg you! [. . .]

With all my heart I wish you health, and for you to see the sun, hear the sea and listen to music.

Your M.

31 December 1939. Moscow
To his sister Yelena

Dearest Lyolya,

I received your letter and hope that you and your family will be recovered soon. And since the New Year is imminent, I send you and the others my best and joyful wishes.

I won't wish anything for myself, since I have noticed that nothing has ever worked out as I wished. [. . .] In fact, neither those who are treating me nor even I can say anything for sure. What will be, will be. I feel happiness at being home. Lyusya and I kiss you.

Mikhail.

From Yelena Sergeyevna's diary
1 January 1940

1939, the most difficult year in my life, has gone, and may God grant that 1940 should not be the same!

15 January 1940

Misha is correcting the novel [*The Master and Margarita*] as much as his strength will allow, and I am copying it out . . .

16 January 1940

42 degrees below zero! [. . .] I believe that he will get better.

24 January 1940. Moscow
To his friend Pavel Popov

Are you alive, dear Pavel? January has turned out uncommonly bitter. I have been completely crippled by the frosts, and feel bad.

Give me a ring!

Your M.

From Yelena Sergeyevna's diary
10 March 1940

16.39. Misha died.

★★★★★★★★★★★★★★★★★★★★★★★★★★★★★

5 January 1961. From Moscow to Paris
From Yelena Sergeyevna to Bulgakov's brother Nikolay

Now I want to tell you in more detail about Misha's death, painful though it is for me to do so . . . [. . .]

When Misha and I understood that we couldn't live without each other (as he put it), he suddenly and very seriously added, 'Just bear in mind that I will die a very painful death; give me your word that you won't hand me over to a hospital and that I will die in your arms.' I smiled without thinking: this was 1932, Misha was just over forty and he was healthy and very youthful . . . Once again he insisted solemnly, 'Give me your word.' And then several times during our life together he reminded me of it.

I insisted that he visit the doctor for X-rays and analyses etc. He did all that and everything was reassuring, but all the same he said it would be 1939, and when the year came he began to speak in a light and joky tone of the fact that this was his last year, his last play, and so on. But since he seemed to be in good health, which had been verified, it was impossible to take his words seriously. Then we went south in the summer, and he became ill on the train. That was on 15 August 1939. We returned the same day to Moscow from Tula: I found a car to take us.

We called out the doctors and he spent a certain time in bed, but then got back on his feet, feeling wretched, and we decided to go and spend some time in Leningrad for a change of air.

We left on 10 September, but came back four days later, because on the very first day on Nevsky Prospekt he realized he was losing his sight. We found a professor there who examined his eyes and said, 'It doesn't look too good.' He insisted I take Misha straight home. In Moscow I called out the best kidney and eye specialists. The first one immediately wanted to transfer Misha into his care in the Kremlin hospital. But Misha said, 'I won't leave her,' and reminded me of my word. And when I was seeing Professor Vovsi out he said, 'I won't insist, because it's only a matter of three days.'

But Misha lived another six months after that. Sometimes he felt worse, then better again. Sometimes he was even able to go out in the street or to the theatre. But he was getting steadily weaker and thinner, and his sight was deteriorating.

Usually we would go to sleep between one and two in the morning. But after a couple of hours he would wake me up, saying, 'Get up, Lyusenka, I will be dead soon, let's talk.' True, he would soon be laughing and joking, and he believed me when I said he would certainly recover, and he'd think up extraordinary sketches for the Moscow Arts Theatre, or the beginning of a new novel, or some other humorous piece. And then, reassured, he would go back to sleep.

As a doctor he knew everything that would happen to him. [. . .]

His legs ceased to obey him. My place was on a cushion on the floor next to his bed. He held my hand all the time, right up until the last second.

On 9 March at about three in the afternoon the doctor said that he wouldn't live more than another two hours. Misha was only semi-conscious. The previous day he'd been suffering dreadfully, his whole body was in pain. He asked for Seryozhka and put his hand on his head. He said, 'Light!' So we switched on all the lamps. But on the 9th, several hours after the doctor had pronounced his sentence, he came to. He pulled me by the hand towards him. I leaned over to kiss him. And he held me there for a long time, it seemed an eternity, and his breath was cold as ice: the last kiss.

The night passed. On the morning of the 10th he was sleeping or slipping in and out of consciousness, and his breathing became faster, warmer and more even. And I suddenly thought and believed, like a madwoman, that the miracle I had kept promising myself had come to pass . . . The miracle I had kept forcing him to believe in . . . [. . .]

Some time later I left the room, and suddenly Zhenechka [her elder son] came running to fetch me: 'Mummy, he's groping for you with his hand.' I ran back and took his hand . . .

Misha began to breathe faster and faster, then suddenly opened his eyes very wide and sighed. There was astonishment in his eyes, and they were filled with an unusual light.

And he died. This was at 16.39, as I noted it down in my diary . . .

A NOTE ABOUT NAMES

All Russian names are made up of three elements: the first name, the patronymic, and the surname. The patronymic is a form that is always derived from the father's name. For example, because Bulgakov's father's first name was Afanasy, Bulgakov and his brothers have the patronymic Afanasyevich, while all his sisters have the patronymic Afanasyevna.

The surname sometiems has a masculine and a feminine form: for example, Popov and Popova. Married women sometimes take over their husband's surname, or they retain their own surname, or they use both at once: Lyudmila Nikolayevna Zamyatina (married to Zamyatin), Olga Sergeyevna Bokshanskaya (married to Kaluzhsky) and Anna Ilyinichna Tolstaya–Popova (married to Popov) are examples in this book of all three practices.

Another characteristic of Russian names is that diminutive forms are very often used instead of the full name. The following are some examples:
– Lyubov Yevgenyevna Belozerskaya (Bulgakova): Lyuba, Lyu-banya, Lyubasha, Lyubinka, Lyubochka.
– Olga Sergeyevna Bokshanskaya: Olya.
– Ivan Afanasyevich Bulgakov: Vanechka, Vanya.
– Konstantin P. Bulgakov: Kostya.
– Mikhail Afanasyevich Bulgakov: Mak, Maka, Misha, Mishenka.
– Nikolay Afanasyevich Bulgakov: Kolya, Nikol, Nikolaychik.
– Nadezhda Afanasyevna Bulgakova: Nadya.

- Varvara Afanasyevna Bulgakova: Varya.
- Yelena Afanasyevna Bulgakova: Lyolya.
- Yelena Sergeyevna Bulgakova: Helen, Lyu, Lyusenka, Lyusetta, Lyusi, Lyusya.
- Aleksandr Gdeshinsky: Sasha.
- Yevgeny Kaluzhsky: Zhenya.
- Tatyana Nikolayevna Lappa (Bulgakova): Tanya, Tanyusha, Taska, Tasya.
- Nikolay Lyamin: Kolya.
- Pavel Popov: Patya.
- Anna Tolstaya-Popova: Annushka.
- Nikolay Radlov: Kolya.
- Nadezhda Radlova: Dina.
- Sergey Yevgenyevich Shilovsky: Seryozha, Seryozhka.
- Yevgeny Yevgenyevich Shilovsky: Zhenechka, Zhenichka, Zhenya.
- Sergey Yermolinsky: Seryozha.
- Yevgeny Zamyatin: Zhenya.

Bulgakov and his family and close friends also used a great many nicknames, some of which are not really diminutives at all:

- Lyubov Yevgenyevna Belozerskaya (Bulgakova): Topson.
- Mikhail Afanasyevich Bulgakov: Afanasyevich, Molière Afanasyevich, UncMich.
- Yelena Sergeyevna Bulgakova: Ku, Madeleine Cowardy the Unreliable, Masya, Mysya, Puzanovsky.
- Sergey Topleninov: Topi.

INDEX

INDEX

INDEX

INDEX

p-45 Flat # 50
29 - descrip of Heart of a Dog